MASTERING
PASCAL PROGRAMMING

ERIC HUGGINS

MACMILLAN

First published 1983
Reprinted 1985, 1987, 1988

Published by
MACMILLAN EDUCATION LTD
Houndmills, Basingstoke, Hampshire RG21 2XS
and London
Companies and representatives
throughout the world

Printed in Hong Kong

ISBN 0-333-32293-2 (hardcover)
ISBN 0-333-32294-0 (paperback — home edition)
ISBN 0-333-35460-5 (paperback — export edition)

CONTENTS

CONTENTS

detail of part of the mechanism of the calculating machine designed and made by Blaise Pascal, then aged 19, in 1642; the drums were approximately 2 cm in diameter; this was the earliest computing machine on which all four arithmetical operations could be carried out; in the remaining 20 years of his life, Pascal became eminent as mathematician and philosopher; the computing language was named after him. Facsimile courtesy of the Science Museum, London

PREFACE

The use of Pascal has been expanding rapidly during the past few years. The spectrum of users, and potential users, is wide indeed. It now ranges from those who had never previously written computer programs to those who have had considerable computing experience with other languages. Pascal is being used in science and mathematics, in business and commerce, for simulation and games, for process control in real time as well as for Wirth's primary purpose as an introduction to good programming practice. Thus, the potential readership of this book is probably drawn from a broad field with widely differing interests.

My aim has been to meet the needs both of the newcomer to computing and of the reader who has some programming experience but none of Pascal. I have tried to keep the main text virtually 'non-mathematical', though a knowledge of arithmetic and of elementary algebra is essential to any understanding of computers. An optional chapter on mathematical applications of Pascal is introduced at an early stage.

On the assumption that most readers have access, or are hoping to have access, to a small computer or a terminal, the book has been designed to allow early 'hands on' experience. Previous experience with computers is not assumed.

I have tried to structure the book in a way that will encourage selective reading according to individual needs. The Pascal language itself is covered in two separate parts. The first part (Chapters 2–9 inclusive) covers approximately the same ground as the working subset of the language, Pascal-S. To help those whose applications may be business or commercial I have included text files in this first section. After studying this first part most readers should have assimilated enough of the language to be able to write useful programs to suit their particular interests.

The remainder of the language, up to Level 0 of BS 6192:1982, is covered towards the end of the book (Chapters 14–17). Between the two parts there are optional chapters on sorting, top-down design, simulation and graphics. Chapter 18 is an optional chapter on the use of Pascal in real time. The book starts with a chapter on computing fundamentals for those new to the art and ends with a set of practical hints based on practical experience.

Each optional chapter has an opening paragraph, marked with the symbol □, that guides the reader to his next step.

I have taken the view that it is counter-productive to put exercises at the end of every chapter just for the sake of having exercises. Keen programmers will find plenty of their own problems to program. Most of the exercises either help to give a better understanding of the implementation being used or they are referred to in subsequent chapters.

The use of INPUT in interactive operation is discussed at length, since the authors of different compilers have different interpretations of what constitutes the INPUT file in interactive mode.

All the full programs (and many of the skeleton ones after 'fleshing out') have been tested either on my TRS-80 using the Bourne/Molimerx compiler, version 5.0, or by Texas Instruments Ltd using their Microprocessor Pascal development system, version 3.0. I hope that they are thus bug-free. Since, at the time of writing, neither compiler claims complete conformity with the new British Standard and since transcription errors may have occurred, I should be most grateful to be advised of any errors or discrepancies that are discovered.

Finally I should like to express my sincere thanks to the many people who gave useful help and valid criticism during the preparation of this book. It would be invidious to mention anyone specifically since much of the most helpful criticism came from people whom I do not know even by name. I have thanked those that I do know. If the others should chance to see this book, I hope they will appreciate how much their comments on the original drafts have been taken to heart.

August 1982   ERIC HUGGINS

CHAPTER 1

KNOW YOUR COMPUTER

□ This chapter is addressed to newcomers to computing. If you have already had some experience of using computers and of programming them in some other language, you will wish to skip to Chapter 2 where Pascal really starts. On the way, you might like to glance at the section at the end of this chapter headed 'Software', because the method used to translate a Pascal source into an executable program is often different from that of other languages. □

1.1 INTRODUCTION

There was a time (roughly from 1940 to 1965) when the world was divided into two: computer specialists and the rest of us. Only the specialists were allowed to approach those sacred and somewhat sinister electronic giants which consumed vast quantities of energy and were carefully locked away in their air-conditioned rooms. The rest of us looked on in awe, and had little option but to accept everything the specialists said and did. They used to disappear into their inner sanctum with packs of punched cards or rolls of punched paper tape, and come back hours or even days later with a great wad of paper which they assured us was the answer to our problem. Either we accepted it, or we didn't. And if we didn't, there was not much we could do about it; they were the experts and the only people who knew how to talk to the computer in the only language it understood.

But all that has now changed. Most readers of this book will have access to a computer with which they are able to communicate directly. By the time that they have finished this book they should be able to 'talk' to the computer in a language, Pascal, which they and the computer both understand and the answers to their problems will come back, not in hours, but in seconds or less.

Such access is likely to be achieved in one of three ways which are exemplified in Figs 1.1–1.3.

Figure 1.1 shows a *teletypewriter terminal*. This consists essentially of a keyboard and a printer and is very similar to the well-known Telex machine. In this type of installation there is usually no computing power

Fig 1.1 *a teletypewriter terminal (photograph reproduced by courtesy of the Westrex Company Ltd)*

in the terminal itself, in which case it is described as a *dumb* terminal. All the computing power is in a *remote* computer to which the terminal is connected. 'Remote' in this context does not necessarily indicate a great distance. It means rather that the computer is not in the same box as the terminal. A remote computer may be situated anywhere. It may be adjacent to the terminal, in the same room, or it could be on the other side of the world, connected by submarine cable or by a space satellite. A remote computer may have several such terminals connected to it, but because it can work at a speed which is many times faster than·that of the terminals and the people using them, it is able to share its time between them. The terminal user seldom suffers any inconvenience from the fact that other terminals may be using the computer at the same time.

Figure 1.2 shows a *visual display terminal*. Like the terminal in Fig. 1.1

Fig 1.2 *a visual display unit (VDU) terminal (photograph reproduced by courtesy of Systime Ltd)*

it has a keyboard but, unlike Fig. 1.1, the output appears on a cathode ray tube screen instead of a roll of paper. Like teletypewriters, visual display terminals are connected to remote computers, but sometimes they incorporate some computing power of their own. When they do, such terminals are called *smart* or *intelligent* as opposed to dumb. (The terms are used synonymously in this book, although a smart terminal is often considered to be rather less smart than an intelligent terminal and an intelligent terminal to be more intelligent than a smart one.) The main advantage to the user of having an intelligent terminal is that it usually appears to work faster, because the amount of information that has to be passed between the terminal and the remote computer is often much reduced, thus avoiding delays in the communication network.

The third type of access that the reader might have is a self-contained *minicomputer* or *microcomputer*. Figure 1.3 shows the author's microcomputer on which the whole text of this book has been written and most of the programs have been tested.† There is no direct connection between this installation and any other computer.

†The author's implementation does not cover one feature of the language, records. Those programs have been tested on another installation.

Fig **1**.3 *the author's installation: this installation is independent and not connected to any other installation*

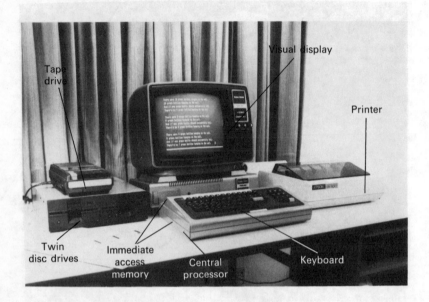

By comparison, Fig. 1.4 shows a large commercial computing installation which has the same features as those in Fig. 1.3 but has many times the computing power.

Whichever type of terminal or computer is used, the general principles of operating are the same, but there will be differences of detail. It is beyond the scope of this book to describe operating procedures (how to switch on, how to load programs, etc). The reader must find out how to operate his own installation (by studying the manuals supplied with the equipment and/or by discussion with people who have already had some experience in using it). However, the following description may help to give the beginner a better overall picture.

All digital computing systems, whatever their size, have essentially the same components, connected together in essentially the same way. This typical layout is shown diagrammatically in Fig. 1.5. The heart of the system is the *central processing unit*. This is where all the arithmetic is carried out and where all the logical decisions are made to control the routing of every single item of data or information within the whole system. Although it has been drawn rather large, as befits its importance, it is nowadays often physically the smallest component of the system. In a minicomputer or microcomputer it is usually a single chip or wafer of silicon measuring about 5 mm square.

Fig 1.4 *a fairly large commercial installation comprising the same elements as shown in Fig 1.3; in such an installation most of the input data would be provided from remote terminals or from tapes or discs prepared 'off-line' (photograph reproduced by courtesy of International Computers Ltd)*

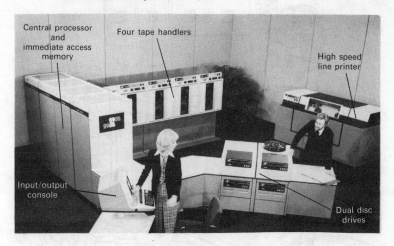

Central processor and immediate access memory

Four tape handlers

High speed line printer

Input/output console

Dual disc drives

Fig 1.5 *the 'architecture' of a computer: all information and data are routed through the central processing unit (CPU), wherein all arithmetical calculations and logical decisions are undertaken; in mini- and microcomputers the CPU is usually a silicon chip about 5 mm square*

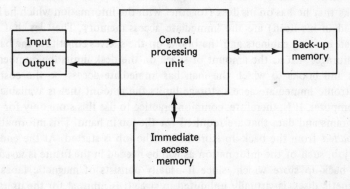

Memory is the storage area where all data, programs and other information necessary for the operation of the computer are stored. It is split into two types: *immediate access* and *back-up*. To understand the difference beween these two types of memory it sometimes helps to consider how a 'human computer' might work (see Fig. 1.6). The man himself is the

Fig 1.6 *a 'human computer' at work: the files on the desk represent the immediate access memory; the files in the filing cabinet and the books on the shelves represent the back-up store*

equivalent of the central processing unit. The papers, files and reference books that he has on his desk (together with the information which he has stored in his head) are the immediate access memory. The files that are stored in filing cabinets and the books on the shelves constitute the back-up storage. Just as the amount of space on the desk limits the number of files and books to which the man has immediate access, so the cost of electronic immediate access storage limits the amount that is available to a computer. It is, therefore, common practice to use this store only for the programs and data that are required for the job in hand. This information is *loaded* from the back-up store before the job is started. At the end of the job, such of the information as will be needed in the future is *saved* in the back-up store which, since it usually consists of magnetic tapes or magnetic discs, is virtually unlimited in size. It is unusual for the users of terminals (Figs 1.1 and 1.2) actually to handle these magnetic media since their back-up stores are normally kept alongside the remote computer, but users of minicomputers or microcomputers will have to ensure that the correct tape, cassette or disc is inserted into the relevant tape or disc drive unit before attempting to gain access to the file. In fact the necessity to handle their own back-up storage media is often the most important difference that users will see between working at a terminal and using a stand-alone computer.

Input (in Fig. 1.5) will almost invariably be from a keyboard of the 'QWERTY' type (Fig. 1.7) and output will be either to a printer or a visual display. In some installations, both types of output will be available, to be selected at the discretion of the user.

Fig 1.7 *a typical terminal keyboard: the key layout is often referred to as 'QWERTY', from the first row of alphabetical keys*

Figure 1.8 shows diagrammatically the layouts for installations employing, respectively, (a) a dumb terminal, (b) an intelligent terminal, (c) a stand-alone mini- or microcomputer.

The immediate access memory can be considered as consisting of a series of slots or pigeonholes in each of which it is possible to store one number. Under instructions from the program, the central processing unit can select a particular slot and either 'write' a new number into the slot (in which case the old number is deleted and cannot be used again) or 'read' the existing number and use it in calculations (in which case the number that is in the slot remains unchanged). A Pascal program is able to give a separate name to each of the memory slots which are to be used for the storing of data. Let us suppose that we have given three such slots the following names: BOYS, GIRLS, PUPILS. We could then have the following program instructions:

```
BOYS   := 7 ;
GIRLS  := 5 ;
PUPILS := GIRLS + BOYS ;
```

where the sign ':=' means 'take the value of' or 'becomes'

8

After this program fragment has been carried out ('executed', in computer parlance), the three slots would contain the numbers 7, 5 and 12 respectively. You will see that, although the computer has had to collect the numbers from the BOYS and GIRLS slots in order to calculate the

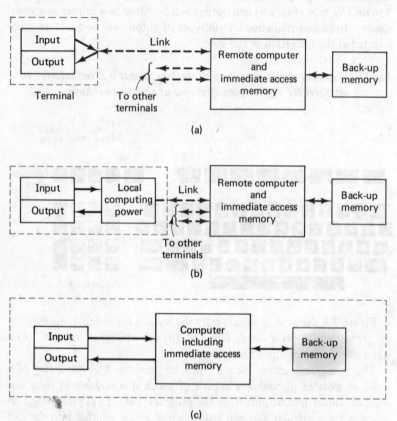

Fig 1.8 *(a) a 'dumb' terminal operating to a remote computer – the link may be by a short wire, a land line, a submarine cable, a radio link (perhaps via a satellite) or any combination of these; (b) an 'intelligent' terminal – the local computer may incorporate immediate access and back-up memory; (c) a 'stand alone' system*

number of pupils, these numbers have not been changed by the calculation in the last line and would still be available for any further calculations. In fact the only way to change the number in any slot is to give an instruction where the name of the slot appears on the left hand side of the : = sign. We shall deal with this more fully in the next chapter when we discuss programming in more detail.

It is not only numbers that can be stored in computer memories. Letters of the alphabet, mathematical symbols, punctuation marks and any of the other characters which are available on the keyboard, printer or visual display can be handled by the computer. An important modern application of this facility is the *word processor* or *text editor* where the text is 'written' into the computer's memory and where amendments can easily be made and mistakes corrected before the text is finally printed.

A computer program is a special example of text that can be stored in a computer's memory and, in fact, the computer is unable to function until there is a program in the part of the immediate access memory that is earmarked for this purpose. But programs can be treated just like other text: they can be composed and edited on the computer. When this is being done there will effectively be two quite different programs in the memory: the program that is being edited and the program (often called an *editor*) which enables the computer to be used as a text editor. This idea of using one computer program to modify another one is an important concept for Pascal users to understand, because they will meet it later in another context. However, we must first consider programming *languages* in greater detail and it may help if we consider an apparently unrelated analogy.

A sheepdog can be trained to obey a few simple verbal or whistled commands which mean, for example, 'wait', 'go forward', 'go left', 'go right', etc. The shepherd, by issuing a series of these instructions in the correct order, is able to make the dog go where he wants it to. Despite the limited vocabulary of communication between shepherd and dog, very complicated manoeuvres can be achieved, as anyone who has seen a sheepdog trial will know. Only the shepherd who has worked with the dog can get the best results from it. Someone else, the farmer for instance, who wants some sheep brought from a hillside and put into a pen, could tell the shepherd that that is what he wants and the shepherd would have to interpret or translate that instruction into the series of shouts and whistles that the dog understands. Two different languages are in use here: the one the farmer speaks and the one the dog understands. Such languages are sometimes thought of in two different *levels*. The normal speech that the farmer speaks can be called a 'high level language'. The one that the dog understands can be called a 'low level language'.

It is the same with computers. A computer is designed and constructed to understand a fairly simple, low level language with a restricted vocabulary, usually consisting of a series of numbers. It is quite possible for programmers to write programs in this low level language (often called *machine code* because it is the language of the computing machine) but such programming is tedious and errors are easily made and hard to find.

Thus most programs are written in high level languages, of which Pascal is one, which human beings find very much easier to write and to understand.

Another advantage of using a high level language is the fact that it is largely 'machine independent'. Different makes and type of computers have different machine code languages. A machine code program written for one computer might have to be completely re-written before it could be run on another. On the other hand, programs written in standard Pascal should need, at worst, only minor alterations to enable them to be run on most other computers.

With such obvious advantages, there must be a snag. Of course there is. Just as the farmer's instruction has to be translated by the shepherd into 'dog's language', so also must the high level language be translated into machine code before the computer can obey it. Fortunately this is not a very serious problem because we can get the computer itself to do the translation. The program to do the translation is usually called a *compiler* or an *interpreter* and it must be written by an expert. But once a compiler has been written for a particular computer it can be stored on tape or disc. Copies can then be made and sold commercially (subject to copyright restrictions) to anyone who has a similar computer. It can then be used to translate *any* Pascal program into machine code for that machine.

Before we go on, there are two definitions that are in common use, a knowledge of which will help in understanding the subsequent discussion:

(1) A *source program* is the program as originally written. It is implicitly written in a high level language, in our case Pascal.

(2) An *object program* is the translated version of the source program in the language that the computer understands. It is thus, implicitly, in machine code.

You will by now have realised that to run a computing system properly you will need not only the computer and its associated equipment (visual display, printer, tape or disc drive, etc.), but also the necessary programs (compilers, etc.) on which the system operates. Computer jargon has adopted two terms, *hardware* and *software*, to differentiate between these two aspects. Before you start trying to run Pascal programs on your computer or terminal, you must be sure that you have the necessary software available and that you know how to use it.

1.2 SOFTWARE

Clearly, if Pascal is to be a universal language, it must not vary. A British Standard (6192: 1982) has recently been published and it is expected that this will form the basis for an international standard. The syntax in this book follows that Standard. But there are certain aspects that are not covered in the Standard. For example, the precise method of translation from source program into object program is left to the discretion of the person who writes the software. Furthermore, there are certain features of the defined language that may need to be modified slightly because of hardware limitations. For example, the Pascal language calls for the use of curly brackets (sometimes called 'braces') and square brackets in certain circumstances (see Chapters 2, 9 and 16). Since many computer keyboards have not got such brackets, standard Pascal defines the alternatives that may be used. Other limitations may be caused by shortcomings in the software. For example, a compiler that can cope with the whole vocabulary of the Pascal language can be a very long and complicated program. It could thus be expensive and it may need a large computer to operate on. For this reason many compilers are available which will accept a *subset* of the language. This is seldom a serious limitation. In just the same way as it is possible to carry on a useful and intelligent conversation in a foreign language with a limited vocabulary, so also is it possible to write complicated and efficient Pascal programs without a full vocabulary.

Variations, due to either software or hardware, are dependent on the *implementation* being used. A 'Pascal implementation' for any particular installation, is a function of both the hardware and the software that is used for the translation of the Pascal source program into the object program, and can affect many different aspects, ranging from the size of the immediate access memory to the type of input/output devices, or from the method that is used to translate the source program into the object program to the maximum value of the numbers that the program will handle. For example, two computers having identical hardware but using different software are almost certain to have implementation differences and the same is likely to be true when using similar software on different types of computers. It would be quite impracticable to describe all the possibilities in this book. All that can be done is to describe typical systems and to highlight those aspects that may be *implementation dependent,* that is to say things that are known to vary between different implementations. The handbooks that are supplied with the computer and with the software (often called the *documentation*) will usually give the user the information he needs but, regrettably, some documentation is not as helpful as it should be. The user may have to find out some things by trial and error.

The simplest system of translation to describe is the straight compiler. With this, the source program is translated directly into the object program. To use the compiler it must first be loaded into the immediate access memory. The compiler will then call for the source program and will translate it, checking for errors as it does so, into the object program. There will thus be three different programs in the memory at the same

Fig 1.9 *stages in compiling, translating and interpreting: (a) a straight compiler – the source program is translated into the object program in one pass and the object program may be executed whenever desired; (b) an interpreter – the source program is translated into object codes which are executed, and object codes are not retained after execution; (c) Pascal programs are often translated in two stages – first into an intermediate P-code program which can be either translated for immediate execution or translated into an executable object program*

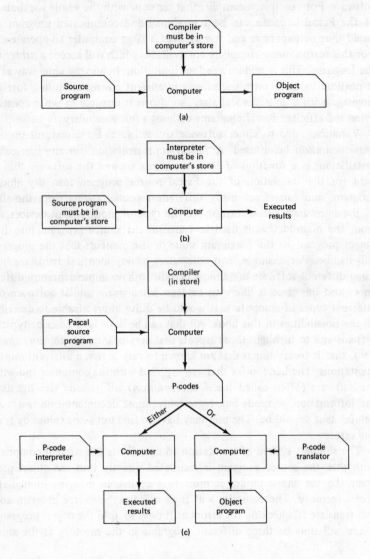

time: the compiler, the source program and the object program. The first must be in the immediate access memory, the others, depending on implementation, will be either in immediate access or in back-up memory. It will be realised from this description that the whole source program must be translated into the object program before it is possible to execute the program. This takes time (typically, several milliseconds up to one second per instruction), but once the object program has been successfully compiled, it can be saved in back-up store and used on subsequent occasions without such delay.

Another method that can be used for translating high level languages into object code is the interpreter. Note that the expression 'object code' rather than 'object program' was used in the last sentence. This is because an interpreter translates each instruction in turn into the object code for that instruction and then causes it to be executed immediately, before moving on to the next instruction. The interpreter and the source program have to be in the immediate access store the whole time that the program is being executed, but the object code is lost as soon as the instruction has been executed. Although this type of interpreter is commonly used with some other high level languages, it is not, at the time of writing, generally available for Pascal.

An interpreter for Pascal is generally used somewhat differently. Translation is in two stages. In the first stage the source program is translated by a compiler which produces a program in a new intermediate language (usually called 'P-code'). This intermediate program is then translated into machine code either by a *translator* or by an *intermediate code interpreter*. The two types of software are similar in that each translates from the intermediate code into machine code, but the former does it in the same way as a compiler (that is, by producing a self-standing object program which can be subsequently executed), while the latter operates in exactly the same way as described in the last paragraph.

Figure 1.9 shows these different approaches in diagrammatic form.

EXERCISE

If you have access to a computer or terminal with Pascal capability, you should now get acquainted with it, its operating system and the details of the specific Pascal implementation which it uses.

CHAPTER 2

INTRODUCTION TO PROGRAMMING IN PASCAL

By way of introduction, we start with a comparatively simple Pascal program, one to evaluate the area of a circle from its radius, using the well-known formula

$$area = \pi \times radius^2 .$$

Here it is:

```
PROGRAM CircleArea (INPUT,OUTPUT);

CONST
  pi = 3.14159;

VAR
  radius, area : REAL;

BEGIN
  WRITE ('What is the radius (millimetres) ? ');
  READ (radius);
  area := pi * radius * radius;
  WRITELN ('Area is ', area, ' sq mm')
END.
```

In due course we shall be studying this program line by line. In the meanwhile there are some general points to be made.

It will be seen that a Pascal program consists of words, numbers, punctuation and other symbols.

The words fall naturally into two categories: those which form part of the vocabulary of the Pascal language and those that are chosen or created by the programmer.

Those that form the vocabulary of the Pascal language are shown in this book, both in the programs and in the text, in upper case (BLOCK CAPITALS). These words fall into two distinct classes:

(1) Some (**PROGRAM, CONST, VAR**, etc.) are the *word symbols*, also called *reserved words*, of the language. These words, and some 30

others that we shall meet later, have all been assigned special meanings in Pascal and must never be used for any other purpose. In order to help you to recognise them they are printed in programs not only in capitals but also underlined. This is one of the conventions adopted in this book. Neither the underlining nor the use of upper case is a requirement of the Pascal language. In the text, such words are shown in **BOLD TYPE**. A full list of all reserved words is given in Appendix I.

(2) Others (INPUT, OUTPUT, READ, WRITE, etc.) are standard words, also called *required identifiers*, that have also been assigned special meanings in the language but, unlike reserved words, they can be redefined by the programmer if he wishes to do so. However, the beginner is well advised to treat all such words as though they too were reserved and not to use them for any other purpose. In this book they always appear, both in programs and in the text, in upper case normal type.

The words that the programmer has selected or created specifically for this particular program are shown wholly or partly in lower case. They also fall into two categories. Those that appear within single quotation marks are the messages that are to be displayed on the output device of the computer. The use of single quotes here is a requirement of the language. The others in lower case (*pi*, *radius*, *area*) are the names that we have selected to represent certain items of data. These names are usually referred to as *identifiers*. In the text they will appear in *italics*. Such identifiers can also be used to identify certain parts of the program and the program itself (*CircleArea*).

It must be emphasised that these typographical distinctions are made in this book to assist the beginner. They are not an essential part of the language. You may well find that your particular implementation does not allow you to use lower case and you will have to key all words in upper case, irrespective of their meaning. However, if you are allowed both upper and lower case, then you may find it helpful to use lower case for the words you choose yourself and upper case for reserved and standard words. You may also find it helpful, when you are drafting your programs, always to follow these conventions and to underline the reserved words until you are so familiar with them that you recognise them subconsciously.

The programmer has considerable freedom in the selection of words or pseudo-words as identifiers. There are two simple rules:

(1) No identifier may have the same spelling as any word symbol or other identifier.

(2) Every identifier must be composed entirely of letters and numerals (punctuation marks and other symbols are not acceptable) and the first, or only, character in the word must be a letter.

There is no restriction on the number of characters in a name, but it is good practice to keep names as short as possible provided that their meaning can immediately be recognised.

The following names are valid:

> *number*
> *VAT69*
> *Hastings1066*
> *rs1300gt*
> *anIdentifierOfConsiderableLength*

The following names are invalid for the reasons given:

39steps	does not start with a letter
half-year	only letters and numerals permitted
wage rate	space not permitted
begin	Pascal reserved word

Furthermore, in some implementations the computer takes note only of the first eight characters of the identifier (and in some microsystems this number may be less) and thus would not be able to distinguish between two or more identifiers with identical first eight characters. For example

> *triangleA*   and   *triangleB*

or

> *materialReceived*   and   *materialIssued*

One way round this problem is to abbreviate the first part so that less than the first eight characters are identical:

> *triangA*   and   *triangB*

or

> *matReceived*   and   *matIssued*,

but often a more satisfactory way is to reverse the order of the elements in a name so that the discrete part comes first:

> *aTriangle*   and   *bTriangle*

or

> *receivedMaterial*   and   *issuedMaterial*.

Since no distinction is made between upper and lower case letters it is recommended practice, as above, to use capital letters to indicate the start of a second or subsequent word or pseudo-word in an identifier. This is not mandatory but it does often help to make a long identifier easier to read. In this book there is one further convention: all *constant* and *variable* identifiers commence with a lower case letter. Program names and (as we shall see later) file names start with a capital letter.

We shall have more to say about the choice of names when we discuss programming tactics in Chapter 19.

Numbers are always written in Pascal programs either in the conventional decimal form such as

$$127.19, \quad 82576.5, \quad 0.006, \quad 1982$$

or in what is generally called 'scientific notation' although the correct computer term is *floating point representation*:

$$1.275E5, \quad 0.1E-2, \quad 10E+6.$$

This notation is similar to that now in wide use in pocket calculators. For those unfamiliar with this format, it should be explained that 'E' (or, on some implementations, 'e') has the meaning 'multiplied by 10 to the power of'. Therefore the last three numbers represent, respectively

$$127500, \quad 0.001, \quad 1000000.$$

There are a few limitations put on the representation of numbers in Pascal. It is not permissible to have a decimal point, as it were, 'hanging in the air'. Thus it is not permissible to write

$$.5 \quad \text{or} \quad 1.$$

These must be represented as

$$0.5 \quad \text{and} \quad 1.0 \text{ (or simply as 1).}$$

Also *vulgar fractions* are not permitted. Thus $2\frac{1}{2}$ must be written as 2.5 and 5/8 as 0.625.

The numbers we shall be using in Pascal will normally be of one or other of two *types*. They will either be whole numbers (*integers*) or *real* numbers which contain, or may contain, a decimal point. There are several reasons for making the distinction, but for the moment it is enough to mention that real numbers typically require twice as much storage space in the computer as integers and real arithmetic takes several times as long to perform as integer arithmetic.

Numbers are commonly used as data in computing, though there are other permissible forms of data, as will be shown later. Storage space has to be found within the computer to hold the current value of each item of data. The data used in a Pascal program are of one or other of two different classes – *constants* and *variables*. In the program given at the start of this chapter, π is clearly a constant. Its value will remain at 3.14159 (or whatever more or less accurate value we choose for it) throughout the program. On the other hand, the whole object of the program is that we should be able to assign whatever value we wish to *radius*, so it is clearly a variable and, similarly, the result of the calculation, *area*, for which we shall also require storage space, is also a variable.

The points so far discussed in this chapter are summarised in diagrammatic form in Fig. 2.1.

Fig 2.1 *the elements of a Pascal program*

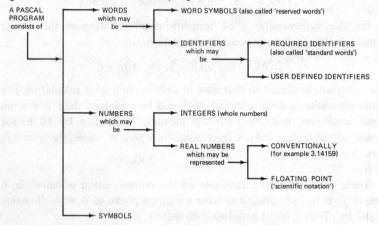

Let us now examine this program more closely:

```
1    PROGRAM CircleArea2 (INPUT,OUTPUT);
2    { The area of a circle, given its radius }
3
4    CONST
5      pi = 3.14159;
6
7    VAR
8      radius, area : REAL;
9
10   BEGIN
11     WRITE
           ('What is the radius (millimetres) ? ');
12     READ (radius);
13     area := pi * radius * radius;
14     WRITELN ('Area is ', area, ' sq mm')
15   END.
```

There are two differences between this program as reproduced here and the original at the start of the chapter. The first is the inclusion of line numbers. Line numbering is not a Pascal requirement as it is of some other languages. In fact it would definitely be unacceptable in a Pascal source program in most implementations. Some compilers, however, have the facility to add line numbers when listing out programs, as an aid to tracing errors (often called 'debugging'). Line numbers have been inserted in the listings in this book wherever they will facilitate cross reference from the text.

Using these line numbers we can now examine this program line by line. A Pascal program consists of a sequence of *definitions*, *declarations* and *statements*. Each of these must be separated from its successor by a *separator* which is usually, but not always, a semicolon. The main exception to this rule is that certain reserved words also act as separators. We shall discuss these as they arise.

Line 1 of the program is the *program heading*. It starts with the word symbol **PROGRAM** followed by an identifier, *CircleArea2*, which is the name that we have given to this program. We are required to give every Pascal program a name even though the name often plays no part within the program. In this case, the name is followed by (INPUT, OUTPUT) which indicates to the computer that it will receive data from its normal input device and will be required to transmit data to its normal output device. INPUT and OUTPUT in this context are known as *program parameters*.

In line 2 we have the second addition since this program first appeared. A description of the program has been added. The text enclosed in curly brackets, { }, (also often called *braces*) is known as a *remark* or *comment*. Such comments are placed in the program to clarify any points that may not be immediately clear to anyone who reads it. They form no part of the program. The braces and all characters within them are ignored by the compiler when the program is compiled, but the liberal use of comments can be of considerable help in understanding programs. Such comments are of assistance not only to outsiders, but also to the programmer himself when returning to his program after an interval.

Comments may be placed anywhere in a program where a space is permitted (that is anywhere except in the middle of words, numbers or special symbols (such as : =). Since many keyboards do not have braces, { }, the double symbols (* and *) are an acceptable alternative and will be used henceforth in this book. Since comments form no part of the program, they may be composed of any combination of alphanumerical or other characters, with the exception that } and *) must not appear in the comment, for reasons that should be obvious.

In line 4 we have one word symbol, **CONST**, which indicates that the following data will define the constants that we shall use. In this program there is only one constant, *pi*, defined in line 5 with its value. Next (line 7) we have another word symbol, **VAR**, which indicates the start of the declarations of the names or identifiers that we shall be using for variable data. There are two such variables, *radius* and *area*. It will be seen that these identifiers are separated from each other by a comma and followed by a colon and standard word, REAL, indicating that both *radius* and *area* may have real values as opposed to integer. All these definitions and declarations must be made at this stage to enable the compiler to reserve the necessary storage space for them.

Having now established all the necessary preliminaries, we can introduce the main part of the program by means of the word symbol **BEGIN** in line 10.

After this there follow four *statements*. Statements are the actual instructions that the computer carries out or 'executes'. They thus differ from definitions and declarations, whose purpose is to give the compiler advance information. The four statements are all instructing the computer to take some action with data.

The first instructs the computer to WRITE a message (*'What is the radius?'*) on the normal output device (usually VDU or teletype). Any series of characters thus enclosed in single quotes is known as a *string* of characters or a *character string*. In this case the string is a message to remind the person using the computer that data is required and the nature of that data. A message of this nature is therefore often called a 'prompt'. Although not always strictly necessary, it is good programming practice to ensure that clear prompts are provided whenever the operator might be in doubt what to do next.

The next statement will READ the number which is supplied to the normal input device (usually a keyboard) and give the value of that number to the variable, *radius*.

In line 13 we have what is known as an *assignment statement*. An assignment statement consists of three parts. On the left is a variable, in the middle the *assignment symbol*, and on the right is some value or *expression*. An expression in Pascal is very similar to an expression in algebra. It consists of numbers or variables connected by mathematical symbols (*operators*) in such a way that the value of the expression can be computed. Its value is then assigned to the variable on the left. The assignment symbol consists of the colon followed by the *equals* sign:

$$: =$$

This is one of several Pascal 'special symbols' in which two single symbols are combined in Pascal to make a third, quite unrelated, symbol. The symbol, $: =$, can be pronounced, 'becomes' or 'takes the value of'. In particular it is important not to confuse the assignment symbol with equality. In algebra, the equation $x = x + 3$ would be imaginary, but in Pascal it is quite permissible and, as we shall see later, quite common to have statements such as

$$x : = x + 3$$

which means that the value of x is increased by 3, the new value of x becoming three greater than the old one.

The other unusual symbol in this statement is the use of an asterisk '*' to indicate multiplication. Since few computer keyboards have a multiplication sign and, in any case, it could easily be confused with the letter x, an asterisk is always used instead.

Line 14 is the instruction to output the result. This is generally similar to the WRITE statement of line 11 but there are one or two differences. First, the instruction is WRITELN and not WRITE. WRITELN is an abbreviation for 'write line'. When the computer has finished outputting the data in the brackets, it will output additional characters (equivalent to the *carriage return* key on an electric typewriter) to ensure that the next message starts on a new line.

Secondly, instead of a single item, there are three separate items of data in the parenthesis brackets. The brackets and their contents are known as a *list* (even when there is only a single item, as there is in the WRITE and READ lists of lines 11 and 12).

The two strings in this list will be output as they stand, but the variable, *area*, which is not in quotes, will be evaluated and its value will be output. This will be made clear shortly when we look at the output from running this program.

Finally, in line 15, we have the single word symbol **END**. Every **BEGIN** in a program must have a corresponding **END**. These two word symbols are known as *delimiters* and they have an important role in Pascal programming. We shall be meeting them frequently. For the present we shall confine ourselves to stating that every Pascal program must have at least one statement or collection of statements so marked.

The following might be the result of running this simple program as it might appear on a VDU or teletypewriter:

```
What is the radius (millimetres) ? 100←
Area is  3.14159E+04 sq mm
```

For the purpose of this book, all the examples of results from running computer programs have been modified in two ways. First, so that you can readily differentiate between information which has been printed by the computer and data which has been entered at the keyboard, the former is in Roman (upright) type and the latter is in *italic* (sloping) type. Secondly, the sign, '←', indicates the pressing of the key that goes under different names on different keyboards ('carriage return', 'return', 'enter', a large left-pointing arrow, etc.). In future this key will always be referred to as '<newline>'. (It is always necessary to press <newline> or <space> at the conclusion of entering a number from the keyboard, as a sign to the computer that entry of the number is now complete and that no further digits are to be expected.)

These typographical features have been added to make it easier for you to identify the data that has been output by the computer. Normal implementations do not make such differentiations.

The result, since it is a real number, has been printed in scientific or floating point representation. In the next chapter we describe how real numbers may be output in the more familiar fixed point representation.

Let us look at the results from running this program again with different data

```
What is the radius (millimetres) ? 1.5←
Area is  7.06858E+00 sq mm
```

and for a very small circle,

```
What is the radius (millimetres) ? 0.05←
Area is  7.85398E-03 sq mm
```

Since $10^0 = 1$ and $10^{-3} = 0.001$, these answers could also be written 7.06858 and 0.00785398 respectively.

The other important aspect of the above program which we have not yet discussed is punctuation. A computer is much less tolerant of mistakes in punctuation than is a human reader. If a comma or even a full-stop has been omitted from the text of this book, it will probably not worry you very much. The human eye is tolerant to such mistakes and often doesn't notice them. But such omissions cannot be tolerated in a computer program. Every punctuation mark in the above program is important, and the program would fail to work without it. So let us look at punctuation more closely.

Commas (lines, 1 8 and 14) are used to separate variables, expressions and other items when they are grouped together; for example, in a declaration or a READ or WRITE list.

Colons (line 8) are used to separate the type identifiers (INTEGER and REAL) from the variable identifiers in declarations (and for other purposes that we shall meet later).

Parenthesis brackets are used to indicate parameters. For example, in line 1 the parameters so indicated are the input/output devices. In READ statements the parameters are the variables to which the input has to be assigned and in WRITE statements they are the items in the WRITE list.

Semicolons are the *separators* which indicate the end of one declaration or statement and the beginning of the next. You will note that there are some lines (4, 7, 10 and 14) that do not end with a semicolon. The delimiters CONST, VAR and BEGIN, not being in themselves definitions, declarations or statements, are not followed by semicolons and any statement that immediately precedes the delimiter END does not require a semicolon since END is considered to be a separator itself. (Some implementations are more tolerant than others of redundant semicolons in this position, but the fact that a compiler accepts them on some occasions does not necessarily mean that it will accept them in all circumstances).

Words (reserved words, standard words or identifiers) must always be separated from each other by at least one space or new line unless a valid non-alphanumerical symbol already intervenes. Examples of positions where such separators are essential are between **PROGRAM** and *CircleArea* in line 1, between **CONST** and *pi* in lines 4 and 5 and between **VAR** and *radius* in lines 7 and 8.

Finally, there is a full-stop at the end of the last line. This apparently insignificant point is very important to the program since it is this, and not the **END**, that indicates the end of the program text.

Since statements are separated by semicolons and words are separated by spaces or new lines it would be permissible to print the above program as follows:

```
PROGRAM CircleArea(INPUT,OUTPUT);CONST pi=
3.14159;VAR radius,area:REAL;BEGIN WRITE
('What is the radius (millimeters) ? ');READ
(radius);area:=pi*radius*radius;WRITELN
('area is ',area,' sq mm')END.
```

but human readers would find it very much harder to understand. There are very good reasons for making sure that our programs are always made as easy as possible to understand. Someone else may want to modify our programs. We ourselves may want to modify them later on. Many a programmer returning to a program after a lapse of time has found that he cannot follow his program, although it was crystal clear to him when he wrote it. It is therefore very important that we make our programs as understandable as possible. One way we can always help is by seeing that our programs are well laid out. When programs are being compiled, blank lines and extra spaces (except in the middle of words, names and compound symbols such as : =) are ignored. You are encouraged to add such spaces and lines as will make the program easier to read.

In the program *CircleArea2* you will notice that lines 3, 6 and 9 have been left blank. The spaces they leave help to distinguish for the reader the difference between the program heading, the constant definition, the variable declarations and the main part of the program. You will also see that each statement between the **BEGIN** and **END** has been indented a couple of spaces. This helps to highlight the sequence of statements and makes it easier, when we have many such statement sequences in a program, to see which **END** pairs up with which **BEGIN**. Some implementations include a program that automatically formats a program in this way for you. If your have access to such a program, you should use it, to ensure some standardisation among the users of the same equipment.

Otherwise, you could do worse than use the programs in this book as a model (with the exception of the horrible example contained in the last paragraph!). It is a good thing to pick up good habits from the start. Bad habits are often difficult to shake off.

Operators used in Pascal expressions are generally similar to the mathematical symbols used in algebra. Thus the symbols + and − indicate *addition* and *subtraction* respectively and we have already met the ∗ symbol which is used for multiplication. It is important to note that Pascal does not permit an implied multiplication symbol as is commonly used in algebra. Thus

$$a := 3b \quad \text{and} \quad a := 24(b + 5)$$

are not allowed. The must be written in full as

$$a := 3 * b \quad \text{and} \quad a := 24 * (b + 5)$$

These three symbols (+, − and ∗) can be used with numbers of type REAL or type INTEGER. It is in the treatment of division that we see some major differences between REAL and INTEGER arithmetic. *Real* division is indicated by the symbol /, which is the exact equivalent of ÷, and will produce a REAL result to the precision which the implementation allows.

INTEGER division uses the operator **DIV** (a reserved word) as a symbol. It may only be used with two numbers of type INTEGER and the result is the integral part (that part which precedes the decimal point) of the quotient and is of type INTEGER. Thus the results of

$$19 \textbf{ DIV } 18 \quad \text{and} \quad 19 \textbf{ DIV } 10$$

will be 1 in each case, although the quotients are 1.056 and 1.9 respectively. Note also that the result of

$$19 \textbf{ DIV } 20$$

will be zero.

There is another operator that can be used with INTEGER division, the reserved word **MOD**. This gives the *modulus* or remainder when one integer is divided by another, the result also being of type INTEGER. Thus

$$19 \textbf{ MOD } 18 \quad \text{gives the result } 1,$$
$$19 \textbf{ MOD } 10 \quad \text{gives the result } 9,$$
$$19 \textbf{ MOD } 19 \quad \text{gives the result } 0.$$

Except when using **DIV** and **MOD**, the operands in an expression can be either REAL or INTEGER, but the result may only be INTEGER if all the operands are of type INTEGER. If one or more of them are REAL the result is REAL and must therefore be assigned to a REAL variable. This is shown explicitly in Table 2.1 and is demonstrated in the following program:

```
PROGRAM NumberTypes (INPUT, OUTPUT);

VAR real2, real3, real4  : REAL;
    int2, int3, int4  : INTEGER;

BEGIN
  READ (real2, real3, int2, int3);
  int4 := int2 + int3;
  int3 := int2 - 79;
  int2 := int4 * int3 + 56;
  int3 := int2 DIV 24;
  int4 := int2 MOD 24;
  real4 := real2 + real3;
  real3 := real2 + int3 - real4;
  real2 := int2 / int3;
  WRITELN (int2, real2, int3, real3,
                          int4, real4)
END.
```

All the above are valid Pascal statements. The following, however, would be invalid with the above declarations:

```
int2 := real2;
int2 := int3 + real2;
int2 := int3 / int4
```

All these are wrong because an attempt has been made to assign a REAL value to an INTEGER variable. On the other hand it is perfectly legitimate to assign an INTEGER value to a REAL variable. The Pascal

Table 2.1 The type of number resulting from different operations with operands of different types

Operator	Operand 1	Operand 2	Result
+, −, *	Integer	Integer	Integer
	Integer	Real	Real
	Real	Integer	Real
	Real	Real	Real
	Integer	Integer	Real
	Integer	Real	Real
	Real	Integer	Real
	Real	Real	Real
DIV, MOD	Integer	Integer	Integer
	Integer	Real	Not valid
	Real	Integer	Not valid
	Real	Real	Not valid

description is 'assignment compatible'. A variable or constant is *assignment compatible* with another variable if they are both the same type and, furthermore, an INTEGER variable or constant is assignment compatible with a REAL variable. A REAL variable or constant is not assignment compatible with an INTEGER variable. The following are all valid:

```
real2 := 25;
real2 := int2;
real2 := int2 DIV int3;
real2 := int2 MOD int3
```

The following would be invalid for a different reason:

```
real2 := int2 DIV 13.75;
real2 := real3 DIV int2;
real2 := int2 MOD real3
```

Their invalidity arises because **DIV** and **MOD** require both operands to be of type INTEGER.

Finally, on the subject of division, any attempt to divide by zero will produce an error when the program is executed. Both the following statements would produce errors:

```
real2 := real3 / 0;
int2 := int3 DIV 0
```

The following could also produce errors if, at the time they were executed, *real4* and *int4* had the value zero:

```
real2 := real3 / real4;
int2 := int3 MOD int4
```

The last two examples are perfectly valid Pascal statements. They only become invalid if *real4* and *int4* have the value zero during execution of the program. There are various other errors of this nature, some of which we will shortly encounter, that can only be identified during the execution of a program. The time of execution is also often called 'run time' and errors that occur then are called 'run time errors'. Errors of syntax, however, will produce 'compile time errors' since they should be identified by the compiler when the program is compiled.

We briefly mentioned 'expressions' earlier and explained that in Pascal they are very similar to expressions in algebra. An expression is any grouping of identifiers, numbers and operators. A *valid* expression is one that can be evaluated to give a single value. Examples of valid expressions are

$$a + b, \quad a * 3, \quad 2 * (a + b)$$

The last example shows that one expression may contain another one, since it was previously indicated that $a + b$ is an expression. Furthermore, $a, b, 3$ and $-a$ are all, by implication, expressions.

With a few exceptions, expressions may be used anywhere that an identifier or value may be used. The two exceptions that concern us at present are as follows. Expressions may *not* appear on the left side (before the : = sign) in an assignment statement, and they may not appear in a **READ** list. They may, however, appear in a **WRITE** list, as the following example shows.

Lines 13 and 14 of the *CircleArea2* program,

```
area := pi * radius * radius;
WRITELN ('Area is', area, 'sq mm')
```

may be combined into

```
WRITELN ('Area is', pi * radius * radius, 'sq mm')
```

EXERCISES

2.1 In the program *NumberTypes* given above, assume that the input was

$$27.83 \qquad 72.17 \qquad 75 \qquad 86$$

What would be the output?

The objective of this exercise is to help you follow through the steps of a program. Therefore you should try to get the answer first by pencil and paper methods. When you have done this, you may, if you like, check your result against the computer. If you get a different result, try to find out why. One way to do this is to insert in the program, after each assignment statement, an additional statement

WRITELN ('variable =', variable)

substituting for each of the words *variable* the actual name of the variable in the immediately preceding assignment statement. This will enable you to trace the program through step by step.

2.2 Write a program that will read in a length in inches (a positive integer not greater than 30 000) and convert it into miles, yards, feet and inches (1 foot = 12 inches, 1 yard = 3 feet and 1 mile = 1760 yards) and display the result on one line of the page or VDU. Each output value should be preceded with the caption 'Miles =', 'yards =', etc.

Use the program to evaluate 345 inches.

Now try to improve the layout of the output by including a number of spaces in the strings.

2.3 Enter and run the following short program:

```
PROGRAM MaximumInteger (OUTPUT);

VAR
  maxi : INTEGER;

BEGIN
  maxi := MAXINT;
  WRITELN ('Maximum integer=', maxi)
END.
```

Your computer should respond with a number. Make a note of the number you get.

CHAPTER 3

SYNTAX, OUTPUT FORMAT AND FOR LOOPS

3.1 SYNTAX

You will have realised from the previous chapter that it is important that all the elements that make up a Pascal program (reserved words, identifiers, punctuation) are correctly used and in the right order. Just as a spoken or written language must be grammatically correct, so must a computer language be correctly constructed. The term used in both cases for this construction is *syntax*.

There are generally two ways of learning correct syntax in a spoken or written language. One is by example and habit so that the correct syntax is used subconsciously. The other is by a study of the rules. When a child learns his native language or mother tongue, he uses the first method almost entirely, only later, perhaps, coming to a detailed study of the rules of syntax. When later he learns a foreign language he is likely to use both methods in parallel, using the syntax rules to supplement what he hears or reads. It is the same with a computer language.

In this book we shall aim to describe Pascal mainly by example, but the syntax rules are also given, since correct syntax is so important in any computer language. Various methods have been developed in order to simplify the description of computer program syntax. In this book we shall use two such methods. One of them, *syntax diagrams*, is apt to be daunting to beginners and has therefore been relegated to Appendix II. The other, which is slightly less daunting though not always so completely precise, will be used in the text. In the main, it is there for guidance and may be skipped at first reading.

The convention is that anything enclosed in triangular brackets, '<' and '>', is considered to have the meaning that has been defined for it in the text. We have, for example, already met '<newline>' as an abbreviation for the symbol that results from pressing the key (marked in various ways) that is the equivalent of the 'carriage return' key on electric typewriters. We could also define an assignment statement as

$$\text{<variable identifier> : = <expression>}$$

where <expression> has already been defined in Chapter 2. However, if you need a more precise definition, you may obtain it by following the syntax diagrams in Appendix II.

Using this notation we can now be rather more explicit about defining <statement>. We have already discussed assignment statements and we have met READ and WRITE statements. If you look in the syntax diagrams, you will not see these last two mentioned. This is because they are special forms of procedure statement, which you will see in the diagram and which we shall be discussing fully later. The term <statement> includes <compound statements> which have the form

$$\text{BEGIN <statement or statements> END}$$

The item <statement or statements> in this definition indicates that any number of statements may appear between the delimiters BEGIN and END. Where there is more than one statement, each must be separated from the next by a semicolon. Any such statement may itself be a compound statement.

Using the same notation, we can now add some further definitions. A *block* in Pascal can be defined for the present as

$$\text{<constant definition part> <variable declaration part>}$$
$$\text{<compound statement>}$$

where <constant definition part> is defined as

$$\text{CONST <one or more constant definitions>;}$$

A <constant definition> can be further defined as

$$\text{<constant identifier> = <constant>}$$

The <variable declaration part> is similarly defined as

$$\text{VAR <one or more variable declarations>;}$$

and a <variable declaration> as

$$\text{<one or more variable identifiers> : <type>}$$

In the above definitions, where there is more than one <constant definition> or more than one <variable declaration>, then each is separated from the previous one by a semicolon. Where there is more than one <variable identifier>, then each is separated from the previous one by a comma.

Also using this notation a program can be defined, quite simply, as

$$\text{<program heading>; <block>.}$$

(Note that the final full-stop in this definition is part of the definition.) We can define <program heading> as

PROGRAM <program name> (<program parameters>)

And, for the present, we can define < program parameters > as

INPUT, OUTPUT

All programs must have an output, and for the present this will always be the normal output device, OUTPUT. Some programs need no external input (for example see *MaximumInteger* in Exercise 2.3 in the last chapter). Where there is no input, INPUT and its associated separating comma may be omitted.

As stated at the introduction to this section, this notation is often difficult for newcomers to computing programming to understand. You should not therefore worry too much if you are at present in this category. You should be aware of the general form of the notation. You will assimilate most of the details as you follow the text and examples in the book. If you have difficulty in following the syntax later or if you find that your programs are rejected for syntax errors when you attempt to compile them, you can refer back to this explanation or you can refer to the syntax diagrams given in Appendix II.

3.2 OUTPUT FORMAT

When you did Exercise 2.2 in the last chapter you probably had an output like this:

```
Miles=    Oyards=    9feet=    1inches=    9
```

In order to improve the layout, you may have tried modifying the 'miles' string (since 30 000 inches is less than 1 mile) and inserting spaces in the other two strings, thus

```
WRITE ('Miles = 0  yards =', yards);
WRITELN ('  feet =',feet, '  inches =', inches)
```

to give an output

```
Miles = 0  yards =     9  feet =     1  inches =    9
```

This shows some improvement, but for a really acceptable layout it would be nice to be able to remove some of the spaces between the '=' sign and the first digit of the value in each case. Pascal enables us to do this by means of *field width parameters*. Thus to output an integer value:

WRITE (<integer expression> : <total field width>)

where <integer expression> is the expression whose value is to be output and <total field width> is any integer expression whose value is greater than zero. The rules for field widths are slightly complicated and are probably best demonstrated by example. Suppose we had the following fragment in a program:

```
WRITELN;
WRITELN ('Value=', value : 4)
```

The following Table 3.1 shows the output we should obtain with different values.

Table 3.1

Value	Output	Output with spaces indicated by 's'
1	Value = 1	Value = s s s 1
12	Value = 12	Value = s s 12
123	Value = 123	Value = s 123
1234	Value = 1234	Value = 1234
12345	Value = 12345	Value = 12345
0	Value = 0	Value = s s s 0
−1	Value = −1	Value = s s − 1
−12	Value = −12	Value = s − 12
−123	Value = −123	Value = − 123
−1234	Value = −1234	Value = − 1234
−12345	Value = −12345	Value = − 12345

From this table it will be seen that if the integer is positive and has fewer digits than the number specified by the field width, it will be printed with leading spaces so that it occupies the width. If it is positive but has the same number of digits as the field width or more, then it will be printed without leading spaces and, if necessary, the right hand digits will overflow past the right of the field. Similar rules apply to negative integers, except that the minus sign always appears to the immediate left of the most significant digit, replacing a space if there is one but otherwise forcing all the digits one space to the right.

It should be noted that all the digits (and the minus sign) of an integer are printed, if necessary over-riding the field width instruction. Apart from the obvious fact that any truncating of an integer would give an incorrect value, there is sometimes a further advantage in this.

```
WRITELN;
WRITELN (value1 : 1);
WRITELN (value2 : 1);
etc.
```

will print a list of values that will be left-justified; for example

```
1
12
123
1234
etc.
```

If a field width is *not* specified in a WRITE list for an integer value, then what is known as a *default field width* is used. The actual value of the default field width is implementation dependent.

It is now possible to modify the program of Exercise 2.2 further by the addition of field widths:

```
WRITE ('Miles = 0      yards =', yards : 5);
WRITE ('feet =' :9, feet : 2);
WRITELN ('inches =' :10, inches : 3)
```

to give an output

```
Miles = 0   yards =    9   feet = 1   inches =   9
```

Real numbers can be printed out in the floating point representation that we saw in the last chapter or in fixed point representation. In default of any field width parameters or with one such parameter,

$$\text{WRITE} (<\text{real value}> : <\text{total field width}>)$$

the output will be floating point. The details of floating point representation are implementation dependent. Therefore this book will not discuss width control with floating point. If you do need to control the width, your documentation should tell you how to do it.

Much more frequently, it is desired to output real values in fixed point representation. This is done by having *two* field width parameters, the first indicating total width and the second the number of digits after the decimal point, thus

$$\text{WRITE} (<\text{real value}> : <\text{total width}> : <\text{decimal width}>)$$

where <total width> includes character positions for the decimal point, a minus sign (if the value is less than zero) and at least one digit (which may be the character zero if appropriate) before the decimal point, and <decimal width> is an integer expression indicating the number (greater than zero) of digits required after the decimal point. Again this is easier to demonstrate than to describe. The examples in Table 3.2 use four values:

```
zero    (0.0)
pi      (π = 3.14159265)
ton     (kilogrammes per imperial ton = 1016.0469)
pound   (kilogrammes per imperial pound = 0.45359237)
```

Table 3.2

Statement				Output
1 WRITE ('zero	=',	zero	: 3 : 1)	zero =0.0
2 WRITE ('zero	=',	zero	: 7 : 5)	zero =0.00000
3 WRITE ('zero	=',	zero	: 10 : 5)	zero = 0.00000
4 WRITE ('+pi	=',	pi	: 7 : 5)	+pi =3.14159
5 WRITE ('−pi	=',	−pi	: 7 : 5)	−pi =−3.14159
6 WRITE ('+pi	=',	pi	: 8 : 5)	+pi = 3.14159
7 WRITE ('-pi	=',	−pi	: 8 : 5)	−pi =−3.14159
8 WRITE ('+pi	=',	pi	: 10 : 5)	+pi = 3.14159
9 WRITE ('−pi	=',	−pi	: 10 : 5)	−pi = −3.14159
10 WRITE ('+pi	=',	pi	: 5 : 3)	+pi =3.142
11 WRITE ('ton	=',	ton	: 5 : 3)	ton =1016.047
12 WRITE ('pound=',		pound	: 10 : 5)	pound = 0.45359
13 WRITE ('ton	=',	ton	: 10 : 5)	ton =1016.04690
14 WRITE ('ton	=',	ton	: 8 : 6)	ton =1016.049600
15 WRITE ('pound=',		pound	: 2 : 1)	pound =0.5
16 WRITE (' −pnd =',		−pound:	2 : 1)	−pnd =−0.5

There are various points to note about this representation:

(a) The number of digits written after the decimal point is always the number specified in the second (<decimal width>) field width parameter.

(b) The final printed digit in the decimal width is rounded up if the succeeding digit of the actual value is 5 or greater (examples 10, 11, 15 and 16).

(c) If, for any reason, the number of significant digits in the decimal width is less than the number specified, then the less significant places are infilled with zeros (examples 13 and 14; also 1, 2 and 3).

(d) If the specified <total width> is less than the width required for the complete representation of the <decimal width>, the decimal point and all preceding characters (including the minus sign where appropriate), then the whole representation is shifted enough positions to the right for its value to be correctly displayed (examples 5, 11 and 13).

(e) Irrespective of the value of <total width> there will always be one digit to the left of the decimal point together with the minus sign if appropriate (examples 15 and 16).

Field width parameters can also be used for strings:

WRITE (<string> : <total width>)

If no field width parameter is given, then <total width> is assumed to have a value equal to the number of characters in the string. If the value of <total width> is greater than the number of characters in the string, then the string characters will be preceded by enough spaces to make up the value. If the value of <total width> is less than the number in the string, then the number of characters, starting with the first, output will be the same as the value. The remainder will be skipped over. Again we have some examples but this time the output is printed immediately below the instruction:

```
WRITE ('String of 23 characters')
String of 23 characters

WRITE ('String of 23 characters' : 43)
                        String of 23 characters

WRITE ('String of 23 characters' :23)
String of 23 characters

WRITE ('String of 23 characters' :19)
String of 23 charact
```

Because a computer is of finite size, it is necessary for the designers to put a limit to the size of numbers which it can handle. If you did the exercise at the end of the last chapter and managed to get a result, it will most likely have been a number such as 32767, 8388607 or something larger. This is because MAXINT is a standard Pascal constant identifier. In any given implementation its value is that of the largest positive integer permitted in that implementation.

Any given implementation will handle integers in the range −MAXINT < 0 < + MAXINT. If, at any time during the execution of a program, the absolute value (the largest value irrespective of sign) of an integer variable exceeds MAXINT, an error message will be displayed and the execution will usually be aborted. This can sometimes happen unexpectedly, as Exercise 3.1 at the end of this chapter is intended to demonstrate.

Real numbers, too, have an implementation-dependent maximum (absolute) value and also a minimum (absolute) non-zero value. The documentation should tell you what these are, but there is another way to find out, as you will see in Exercise 3.2 at the end of this chapter.

3.3 THE FOR LOOP

The programs given in the last chapter were simple 'straight through' programs. The statements were executed, each in turn, in the order in which they had been written. However, one of the major strengths of a computer is its ability to repeat selected statements with different data. One of several *iterative structures* in Pascal is the **FOR** statement or **FOR** 'loop'. The **FOR** statement has the construction

FOR <control var> : = <expr> **TO** <expr> **DO** <statement>

where <control var> is any variable of a type other than real. (Later, we shall be meeting types of variable other than integer and real. Until then, a non-real variable may be considered as being an integer variable.) In each case < expr > is any expression that can be evaluated into a value of the same type as the control variable. <statement> may be any statement. It may thus be a simple statement, a compound statement or another **FOR** statement.

To demonstrate the use of the **FOR** statement, let us look at a slightly simplified version of the task which is carried out every week by thousands of computers all over the world – the compilation of employees' weekly pay.

Let us assume that a certain company has one hundred employees whose gross pay each week is the product of their wage rate multiplied by the hours they have worked. Let us further assume that not all the employees have the same wage rate, nor do they all work the same number of hours. The following program will calculate the weekly pay packet for each employee and at the same time keep a running total of the total company payroll.

```
1    PROGRAM Payroll (INPUT, OUTPUT);
2
3    (* Program to calculate weekly paypacket of  *
4     * each of 100 employees from hours worked    *
5     * and hourly rates. It also keeps a running  *
6     * total displayed at the end of the program  *
7     *            as Total Payroll.               *)
8    VAR hours, wageRate, weeksPay,
                                 total : REAL;
9        num (* employee's number *) : INTEGER;
10
11   BEGIN
12     total := 0;
13     FOR num := 1 TO 100 DO
14     BEGIN
15       WRITE ('Number', num :4, ' Hours? ');
16       READ (hours);
17       WRITE ('Rate? ' : 18);
18       READ (wageRate);
19       weeksPay := hours * wageRate;
20       WRITE ('The pay for number',num :4);
21       WRITELN (' is  £', weeksPay :7 :2);
```

```
22      total := total + weeksPay
23    END;
24    WRITELN;
25    WRITELN
          (' Total wages for week = £', total :9 :2)
26 END.
```

At line 13 we have the **FOR** statement, whose effect will be more readily understood when we have seen the kind of results we might obtain from it.

```
Number     1  Hours? 39.5€
              Rate? 2.86€
The Pay for Number    1 is £ 112.97
Number     2  Hours? 41.0€
              Rate? 2.60€
The Pay for Number    2 is £ 106.60
Number     3  Hours? 40.75€
              Rate? 3.0€
The Pay for Number    3 is £ 122.25
Number     4  Hours? 38.0€
              Rate? 2.50€
The Pay for Number    4 is £  95.00
                    .
                    .
                    .
Number    99  Hours? 22.0€
              Rate? 2.55€
The Pay for Number   99 is £  56.10
Number   100  Hours? 41.5€
              Rate? 3.10€
The Pay for Number  100 is £ 128.65

   Total wages for week = £ 10523.42
```

A glance at the program will show that the compound statement bounded by **BEGIN** at line 14 and **END** at line 23 has been repeated 100 times under the instruction of the **FOR** statement in line 13.

When the **FOR** statement is first encountered, the control variable takes the value of the first expression. Each time the loop is completed, the control variable is *incremented* (increased by 1) and the loop is followed again using the new value of the control variable until the control variable exceeds the second expression. A study of the above program and the results should make this clear.

There are two special cases to be considered. The first is where the two expressions are equal when the **FOR** statement is encountered for the first time. In this case the loop is performed once only, because the next time the control variable will exceed the second expression. The second special case occurs if, on first encounter, the first expression already exceeds the second. In this case the loop will not be executed at all and the computer will run on to the next statement after the loop.

In addition to the **FOR** ... **TO** ... **DO** statement described above, there is another, the **FOR** ... **DOWNTO** ... **DO** statement:

FOR $<$cntrl var$>$: = $<$expr$>$ **DOWNTO** $<$expr$>$ **DO** $<$statement$>$

In this type of **FOR** statement the control variable is *decremented* each time until it is *less than* the second expression. With these two exceptions it is identical to the **FOR** ... **TO** ... **DO** statement. For example

FOR *year* : = 1983 **DOWNTO** 1945 **DO** $<$statement$>$

There are two important points to be made about control variables:

(a) The first is that there must be no program statement within the **FOR** loop that affects the value of the control variable. In other words the control variable must not appear, within the loop, either on the left hand side of an assignment statement or in a READ statement.

(b) Secondly, it is important to note that after the loop has been executed with its final value, the value of the control variable is undefined. This variable must not be used again until it has been assigned a new value.

There are two other points of interest in the above *payroll* program. The first is the instruction in line 12, *total : = 0*. If *total* had had a value other than zero when the statement in line 21 was executed for the first employee, then this value would have been included in the result and the final value of *total* would have been incorrect. The value of any variable is undefined until it has had an actual value assigned to it. Until then the location allocated to it may still contain the residue of a previous program, or it might even have been used for some other purpose in the current program. Thus the initial setting of any variable is essential. This can easily be overlooked before a **FOR** statement.

The second point of interest is the 'empty' WRITELN statement in line 24. This statement is included to help the layout of the results. It prints a blank line before *Total wages* ... to separate it from the previous list and thus improves the readability of the print-out. You may like to examine how a similar WRITELN after line 21 might also improve the layout.

3.4 NESTING OF LOOPS

The following program will write the square of the first twenty integers:

```
PROGRAM Squares (OUTPUT);

VAR number : INTEGER;
```

```
BEGIN
   WRITELN;
   WRITELN ('The square of');
   FOR number := 1 TO 20 DO
      WRITELN
            (number : 2, ' is', (number * number) :4)
END.
```

It will give the following output:

```
The square of
 1 is   1
 2 is   4
 3 is   9
 4 is  16
      .
      .
      .
17 is 289
18 is 324
19 is 361
20 is 400
```

We may prefer to display the results across the screen instead of vertically below each other. The following program will do this:

```
PROGRAM DisplayAcross (OUTPUT);

VAR
   line, position, number : INTEGER;

BEGIN
   WRITELN;
   WRITELN ('The square of');
   FOR line := 0 TO 4 DO
   BEGIN
      FOR position := 1 TO 4 DO
      BEGIN
         number := line * 4 + position;
         WRITE (number :2, ' =',
                     (number * number) :4,'      ')
      END;
      WRITELN
   END
END.
```

This program gives the following output:

```
The square of
 1 =    1        2 =    4        3 =    9        4 =   16
 5 =   25        6 =   36        7 =   49        8 =   64
 9 =   81       10 =  100       11 =  121       12 =  144
13 =  169       14 =  196       15 =  225       16 =  256
17 =  289       18 =  324       19 =  361       20 =  400
```

Not only does this example demonstrate the use of nested loops, but it also shows how output can be neatly laid out using Pascal constructions.

EXERCISES

3.1   Try the following program:

```
1     PROGRAM Exercise31 (OUTPUT);
2
3     CONST
4       k = 9999;
5
6     VAR
7       a, b, c : INTEGER;
8
9     BEGIN
10      b := MAXINT - 100;
11      c := MAXINT - 99;
12      a := b - c + k;
13      WRITELN (a)
14    END.
```

When you have tried this program, try altering the statement in line 12 to

$$a := k + b - c;$$

and running the program again. You should get a different response. Why?

3.2   Now try these two programs:

```
PROGRAM Exercise32a (OUTPUT);

VAR
  a : REAL;
  n : INTEGER;

BEGIN
  a := 1.0;
  FOR n := 0 TO 300 DO
  BEGIN
    WRITELN (n, a);
    a := a * 2
  END
END.
```

```
PROGRAM Exercise32b (OUTPUT);

VAR
  a : REAL;
  n : INTEGER;
```

```
BEGIN
  a := 1.0;
  FOR n := 0 DOWNTO -300 DO
  BEGIN
    WRITELN (n, a);
    a := a / 2
  END
END.
```

Run these two programs and decide what, if anything, they teach you about your implementation?

3.3 In many computer games the computer works so fast that it is necessary to introduce a delay into the program. The **FOR** loop in the following program gives such a delay.

```
PROGRAM delay (OUTPUT);

CONST
  timeconst = 32000;

VAR
  n, a : INTEGER;

BEGIN
  WRITELN ('start');
  FOR n := 0 TO timeconst DO
    a := n; (* Dummy statement.
              Does nothing but fill in time *)
  WRITELN ('stop')
END.
```

Run the above program and note the time interval between the appearance of *start* and *stop*. How can this delay be (a) shortened, (b) made a thousand times as long on an implementation where **MAXINT** is 32767 and (c) made variable in duraction once it has been compiled?

CHAPTER 4

PRECEDENCE OF OPERATIONS. MORE LOOPS

4.1 PRECEDENCE

In Chapter 2 we listed some of the arithmetical operators which are used in Pascal. They can apply to both constants and variables and some of them (+, −, *) are applicable to constants and variables of type real or of type integer while others are restricted to type real (/) or to type integer (**DIV, MOD**). Pascal, in common with most other high level languages, awards precedence to multiplication and division operations over those of addition and subtraction. Those with higher precedence are all performed before those with lower precedence. These rules (and one or two others which we shall meet later) are very simple but, as they are different from those of many pocket calculators, they can be a bit confusing at first. For example

$$2 + 3 * 4$$

gives 14 in Pascal since the multiplication takes precedence and will be performed before the addition. On many pocket calculators the result would have been 20. Similarly

$$12 - 6 \text{ DIV } 3$$

will give 10 in Pascal, not 2.

Where there are two operators of the same precedence in an expression, then the pocket calculator rules are followed: the leftmost is performed first or, if you prefer it, the calculation is performed in the order in which it is written. The technical description of this is *left associative*. Thus

$$3.0 / 6.0 * 2.0$$

gives the result 1.0 and not 0.25. Normally the order in which addition and subtraction are performed makes no difference to the result, but it can be important when dealing with large numbers. The fact that there is a maximum value for integer numbers has already been discussed in the last chapter. Exercise 3.1 at the end of that chapter was designed to demonstrate that it is possible to exceed the maximum permitted value unwittingly when interim values in a calculation are too big. You were asked to perform the same sum on two occasions but with the terms written in different orders. Provided that an implementation produces an answer that is in accordance with the above rules, it does not matter in which order it carries out the evaluation and we should not be concerned with the interim results. But if the implementation is consistent in its order, then it is probable that at one stage, in one of the examples, there would have been an interim value of

$$9999 + MAXINT$$

which we would expect to be too big for the implementation to handle and it could give an incorrect result or an error message 'INTEGER OVER-FLOW' or something similar. If you did get an incorrect result or an error message, then you should be aware of the possibility and take the pre-cautions described in the next paragraph. This applies to any large numbers that may give an interim result greater than MAXINT (or less than −MAX-INT). If you got a correct answer both times then you have probably no need to take precautions. This could be due to one of several reasons (indi-cating that the compiler is either not very efficient or it is super-efficient.)

There is a way in which the programmer can override the above rules or the vagaries of his compiler. That is by the use of brackets as in ordinary algebra or arithmetic. When an expression contains terms enclosed in brackets, the part enclosed in brackets is evaluated first, whatever the precedence of the operators. For example

$$2 * (5 - 4)$$

will give the result 2. Brackets can also be nested as

$$6 - (2 * (5 - 4))$$

to give 4. Whenever you have any doubt, it is always advisable to put brackets in your expressions. Doing so also has the desirable effect of reminding you, and anyone else who reads your program, what you intended. There is nothing wrong in having superfluous brackets in a program (the outer pair of brackets in the above expression are actually superfluous). One such place where brackets can be useful is where there is a risk of integer overflow. In the example we have already discussed

$$a := k + (b - c);$$

would ensure that the two large numbers are subtracted from each other first, to give a small number (in this case, 1) to be added to k.

Real numbers, too, have maximum absolute values, as Exercise 3.2 in the last chapter was designed to demonstrate. You probably got an overflow indication when n was approximately 126 or approximately 255, though if you got a different number it is not particularly significant. The value of a that you got just before overflow is, however, of significance as this is nearly the largest real number that your implementation will handle.

Furthermore, as we shall shortly demonstrate, when real numbers are smaller than a certain (implementation-dependent) absolute value, the computer cannot distinguish them from zero.

These limitations must be borne in mind for all calculations, including intermediate calculations. In addition to the possibility of causing an overflow with large numbers, as in integer arithmetic, there is also the possibility of problems with very small real numbers. If a number has become so small that it is held in the computer as zero, an error will occur if an attempt is made to use it as a divisor.

Another iterative statement in Pascal is the **WHILE . . . DO** statement, the general representation of which is

$$\textbf{WHILE} < \text{expression} > \textbf{DO} < \text{statement} >$$

A typical way of using it might be in a different version of the delay routine that we met in the last chapter:

```
n := 0;
WHILE n < MAXINT DO n := n+1
```

The expression $n < MAXINT$ is what is sometimes called a *Boolean expression*† which can have one of two values only: *true* or *false*. In this case if n is less than MAXINT then the expression is true, but if n is equal to, or greater than, MAXINT, then the expression is false. So long as the expression after **WHILE** is true then the statement after **DO** will be repeated. The sign '$<$' meaning 'is less than' is known as a *relational operator*. Six different relational operators are allowed in Boolean expressions in Pascal. They are

$<$	is less than
$=$	is equal to
$>$	is greater than
$<=$	is less than or equal to
$>=$	is greater than or equal to
$<>$	is not equal to

†After George Boole, a British mathematician of the nineteenth century.

With the exception of '=', which also occurs in other contexts, the use of these relational operators is limited to Boolean expressions but, as we shall see, Boolean expressions are not confined to **WHILE** statements.

The following program is designed to show what is the smallest positive real number that your computer is able to distinguish from zero.

```
PROGRAM SmallestReal (OUTPUT);

CONST
   initialNumber = 1;
   divisor = 2;
VAR
   number, previousNumber : REAL;

BEGIN
   number := initialNumber;
   WHILE number > 0 DO
   BEGIN
      previousNumber := number;
      number := number / divisor
   END;
   WRITELN ('The value of number now is', number);
   WRITELN ('The previous number was',
                             previousNumber)
END.
```

The **WHILE** statement will be repeated until the value of *number* becomes so small that it can only be represented in the computer by zero. The value of *previousNumber* will be very close to the smallest number that your implementation will handle. If you are curious enough to want to find it more accurately, you can run the program again, changing the constants so that *initialNumber* is the value you obtained from the previous run and *divisor* is progressively reduced to 1.1, 1.01, 1.001, etc., but be very careful! As the decimal part of the divisor becomes smaller and smaller, a point will be reached when *divisor* will be represented in the computer as 1.0 and the program will enter an infinite loop.

4.2 REPEAT STATEMENTS

There is another Pascal statement that is very similar to the **WHILE** statement. It takes the form

REPEAT <statement> **UNTIL** <Boolean expression>.

There are two main differences between the two instructions, **WHILE** and **REPEAT**. One is a matter of syntax. **REPEAT** and **UNTIL** act as brackets in the same way as **BEGIN** and **END** do. Therefore any number of statements may appear in a **REPEAT** loop and it is not necessary to mark its start and finish with **BEGIN** and **END**. The **WHILE** statement, on the other hand, controls only one statement. If more than one statement is required in a **WHILE** loop, they must be formed into one *compound statement*, suitably bracketed.

The other main difference between the two types of loops is that in the **WHILE** loop the condition of the Boolean expression is tested *before* the loop is entered, whereas in the **REPEAT** loop the expression is tested *after* execution of the loop. Therefore a **REPEAT** loop will always be executed at least once, even if the condition is false at the start.

As an example of the use of the **REPEAT** statement, let us look again at the *Payroll* program of the last chapter. In that program, you will remember, we made the assumption that there were exactly 100 employees and that their clock numbers ran from 1 to 100. Of course, this never happens in practice. Employees leave, others join and it is often the practice to let the clock number of a departing employee lie in abeyance while a new employee is given a number which is one higher than the last employee that joined. Thus in a factory of 100 employees (more or less) the clock numbers may range from single figures to 1000 or more. Furthermore, since the computer can be programmed to sort the entries into numerical order, as we shall see later in Chapter 10, it is a waste of clerical effort to have them manually sorted beforehand. Thus we want a program that will accept an input of

clock number, hours, rate

for each employee with the clock numbers in any sequence.

We are going to replace the **FOR** loop of the original program with a **REPEAT** loop. This introduces a minor problem that must be resolved before we rewrite the program. Previously, execution of the program was finished after the 100th entry since we knew that there were exactly 100 employees. Now we know that there are approximately 100 employees, so how is the program to know when all the entries have been keyed in, if the total number of entries can vary? The usual way is to have a dummy clock number, a number that is not allocated to any employee but which gives the computer the message 'there are no more entries this week'. Since it is seldom common practice to allocate the number zero to any employee, zero is often used as the dummy or *marker*.

The following program will meet our requirements, using zero as a marker.

```
PROGRAM Payroll2 (INPUT, OUTPUT);

(*   Modification of original 'Payroll' program   *
 *   to allow entries to be made in any sequence,  *
 *        using clock number 'zero' as an          *
 *           'end of entries' marker.              *)
```

```
VAR
     hours, wageRate, weeksPay, total : REAL;
     num (* employee's number *)       : INTEGER;

BEGIN
  total := 0;
  WRITELN
      ( 'Number   Hours   Wagerate      Week''s pay');
  WRITELN;
  REPEAT
    WRITE ('?');
    READ ( num, hours, wageRate );
    weeksPay := hours * wageRate;
    WRITELN (weeksPay :38 :2);
    total := total + weeksPay
  UNTIL num = 0 ;
  WRITELN ('----------' :38);
  WRITELN
      ('Total wages for week = £' :29, total :9 :2);
  WRITELN ('=========' :38)
END.
```

In this program, liberal use has been made of field width parameters. Their effect is shown in the following output:

```
Number  Hours  Wagerate      Week's pay

?27 39.5 2.86€
                                 112.97
?159 41.0 2.60€
                                 106.60
?83 40.75 3.0€
                                 122.25
    .                              .
    .                              .
    .                              .
?351 22.0 2.55€
                                  56.10
?427 41.5 3.10€
                                 128.65
?0 0 0€
                                   0.00
                              ---------
Total wages for week = £ 10523.42
                              =========
```

Note that in addition to entering the dummy clock number of zero, it is also necessary to enter dummy hours worked and a dummy hourly rate for this dummy employee, since the READ statement requires the three entries. Furthermore, note that at least one of the last two entries must also be zero, in order to make the week's pay zero for this dummy employee. If this were not done, a spurious additional wage packet would have been added to the total.

You should by now have had enough experience of loops to be able to follow the operation of the **REPEAT** loop with ease. It is quite straightforward and no further description is necessary.

The **FOR**, **WHILE** and **REPEAT** loops are the only types of loop normally available in Pascal. Very few problems that are worth the programming effort can be done without at least one of them and it is therefore important that you fully understand their operation.

4.3 IF STATEMENTS

Another frequently used statement in Pascal is the **IF** statement. This takes the general form

IF < Boolean expression > **THEN** < statement >

The difference between **WHILE** and **IF** is that whereas the former will reiterate the statement until the conditional expression is satisfied, the latter will not. If the expression following the **IF** is true, then the statement following **THEN** is executed (once only). If, on the other hand, the expression is false, then the statement is ignored and the computer follows on to the next instruction in the program. A couple of examples will explain this.

Suppose in the factory for which we have written the *Payroll* program, overtime is paid on all hours over 40 in one week and that the overtime rate of pay is one and a half times the normal rate. We could insert the following instruction immediately after reading in the hours, etc.:

IF hours > 40 **THEN** hours : = 40 + (hours − 40) * 1.5

The effect of this instruction, after multiplying the new value for hours by the rate, will be just the same as if we had multiplied the 40 hours by the standard rate and the balance of 1.5 times the standard rate.

The second example takes us to the heart of many programs written for games and statistics – the generation of random numbers. More correctly we should say *pseudo-random* or *quasi-random* numbers because normal digital computers cannot generate numbers strictly at random.† The random number generator we shall be describing produces pseudo-random numbers in the range from 1 to 9999 inclusive and works on the following algorithm:

† To ease the minds of holders of British Premium Bonds, it should be explained that ERNIE, the computer that picks the winners, works on a different principle and that its numbers *are* completely random! For a fuller discussion on random numbers, see Huggins (1979, Chapter 18).

Start with any number in the range from 1 to 10036 inclusive. This number is called the 'seed'. In practice the seed is often obtained from the computer's internal clock. One way is to record the time that elapses between first switching on the computer and the depression of the first key. As this time is measured in milliseconds and no human being can judge the time he presses a key to that sort of accuracy, the seed is reasonably random. If the number of milliseconds exceeds the upper limit set for the seed, then only the least significant digits of the time are used. Incidentally it is not desirable to generate subsequent random numbers from the clock, because the program is often running to a rhythm that is tied to the clock and the resulting numbers may not be sufficiently random, with reference to each other, for some purposes.

After that diversion, let us return to our random number generator. After obtaining the seed, it is doubled. If the result is greater than 10037, then 10037 is subtracted from it. The result then becomes the new seed for the next calculation of a random number. Since we do not want our number to be greater than 9999 we ignore any result that is greater than 9999 and immediately generate a new number. The following program will produce 9999 different numbers in a pseudo-random order, before it repeats them all over again. The seed in this case must be supplied manually.

```
PROGRAM Random (INPUT, OUTPUT);

CONST prime = 10037;
VAR start, seed, printPos : INTEGER;

BEGIN
  WRITE ('At what number do you want to start ?');
  READ ( start );
  seed := start;
  printPos := 0;
  WRITELN;
  REPEAT
    seed := seed * 2;
    seed := seed MOD prime;
    IF seed <= 9999 THEN
    BEGIN
      WRITE (seed :5);
      printPos := printPos + 1
    END;
    IF printPos MOD 10 = 0 THEN WRITELN
  UNTIL seed = start
END.
```

The following are the first six lines of output obtained from running this program:

```
At what number do you want to start ?7777←
```

5517	997	1994	3988	7976	5915	1793	3586	7172	4307
8614	7191	4345	8690	7343	4649	9298	8559	7081	4125
8250	6463	2889	5778	1519	3038	6076	2115	4230	8460
6883	3729	7458	4879	9758	9479	8921	7805	5573	1109
2218	4436	8872	7707	5377	717	1434	2868	5736	1435

Before leaving this program it is necessary to say a word about the significance of the value 10037 that has been given to the constant *prime*. This value has been chosen advisedly. It is, as indicated, a prime number, but it is also a prime number with special attributes, one of which is that when used in the above program it generates *every* number from 1 to its own predecessor, before repeating the cycle. It has also been chosen because it is the smallest such number which exceeds the upper limit (9999) of our desired sequence length, thus keeping the wastage of excess numbers to a minimum. If we had wanted a sequence length of 100 or only of 10, then we should have been luckier because both 101 and 11 are prime numbers with the required properties, and we should not have to insert the second **IF** instruction in the program. Such short sequence lengths are usually of little value for statistical work, or even for games, where the sequence order gets learnt (subconsciously, if not consciously) very quickly. If a number of only one or two digits is needed, then it is usually better to generate a four digit number from the above program and reduce it by a **MOD** 10 or **MOD** 100 instruction.

EXERCISES

4.1 Write a program to output the '*n*-times' multiplication tables in the following format which shows the first, last and two intermediate lines:

```
2 x   1 = 2        3 x   1 = 3        4 x   1 = 4
    .        .          .        .          .        .
2 x  12 = 24       3 x  12 = 36       4 x  12 = 48

5 x   1 = 5        6 x   1 = 6        7 x   1 = 7
    .        .          .        .          .        .
8 x  12 = 96       9 x  12 = 108     10 x  12 = 108
```

Note that both the multiplier and the multiplicand are *right-justified* (their right hand digits are vertically in line) whereas the product is to be *left-justified* with only one space between it and the '=' sign.

4.2 In the program *Payroll2*, the printing of the dummy numbers (0, 0, 0, 0.00) is untidy. It is possible to rewrite the above program so that, once clock number *zero* is entered, no further entries are needed and the writing of 0.00 for the week's pay for the final entry is suppressed. This can be done in at least three different ways, using respectively **WHILE**, **REPEAT** and **IF** constructions. What are they?

4.3 The random numbers generated by the *Random* program contain some long sequences of doubled numbers (for example 1 2 4 8 16 32 64 126 etc.) which may be unacceptable in some applications. By selecting only every nth new seed generated it is possible to break up such sequences. Provided that n is not a factor of 10036 there will be no reduction in the total sequence length but the program will take longer to run, by a factor of approximately n. Modify the program so that only every seventh new seed is actually output, retaining 9999 as the upper limit.

CHAPTER 5

APPLICATIONS 1:
MATHEMATICS

□ This chapter is the first of several 'applications' chapters that will be introduced at various stages through the book. No new principles or features of the Pascal language are introduced in any of them. Their purpose is to cater for certain specialist requirements; for example this chapter discusses some mathematical aspects of the language covered to date. Those who do not wish to use computers for mathematics may safely go straight to Chapter 6. □

5.1 SERIES

The evaluation of series is an obvious task for a computer provided that some of the pitfalls are avoided. Let us start with an easy one. The following evaluates e, the base of Naierian or natural logarithms, to the accuracy that your implementation will allow:

```
PROGRAM Napierian (OUTPUT);
VAR
   cum, difference : REAL;
   n : INTEGER;

BEGIN
   cum := 1;
   difference := 1;
   n := 1;
   WHILE difference <> 0 DO
   BEGIN
      difference := difference / n;
      cum := cum + difference;
      n := n + 1;
   END;
   WRITELN ('e is ', cum)
END.
```

This is straightforward because the series converges quite rapidly. If you want to see how many times the **WHILE** loop is repeated you can add a *WRITE (n)* statement at the end of the loop.

The following program would evaluate the series

$$1 - 1/2 + 1/3 - 1/4 + 1/5 - 1/6 + \ldots \text{etc.}$$

which is the formula for ln 2, the Napierian logarithm of 2, to four decimal places:

```
PROGRAM logarithm1 (OUTPUT);

VAR
  logn, term : REAL;
  sign, n : INTEGER;

BEGIN
  logn := 0;
  sign := 1;
  n := 1;
  term := 1;
  WRITELN ('     n       logn        term');
  WHILE term >= 0.00001 DO
  BEGIN
    term := 1 / n;
    logn := logn + term * sign;
    WRITELN (n, logn, term);
    n := n + 1;
    sign := - sign
  END
END.
```

You are not encouraged to try this program if processing time has to be paid for or if someone else is waiting to use the computer. The **WHILE** loop will have to be iterated 100 000 times, which may take over an hour on a small computer! There is a faster method of arriving at the same result, as we shall see shortly. But before we leave this program, you should note the method that is used to get alternate addition and subtraction of the difference. This is a useful device which is often met in programs that evaluate series.

Most mathematical textbooks show how to manipulate a slowly converging series into one that converges more rapidly. One formula often used in computers to obtain Napierian logarithms is

$$\ln a = 2y + 2y^3/3 + 2y^5/5 + \ldots$$

where $y = (a - 1)/(a + 1)$. This is the formula used in the following program.

```
PROGRAM Logarithm2 (INPUT, OUTPUT);
VAR
  a, y, numerator, denominator,
          difference, cum : REAL;
```

```
BEGIN
  WRITE ('Number ? ');
  READ (a);
  y := (a-1) / (a+1);
  numerator := 2 * y;
  denominator := 1;
  difference := numerator / denominator;
  cum := 0;
  WHILE difference <> 0 DO
  BEGIN
    cum := cum + difference;
    numerator := numerator * y * y;
    denominator := denominator + 2;
    difference := numerator / denominator
  END;
  WRITELN
        ('The natural logarithm of', a, ' is', cum);
END.
```

This program is executed reasonably rapidly for small values of y, but the nearer the absolute value of y approaches unity, the longer it will take. For values of a between 1 ($y = 0$) and e ($y = 0.462$) or between 1 and 1/e ($y = -0.462$), the decay of *difference* is quite rapid, but for larger values an alternative strategy must be used. A logarithm consists of a fractional part or *mantissa* and an integer part or *characteristic*. The characteristic of a Napierian logarithm of a number, a, can be described as the number of times that a may be successively divided by e until the result becomes less than e. The mantissa is then the logarithm of that result. An algorithm to achieve this appears in the program below.

Meanwhile, there is another point arising from the above program which should be considered. If you try this program with e as the input you may well find, depending on your implementation, that the answer you get is just less than 1. This is due to rounding errors when adding small numbers to large ones. The computer will work to a finite number of significant digits. In practice these digits are usually binary digits, but the effect can be demonstrated in decimal. Suppose, to make the example simple, we had a computer operating to only four decimal digits, then we should have the following addition steps:

$$
\begin{array}{r}
0.9242 \\
0.06679 \\
\hline
0.9900 \\
0.008430 \\
\hline
0.9984 \\
0.001285 \\
\hline
\end{array}
$$

0.9997

0.0002135

0.9999

0.00003732

0.9999

0.000006743

0.9999

The addition of further terms would not affect the result. Let us now reverse the process:

0.000006743

0.00003732

0.00004406

0.0002136

0.0002577

0.001286

0.001544

0.008430

0.009974

0.06579

0.07576

0.9242

1.0000

These two aspects, ensuring a rapid convergence and avoiding rounding errors, are both covered in the following program:

```
PROGRAM Logarithm3 (INPUT, OUTPUT);

CONST e = 2.71828;

VAR
  a, x, numerator,
  bal, difference, cum : REAL;
  n, denominator, characteristic : INTEGER;

BEGIN
  WRITE ('Number ? ');
  READ (a);
  characteristic := 0;
  bal := a;
  WHILE bal > e DO
```

```
BEGIN
  bal := bal / e;
  characteristic := characteristic + 1
END;
WHILE bal < 1 DO
BEGIN
  bal := bal * e;
  characteristic := characteristic - 1
END;
x := (bal-1) / (bal+1);
numerator := 2 * x;
denominator := 1;
cum := 0;
REPEAT
  numerator := numerator * x * x;
  denominator := denominator + 2;
  difference := numerator / denominator;
UNTIL difference = 0;
WHILE denominator >= 1 DO
  BEGIN
    cum := cum + numerator / denominator;
    numerator := numerator / (x * x);
    denominator := denominator - 2;
  END;
  WRITELN ('The natural logarithm of', a, ' is',
                  characteristic + cum)
END.
```

Of course, you are unlikely to need to use a program written in Pascal for the calculation of logarithms, since there is a standard function, LN (see Chapter 7), in the Pascal language, and on most implementations this will be executed in machine language which will be far faster than compiled Pascal. However, it is worth while studying these programs because the lessons to be learnt from them apply to series generally.

5.2 OTHER ITERATIONS

The evaluation of series is one example of the way in which the high computational speed of a computer can relieve the monotony of repeated re-calculation. In fact this high speed has brought a new lease of life to mathematical methods that previously either had a largely academic interest or were considered to be 'methods of last resort'. An example is the finding of the roots of an equation or of the zero of a function.

Where it is convenient to find the first differential of a function, the Newton-Raphson method (described in many books on applied calculus) can be used. This method says, in effect, the following:

If x_n is a good approximation to the value of x when $f(x)$ is zero, then x_{n+1} is a better one where

$$x_{n+1} = x_n + \delta x$$

and

$$\delta x = -(f(x))/(f'(x))$$

Let us illustrate this with a specific example. Let us find the root of the equation

$$x^3 + 13.7x - 21 = 0.$$

We can define the following REAL variables for a Pascal program: *xn* is the approximate value of *x* at any given moment; *functXN* is the value of the expression, $x^3 + 13.7x - 21$, when *xn* is substituted for *x*; *diffXN* is the first differential of the same expression with *xn* substituted for *x*. We can now incorporate them in the following program:

```
PROGRAM NewtonRaphson (INPUT,OUTPUT);

VAR xn, functXN, diffXN, delta, epsilon : REAL;
    n, places : INTEGER;

BEGIN
  WRITE ('How many places of decimals?');
  READ (places);
  epsilon := 0.1;
  FOR n := 1 TO places DO
                        epsilon := epsilon / 10;
  xn := 1  (* first guess *);
  REPEAT
    functXN := (xn * xn * xn) + 13.7 * xn - 21;
    diffXN := 3 * (xn * xn) + 10;
    delta := - functXN / diffXN;
    xn := xn + delta
  UNTIL ABS(delta) < epsilon;
  WRITELN ('Root is ',xn :15 :places)
END.
```

Sometimes it is convenient to rearrange the expressions to make the problem more easily manageable. For example,

$$x^2 = k$$

is better rearranged as

$$x^2 - k = 0$$

As an exercise you can rewrite the *NewtonRaphson* program to give the square root of *k*. Once again, you would not normally use this method to find a square root, since there is a standard Pascal function SQRT (see Chapter 7) which, being in machine code, operates faster, although it uses the same algorithm in most implementations. However, you may have to resort to a Pascal solution to find, say, the cube root of a number.

An alternative to the Newton-Raphson method, and one that is useful when the differential of the function is not easy to obtain, is the 'binary ranging' method. It is necessary first to decide what are the minimum and maximum values of x within which the root lies and what will be the sign of the function at each of these values. The function is then evaluated at a point half way between these two values. If the sign of this evaluation is the same as, say, the minimum, the next evaluation will be undertaken with a value of x that is half way between the mid-point and the maximum (that is at the 'three-quarter' position). The process is repeated until x 'homes in' on the root. This condition is indicated when *delta* is so small that it not longer affects the result.

For example, examination of the following function shows that it is negative when $x = 0$ and positive when $x = 1$:

$$\frac{9x + 1}{2x^2 - x + 3} - 2$$

The following program will evaluate the function to three places of decimals:

```
PROGRAM BinaryRanging (INPUT, OUTPUT);

CONST epsilon = 0.0001;
      min = 0;
      max = 1;

VAR y, x, delta, d : REAL;

BEGIN
  delta := max - min;
  x := min;
  y := (9 * x + 1) / (2 * x * x - x + 3) - 2;
  WHILE delta > epsilon DO
  BEGIN
    delta := delta / 2;
    d := delta;
    IF y > 0 THEN d := - d;
    x := x + d;
(*       The last three statements could be         *)
(*    improved by using the ELSE construction       *)
(*             given later (Chapter 6)             *)
    y := (9 * x + 1) / (2 * x * x - x + 3)  - 2;
    WRITELN (x :7 :4)
  END;
  WRITELN ('Root is ', x :6 :3)
END.
```

It lists the successive steps as follows:

```
0.5000
0.7500
0.6250
0.5625
0.5938
0.5781
0.5703
0.5742
0.5762
0.5752
0.5747
0.5745
0.5746
0.5746
Root is   0.575
```

The examples in this chapter are simplified. There are many pitfalls for the unwary. For example, as it is written the program *NewtonRaphson* will not work if the first guess is negative nor will *BinaryRanging* if there is more than one root between the set limits. However, the objective of this chapter is not to give you definitive library programs, but rather to indicate certain principles which you can develop for further use.

CHAPTER 6

TYPES 'CHAR' AND 'BOOLEAN'. BOOLEAN OPERATORS

6.1 INTRODUCTION

So far, we have formally introduced two types of data. Both of them are numerical: INTEGER and REAL. We have also discussed and demonstrated the output of *strings* (or, to be more specific, *character strings*) of which *characters* are the single elements (letters of the alphabet, decimal digits 0-9, punctuation marks, mathematical signs and other symbols). The ability to handle characters and strings of characters is a powerful feature of computers. It makes word processing possible and it has many other uses. In fact the world's first digital electronic data processing machine, 'Colossus', designed by the British Post Office in 1943 to assist in cracking enemy codes, was a character processor and had no numerical computing facilities.

We shall be discussing the handling of strings in Chapter 10. For the present we shall be dealing with single characters. The range of different characters that any implementation can handle is called its *character set*. The *minimum* character set required for a Pascal implementation consists of the following items:

(a) the letters of the English alphabet either upper or lower case
(b) the ten decimal digits, 0 to 9
(c) punctuation marks . , : ;
(d) arithmetical operators + − * /
(e) relational operators = < >
(f) parenthesis brackets ( )
(g) apostrophe or single quote '
(h) up arrow ↑ or commercial *at* @
(i) Space or blank character.

In practice, the character sets available to most implementations are more extensive than the minimum. For example, many have both lower case and upper case letters.

Within the computer each character is represented by a discrete number. The actual code used to correlate each character with its internal representation is implementation dependent, although very many computers use the ASCII code or slight variants of it. ASCII (pronounced 'askey') stands for American Standard Code for Information Interchange and is listed in Appendix IV.

Standard Pascal does not require the use of this or any other specific code. It does, however, insist that the code used for certain characters shall bear certain relationships to each other. The rules are as follows:

(a) The internal representations of each of the digits '0' '1' '2' ... '8' '9' must all be related to each other so that the value of each is *one greater* than that of its predecessor in the list. Thus if the representation of the digit '0' is n, then the representation of the digit '1' must be $n + 1$ and the representation of the digit '7', say, must be $n + 7$.

(b) The representations of the upper case letters of the alphabet 'A' 'B' 'C' ... 'X' 'Y' 'Z' must bear such a relationship *to each other* that the value assigned to each letter is *greater* than that assigned to its predecessor in the alphabet, but it need not be contiguous. Thus, the representation of 'B' must be greater than the representation of 'A' but, if the representation of 'A' is n, then the representation of 'B' is not necessarily $n + 1$.

(c) The same rules apply to the representation of the lower case letters 'a' 'b' 'c' ... 'x' 'y' 'z' as apply to upper case.

It should be noted that these three groups are quite separate and that no group has any defined relationship to any other group.

We have already seen how a variable can be declared to have type INTEGER or type REAL. It can also be declared as a *character* variable of type CHAR.

The following program shows how single characters may be input and output:

```
PROGRAM Characters (INPUT, OUTPUT);

VAR
   ch : CHAR;
BEGIN
   WRITELN ('Write a message');
   REPEAT
     READ (ch);
     WRITE (ch)
   UNTIL ch = '.'
END.
```

The actual output that you will get from running this program will depend on your implementation, but it should show you how a single character can be read and immediately rewritten.

If we wish to refer to a specific character within the program text, then we do so by placing the character within single quotes, 'A' or 'f' or '5', for example. We treat it, in effect, as a string of a single character, which is exactly what it is. Any character of the available character set may thus be represented in single quotes (for example '+' '.' '>') but if the character to be so represented is a single quote itself, we must do this by repeating it, so that we get ' ' ' '.

Characters and strings may be treated as constants. The program

```
PROGRAM CharString (OUTPUT);

CONST
        firstLetter = 'A';
        lastLetter  = 'Z';
        quote       = '''';
        string      =
                ' is the first letter and the last is ';

BEGIN
   WRITELN (quote, firstLetter,
                           quote, string, '''Z.''');
   WRITELN ('A', string, lastLetter)
END.
```

produces the following output:

```
'A' is the first letter and the last is 'Z.'
A is the first letter and the last is Z
```

It is important to appreciate the difference between '3' as a CHAR variable, and 3 as an INTEGER or REAL variable. They are quite different. The following program fragment will help to show the difference:

```
VAR number : REAL;
   digit1, digit2, digit3 : CHAR;
. . . .
 WRITELN ('Write three digits');
 READ (digit1, digit2, digit3);
 WRITELN ('Write a number');
 READ (number);
 WRITELN;
 WRITE ('digit1 = ', digit1, '  digit2 = ', digit2);
 WRITELN ('  digit3 = ', digit3,
                    '  number = ', number :3 :1)
. . . .
```

If, in response to the two READ instructions, we keyed in *2.7* (characters *two, full-stop, seven*) on both occasions, the output would be

```
digit1 = 2  digit2 = .  digit3 = 7  number = 2.7
```

There are occasions when it is desirable to know or find out the actual value that is used for representing a CHAR type within the computer. This can be done by means of the function ORD. 'ORD' is an abbreviation for *ordinal* and, when applied to a character, gives the ordinal position (an integer value) that character has in the character set. For example, in the ASCII character set (Appendix IV) the value of ORD ('A') is 65 and of ord ('2') is 50.

There is another function, CHR, that operates in the opposite way.

$$CHR (<\text{integer expression}>)$$

will give the character whose ordinal position is the specified integer value, provided that such character exists. Thus in the ASCII character set CHR (65) is 'A' and CHR (50) is '2'. Hence CHR (ORD ('A')) is 'A' and ORD (CHR (65)) is 65.

In the ASCII character set, where all the letters in upper case and lower case are respectively contiguous to each other, or in other any character set where upper and lower case letters bear the same ordinal relation relationship to each other, these functions can be used to convert one case to the other, thus (where *ch* is a CHAR variable)

```
READ (ch);
IF (ch >= 'a') AND (ch <= 'z') THEN
    ch := CHR ( ORD (ch) + ORD ('A') - ORD ('a'))
```

6.2 BOOLEAN OPERATORS

This last program fragment introduced a new Pascal reserved word, **AND**. AND is called a *Boolean operator*. The statement says, in effect, perform the operation if, and only if, it is true that *ch* is 'a' or greater *and* it is *also* true that *ch* is 'z' or less.

Another such Boolean operator is **OR**. Suppose that, having read a character, we want to ensure that it was an upper case letter. We could have the following statements:

```
READ (ch);
IF (ch < 'A') OR (ch > 'Z') THEN
    WRITE ('Error')
```

There is a third Boolean operator in Pascal, **NOT**, whose use is demonstrated in the next fragment:

```
WRITELN ('Do you want to play this game?');
WRITELN ('Answer ''Y'' for yes, ''N'' for no');
READ (reply);
IF NOT ((reply = 'Y')
                    OR (reply = 'N')) THEN
    WRITE ('Bad reply')
```

The above **IF** statement could also have been written as

```
IF (reply <> 'Y')
              AND (reply <> 'N') THEN
  etc.
```

It is a matter of personal preference which is used. Boolean statements are sometimes hard to follow, especially when there are two or more negatives. Their correctness can readily be checked by examining what happens when the individual expressions are true and false. Suppose, in the last example, that the letter 'A' is entered where 'Y' or 'N' is expected. The variable *reply* will have the value 'A'. Therefore the expressions *(reply < > 'Y')* and *(reply < > 'N')* are both true, the **IF** condition is satisfied and the error message is output. If 'Y' or 'N' is keyed, then one of these expressions will be false and so will the **IF** condition. The input would thus be accepted. You can subject the **NOT** version to similar reasoning.

AND, **OR** and **NOT** are the only Boolean operators used in Pascal.

Let us now introduce a diversion. Suppose that we wish the computer to simulate a roulette wheel. Roulette is a game of chance in which a ball rattles around in a wheel that is spinning. When the wheel comes to a halt, the ball drops into one of 37 compartments (numbered from 0 to 36). Anyone who has bet on the winning number gets paid 36 times the amount he has staked. No bets are permitted on zero. The banker always wins when the ball lands on zero.

Simulation of a roulette wheel on the computer is very easy. We use the random number generator of the last chapter, modified as in Exercise 4.3, together with the necessary input and output statements.

The steps in the program are as follows:

(1) Send message 'Are you ready to start?'
(2) Check that answer is either 'yes' or 'no'. If not, demand repeat.
(3) If answer is 'no' then repeat steps (1) and (2).
(4) Introduce delay (if desired).
(5) Generate a random number in the range from 0 to 36.
(6) Display the winning number.
(7) Introduce further delay (if desired).
(8) Send message 'Do want you to play again?'
(9) Check that answer is either 'yes' or 'no'. If not, demand repeat.
(10) If the answer is 'yes', then repeat steps (4)–(10).
(11) Otherwise end the game.

The delays are not essential to the game and are omitted in the following program:

```
PROGRAM Roulette (INPUT,OUTPUT);

CONST prime = 10037;
        limit = 10027;
               (* max random number = 10026*)
        skip = 7;
               (* accept every seventh number *)
(* The above are used by
                    the random number generator *)

VAR number, seed, n : INTEGER;
            reply : CHAR;

BEGIN
  WRITE ('What is the starting seed (1 to 9999)');
  READ (seed);
  REPEAT
    WRITE ('Are you ready to start?  Y or N ');
    REPEAT
      READ (reply);
    (* Convert reply to upper case if necessary *)
      IF reply = 'y' THEN reply := 'Y';
      IF reply = 'n' THEN reply := 'N';
      IF (reply <> 'Y') AND (reply <> 'N')
          THEN WRITE ('Bad Reply.  Enter Again');
    UNTIL (reply = 'Y') OR (reply = 'N')
  UNTIL reply = 'Y';
  REPEAT
    REPEAT  (* generate random numbers,
                                  0 to 36 *)

      FOR n := 1 TO skip DO
      BEGIN
        seed := seed * 2;
        seed := seed MOD prime
      END
    UNTIL seed < limit;
    number := seed  MOD 37;
    WRITELN ( 'The winning number is ', number);
    WRITE ('Do you want to play again?');
    REPEAT
      READ (reply);
      IF reply = 'y' THEN reply := 'Y';
      IF reply = 'n' THEN reply := 'N';
      IF (reply <> 'Y') AND (reply <> 'N')
          THEN WRITE ('Bad Reply.  Enter Again');
    UNTIL (reply = 'Y') OR (reply = 'N');
    IF reply = 'Y' THEN
          WRITELN ('Starting again')
          ELSE WRITELN ('Thank you for playing')
  UNTIL reply = 'N'
END.
```

You will see that several constants have been declared at the head of this program. This is not essential to the operation of the program, but it has two advantages. The first is that it makes for clarity when reading the program. It avoids a lot of head scratching when later encountering, for example, the number 10037 in the program and wondering why it is there. To demonstrate this, the number 37 has been left in the body of the program. Reading it now, it is obvious, because we have just been discussing it, that 37 is the number of compartments in the roulette wheel, but it might not be so obvious later. For this reason it is also useful to expand on the significance of constants by comments, as in this example.

Another good reason for bringing constants to the head of the program is that it makes any subsequent change to their values much easier, especially if they are used more than once in the program.

You may wonder why the limit has been raised to 10027. This is because later in the program we are going to divide the value of *seed* by 37, and use the remainder as our *number*. To make sure that every number has an equal chance of turning up, the *limit* must be a multiple of 37, and 10027 is the highest such multiple that is less than *prime*.

Before going further, let us admit at once that there is one major strategic shortcoming in the above program – the way of entering the starting seed. In Chapter 4 it was suggested that the best way of initialising *seed* was to obtain a completely arbitrary number from the computer's internal clock. Many implementations of Pascal include facilities for gaining access to this clock from a Pascal program, but the standard language gives no such facility. So we have to use the only method that the standard language allows – to enter the starting seed manually from the keyboard. An unscrupulous player could quickly learn the sequence that followed from several different starting seeds and turn the knowledge to his advantage. The author disclaims any responsibility for consequential losses resulting from use of this program!

The objective of this program, however, is not to encourage gambling, whether straight or crooked, but to demonstrate some of the features that we have been discussing and to introduce a new one.

This new feature is the **ELSE** that forms part of the final **IF** statement. Its use in this context should be fairly obvious. It gives an alternative line of action. If the condition following the **IF** is satisfied, then we write 'Starting again', but if it is not satisfied, then we write 'Thank you for playing'. We could have achieved the same result in a different way:

```
IF reply = 'Y' THEN
    WRITELN ('Starting again');
IF reply = 'N' THEN
    WRITELN ('Thank you for playing')
```

Clearly the **ELSE** construction gives a neater program, although on this occasion there is an alternative construction. Sometimes, however, there is no simple alternative. We can demonstrate this by bending the rules of roulette slightly. Suppose that there is a system of graded prizes paid out as follows:

(a) First prize is paid on number 36.
(b) Second prize is paid on numbers 6, 12, 18, 24 and 30.
(c) Third prize on numbers 3, 9, 15, 21, 27 and 33.

This could be expressed differently as

Provided only one prize is paid these rules apply:
If number = 0 then lose.
If number = 36 then first prize.
If number **MOD** 6 = 0 then second prize.
If number **MOD** 3 = 0 then third prize.

The following program fragment meets these requirements:

```
WRITE ('You win ');
IF number = 36 THEN WRITELN ('first prize')
ELSE
IF number MOD 6 = 0 THEN WRITELN ('second prize')
ELSE
IF number MOD 3 = 0 THEN WRITELN ('third prize')
ELSE WRITE ('nothing. Bad luck!')
```

If you try writing this fragment in any other way using the language so far discussed, you will find that it will be much more lengthy than this. As we shall see presently, there is another convenient and equally short way of achieving the same result using a new construction. First there are some important points of syntax concerning the use of **ELSE**. **ELSE** is an optional part of the **IF** statement. In standard Pascal it cannot be used in any other construction. The general syntax of the **IF** statement is

IF <expression> **THEN** <statement>

or

IF <expression> **THEN** <statement> **ELSE** <statement>

Therefore it follows that there must not be a semicolon before **ELSE**. (This is an easily made mistake.)

There is no ambiguity in having two or more **IF** statements following each other, one or more of which has an **ELSE**, provided that careful attention is paid to the following rules. As an example, consider the following:

```
1  IF <expression> THEN
2     IF <expression> THEN <statement>
3     ELSE <statement>
```

The **ELSE** in line 3 is paired with the **THEN** in line 2. It has no connection with the **THEN** in line 1. But in

```
1  IF <expression> THEN
2     IF <expression> THEN <statement>
3     ELSE <statement>
4  ELSE <statement>
```

the pairing is lines 2 and 3 and lines 1 and 4.

The rule is that **ELSE** is paired with the nearest preceding otherwise unpaired **THEN**.

As an example of how incorrect use of **ELSE** can lead to unexpected results, consider the following program:

```
PROGRAM IfElse (INPUT,OUTPUT);

VAR
   ch : CHAR;

BEGIN
   READ (ch);
   IF (ch >='0') AND (ch <='9') THEN
            WRITE ('digit');
   IF (ch >='A') AND (ch <='Z') THEN
     IF (ch = 'A') OR (ch = 'E')
       OR (ch = 'I') OR (ch = 'O')
       OR (ch = 'U') THEN WRITE ('vowel')
     ELSE WRITE ('consonant')
   ELSE WRITE ('error')
END.
```

If the input is a digit, the output will be

digiterror

which is probably not what was intended. You will be asked to emend this program in an exercise at the end of this chapter.

6.3 CASE STATEMENTS

There is a common type of computer game where some vehicle, perhaps a spacecraft, has to be guided by a player at the keyboard. Instead of the two possible values of input ('Y' or 'N') that we had in *Roulette*, we might have four ('N', 'E', 'S' or 'W') representing the four cardinal points of the compass. In such a game we may find ourselves having to write a series of statements such as

```
IF reply = 'N' THEN y := 1;
IF reply = 'E' THEN x := 1;
IF reply = 'S' THEN y := -1;
IF reply = 'W' THEN x := -1
```

The repetition of

$$IF \text{ } reply = \ldots THEN \ldots$$

is somewhat ungainly and would become increasingly more so if the number of possible values of *reply* were to increase. However, when all the conditions depend on the value of the *same* variable, Pascal offers us a neater construction:

```
CASE reply OF
   'N' : y := 1;
   'E' : x := 1;
   'S' : y := -1;
   'W' : x := -1
END
```

The constants ('N', 'E', 'S' and 'W') before the colons are the possible values of *reply* and are known as *case labels*. According to the value of *reply* only the statement after the appropriate colon is executed.

The general form of the **CASE** statement is

$$\textbf{CASE} <\text{case index}> \textbf{OF}$$
$$<\text{case list element or elements}> \textbf{END}$$

The item <case index> may be any expression whose value is not REAL, and <case list element> consists of

$$<\text{case label}> : <\text{statement}>$$

and may be repeated as often as desired. Each <case list element> must be separated from the next one by a semicolon. Every **CASE** statement must finish with **END**. Standard Pascal now permits an optional semicolon before the **END** although this was not permitted in earlier versions of the language. Some implementations, therefore, do not accept a semicolon in this position and you are well advised to omit it.

The item <case label> must be one or more constants of the same type as <case index>. If there are two or more constants in one case label, then each must be separated from its predecessor by a comma. Obviously, the same constant may not appear in more than one case label.

Standard Pascal requires that <case index> when evaluated shall have the same value as one of the constants in the case labels. For example it would be a run-time error in the above fragment if *reply* had any value other than 'N', 'E', 'S' or 'W' on entry into the **CASE** statement. However, some implementations do not insist on this and they allow the execution to proceed to the next statement in the program if the appropriate constant is not found.

Some implementations go even further and allow a construction of the following type using **ELSE** to allow a default action.

```
. . .
VAR . . . , ok : INTEGER;
  reply : CHAR;
. . .
ok := 1;
REPEAT
  WRITELN ('Which direction do you wish to go,');
  WRITE ('N, S, E, W ?');
  READ (reply);
  CASE reply OF
    'N', 'n' : y := 1;
    'E', 'e' : x := 1;
    'S', 's' : y := -1;
    'W', 'w' : x := -1
    ELSE ok := 0
  END
UNTIL ok = 1
. . .
```

Some implementations use a different word, such as *OTHERWISE* instead of **ELSE** in this construction. Whichever word is used, some implementations put it after the **END** rather than before. So, before you attempt to use this very convenient construction, do make sure that it is available on your implementation and find out the *exact* syntax, including the acceptance of semicolons before either **END** or **ELSE**.

This last program fragment, incidentally, includes a convenient way of permitting *reply* to be in either upper or lower case. Such a device is useful because different keyboards are apt to respond in different ways. You will have noticed that this was achieved in a slightly different way in the *Roulette* program.

6.4 BOOLEAN VARIABLES

In the last skeleton program, we used the device of setting an integer variable, *ok*, to 1 before reading *direction* and changing it to zero if an invalid character were read in:

```
. . .
VAR . . . ok : INTEGER;
  direction : CHAR;
. . .
ok := 1;
```

```
REPEAT
   . .
   CASE direction OF
      . .
      ELSE ok := 0
   END
UNTIL ok = 1
. . .
```

Let us assume that *ok* is used only in this part of the program (and, perhaps, in other similar parts) where its sole purpose is to be set to 1 if a desired condition has been met or to zero if it has not. These two values can be considered as representing respectively 'true' (1) and 'false' (zero). Thus *ok* is effectively acting as though it were a Boolean variable. Pascal, in fact, allows us to declare a variable of type BOOLEAN, thus

```
VAR ok : BOOLEAN
```

which gives certain advantages in programming.

A variable of type BOOLEAN may be assigned a value of *either* TRUE *or* FALSE and *no other*. A Boolean variable can be assigned its value TRUE by means of an assignment statement

```
ok := TRUE
```

where the right hand side of the statement may be TRUE, FALSE or any Boolean expression. For example, in the statement

```
ok := x = y
```

ok takes the value TRUE if x is equal to y and FALSE otherwise. This statement has the same effect as the statement

```
IF x=y THEN ok := TRUE ELSE ok := FALSE
```

which is not only much more involved, but also takes longer to execute.

Another advantage of using Boolean variables is that they may be referred to logically:

```
IF ok THEN . . .
```

which is equivalent to

```
IF ok = TRUE THEN . . .
```

and

```
UNTIL NOT ok
```

which is equivalent to

```
UNTIL ok = FALSE
```

A Boolean expression need not be a simple expression. For example

```
WHILE same OR NOT ( ok AND done ) DO <statement>
```

will be repeated so long as *same* is true or either *ok* or *done* is false.

The statement

```
result := (( a = 1 ) = ( b = 1 ))
```

is the equivalent of

```
IF ((a=1) AND (b=1))
   OR (a<>1) AND (b<>1))
      THEN result := TRUE
         ELSE result := FALSE
```

Involved Boolean expressions are best avoided if possible. Faulty conditional statements are a common, probably the most common, cause of program malfunction. All such statements should be carefully checked by examining carefully what happens with every possible combination of the values TRUE and FALSE for each Boolean expression.

Within the computer TRUE is represented as 1 and FALSE as 0. This may be demonstrated by the following program which uses the standard function **ORD**, discussed in the next chapter

```
PROGRAM TrueFalse (OUTPUT);

BEGIN
  WRITELN ('True  = ', ORD (TRUE) :1);
  WRITELN ('False = ', ORD (FALSE) :1)
END.
```

which gives the output

```
True  = 1
False = 0
```

ORD may also be used with a Boolean expression:

```
WRITE (number * ORD (number > 0))
```

will output positive values of *number* but a zero for zero and negative values.

EXERCISES

6.1 Write a program that will repeatedly read a character input from the keyboard and output both the character and its internal representation (ordinal value). The final iteration is to take place when the ordinal value of the full stop has been displayed. Use it to prepare a list of the ordinal values of all the character keys (both with and without the <shift> key depressed) on your keyboard. Compare your list with the ASCII character set of Appendix IV.

6.2 Rewrite the IfElse program so that the 'error' message appears only when the incoming digit is neither a digit nor an upper case letter.

6.3 We discussed the following program fragment earlier in this chapter:

```
WRITE ('You win ');
IF number = 36 THEN
   WRITELN ('first prize')
ELSE
IF number MOD 6 = 0 THEN
   WRITELN ('second prize')
ELSE
IF number MOD 4 = 0 THEN
   WRITELN ('third prize')
ELSE WRITE ('nothing.  Bad luck!')
```

Rewrite it using a **CASE** statement in standard Pascal (that is without an **ELSE** option at the end of the **CASE** statement).

CHAPTER 7

FUNCTIONS AND PROCEDURES

7.1 INTRODUCTION

In the *Roulette* program in the last chapter there is a set of eight lines that appear twice in the program. These are the lines that check that the character that is input from the keyboard is either 'Y' or 'N':

```
REPEAT
  READ (reply);
  IF reply = 'y' THEN reply := 'Y';
  IF reply = 'n' THEN reply := 'N';
  IF (reply <> 'Y') AND (reply <> 'N') THEN
     WRITE ('Bad Reply.  Enter Again')
UNTIL (reply = 'Y') OR (reply = 'N')
```

We can avoid having to write out these eight lines twice if we make use of the Pascal construction called a *function*. The use of functions can be demonstrated by rewriting the *Roulette* program as follows (the original comments have been omitted to save space in this text):

```
1  PROGRAM NewRoulette (INPUT,OUTPUT);
2
3  CONST prime = 10037;
4          limit = 10027;
5          skip = 7;
6
7   VAR number, seed, n : INTEGER;
8                restart   : CHAR;
9
10  FUNCTION yesNo :CHAR;
11
12  (* Reads in character from INPUT. Rejects all *
13   * characters except 'Y', 'y', 'N', and 'y'.  *
14   *  'y' and 'n' are converted to upper case.  *)
15
16  VAR reply : CHAR;
17
```

```
18    BEGIN (* Function yesNo *)
19      REPEAT
20        READ (reply);
21        IF reply = 'y' THEN reply := 'Y';
22        IF reply = 'n' THEN reply := 'N';
23        IF (reply <> 'Y') AND (reply <> 'N') THEN
24            WRITE ('Bad Reply.  Enter Again');
25      UNTIL (reply = 'Y') OR (reply = 'N');
26      yesNo := reply
27    END (* Function yesNo *);
28
29    BEGIN
30      WRITE
          ('What is the starting seed (1 to 9999) ?');
31      READ (seed);
32      REPEAT
33        WRITE ('Are you ready to start? Y or N ')
34      UNTIL yesNo = 'Y';
35
36      REPEAT
37        REPEAT
38          FOR n := 1 TO skip DO
39          BEGIN
40              seed := seed * 2;
41              seed := seed MOD prime
42          END
43        UNTIL seed < limit;
44        number := seed   MOD 37;
45
46        WRITELN
            ( 'The winning number is ', number :3);
47        WRITE ('Do you want to play again?');
48        restart := yesNo;
49        IF restart = 'Y' THEN
50            WRITELN ('Starting again')
51            ELSE WRITELN ('Thank you for playing')
52      UNTIL restart = 'N'
53
54    END.
```

Apart from the line numbers, this program has one major difference from the original *Roulette* program of Chapter 6.

In line 10, you will see

FUNCTION yesNo : CHAR;

followed by 17 lines that look rather like a small program on its own. If you examine it carefully you will see that it is very similar to the fragment quoted at the beginning of this chapter (the one that appeared twice in the original *Roulette* program).

All the program from

```
10   FUNCTION yesNo : CHAR;
```

to

```
27   END (* Function yesNo *);
```

constitutes what is known in Pascal as a *function declaration*.

In line 34 you will see

```
UNTIL yesNo = 'Y',
```

and at line 48

```
restart := yesNo.
```

You can now gain an understanding of what a function does if you imagine that immediately before these two statements, the whole part of the program from

```
18   BEGIN (* Function yesNo *)
```

to

```
27   END (* Function yesNo *);
```

had been written out in full. (Ignore, for the moment, the fact that *yesNo* is being treated like a variable although it has not appeared in a **VAR** list.) By the time that we get to lines 34 and 48 respectively, *yesNo* will have, on each occasion, a value, either 'Y' or 'N', that has been entered from the keyboard. This is because each time that *yesNo* is encountered in the main program, the function of that name is 'called'. When a function is called, that part of the program contained in the function declaration is executed. One result of executing this particular program is that at line 26, *yesNo* is assigned a value. At the end of this sub-program, at line 27, this value is 'returned'. The assigned value is given to *yesNo* and the program continues from the point at which it was called.

By writing the function out once only, we can call it as often as we need it in a program by putting it on the right hand side of an assignment statement or by using it in a Boolean expression.

The full set of rules for the syntax of functions is dealt with later in this chapter, but meanwhile two points must be made. The first has already been mentioned. When it appears in assignment statements *yesNo* is treated as though it were a variable. It is *not* a variable. It is actually a *function*. This fact is made clear by the entry of the name *yesNo* immediately after the reserved word **FUNCTION** in the heading of the declaration.

Furthermore, since *yesNo* is to be given a value, the *type* of that value must also be defined. This, you will see, is done in the declaration heading in the same way as it is in variable declarations, by following *yesNo* with ': CHAR'.

Avoiding having to repeat a sequence of identical statements within the same program is not the only advantage of a function. The requirement to enter 'Y' or 'N' from the keyboard is a common feature of very many programs. From now on, whenever you write a program with that requirement, you can incorporate the above function in it without having to re-invent it. Until you next need it you can file the declaration program away somewhere in your own personal library of programs. That is why such frequently used functions are often called *library programs*.

7.2 PROCEDURES

In Chapter 6 it was indicated that the *Roulette* program might be enhanced by introducing a run-time delay at a couple of points. To economise on space, such delays were omitted in *Roulette* and also in *NewRoulette* but, if we had needed them, they would have been similar to the program in Exercise 3.3 in Chapter 3. Since such delays are often needed in programs, a sub-program to introduce one would be a useful one to have in our library. There is one major difference between the requirements for **FUNCTION** *yesNo* and the requirements for a delay sub-program. *yesNo* was required to return a result ('Y' or 'N'), but the delay is not required to do this. A sub-program that is not required to return a result is called a *procedure*. The following procedure will produce a delay of, probably, several seconds, depending on the implementation:

```
PROCEDURE delay;

VAR n : INTEGER;

BEGIN
    FOR n := 1 TO 32000 DO;
END;
```

When this procedure is called from the main program by the simple statement

```
delay
```

it can be said 'to do nothing' 32 000 times. In practice it repeats a 'null statement' each time. Each iteration of the loop takes a finite number of microseconds and the main program is resumed after 32 000 iterations.

In most respects a procedure behaves in the same way as a function. The major difference is that a function returns a value and a procedure does not. This difference leads to differences in the method of calling (a function has a value which must be assigned) and in the declaration heading (for a function the type of the value must be shown, for the same reason).

7.3 PARAMETERS

In practice, it is unlikely that you will always want a delay that lasts 32 000 or any other constant number of cycles. You are much more likely to want to vary the delay to suit the requirements of the main program at the time of call. The following revised version of *delay* enables this to be done:

```
PROCEDURE delay (numCycles : INTEGER);

    VAR n : INTEGER;

    BEGIN
        FOR n := 1 TO numCycles DO;
    END;
```

This procedure will cause a delay of an, as yet unspecified, number of cycles *numCycles*. *numCycles* is known as a *parameter* of the procedure, *delay*. The heading of a procedure or function may include any number of such parameters in parenthesis brackets after its name. Parameters that appear thus in the procedure heading are known as *formal* parameters.

The actual values that will be assigned to these parameters when the procedure is called are specified in the calling statement. Thus a statement

```
delay(5000)
```

will cause the value 5000 to be assigned to *numCycles* as soon as the execution of *delay* starts. The parameters that appear in the calling statement are known as *actual* parameters.

The inclusion of *numCycles* in the procedure declaration heading constitutes its own declaration as a parameter and it must therefore have its type (in this case, INTEGER) declared in the usual way. The actual parameter and the formal parameter must both be of the same type. If the actual parameter had been a REAL variable or a REAL constant (37.2, for example), then the calling statement would have been rejected.

There is no limit to the number of parameters that a function or procedure may have. For example, revising *delay* as follows can enhance its flexibility:

```
PROCEDURE delay
                (innerCycles, outerCycles : INTEGER);

    (*        Introduces a delay of      *
     *      'innerCycles x outerCycles'   *
     *                cycles.             *)

    VAR m, n : INTEGER;
```

```
BEGIN
  FOR m := 1 TO outerCycles DO
    FOR n := 1 TO innerCycles DO;
END;
```

If the approximate number of cycles per second on your implementation were known to be, for example, 5000, then a call

```
delay (n, 5000)
```

would give a delay of approximately *n* seconds and

```
delay (1, 5)
```

would give a delay of approximately 5 milliseconds.

Another useful library program is a function to generate random numbers:

```
FUNCTION random (max : INTEGER ) : INTEGER;

(*          Returns a new pseudo-random value          *)
 *             in the range 0 to 'max'.                 *
 *        'max' must be > zero and < 'prime'.           *
 *           'Seed' must be declared globally.          *)

CONST prime = 10037;
       skip = 7;

VAR limit, n : INTEGER;

BEGIN (* Function 'random' *)
  limit := prime - (prime MOD (max + 1));
  REPEAT
    FOR n := 1 TO skip DO
      BEGIN
        seed := seed * 2;
        seed := seed MOD prime
      END
  UNTIL seed <= limit;
  random := seed MOD (max + 1)
END;
```

As before, the type of the function itself must also be declared. When the function has parameters, the function type appears *after* the closing bracket.

Note that this declaration includes a constant definition list and a variable declaration list. The names used in these lists, together with any names of formal parameters, are *local* to the function and have no significance outside it. They can therefore be assigned values within the function without any effect on any variables that may happen to have the same name within the main program. This means that, in this case for example, *prime*, skip, limit and n could all be used in an outer program quite independently. This has the great advantage that library programs may be taken straight off the shelf without our having to worry whether any names have been duplicated. It also means that you can incorporate, in your own programs, functions written by other people.

You will remember that, in the original *Roulette* program, we made *limit* a constant, the highest whole multiple of 37 that was less than *prime*. This time it has been calculated by the program. Quite apart from the fact that it makes sense to let the computer do the work, there is a more important reason for doing this. Until this function is called, we have no knowledge of the value that will be assigned to *max*. Therefore the evaluation of *limit* must be included as part of the function preliminaries.

Any values that are assigned to parameters or local variables during the call of a function are valid only for the duration of the call. In function *random*, the value of *limit*, for example, will be lost on the return to the main program. Next time *random* is called, the value of *limit* will be undefined until it is reassigned by the first statement in *random*. Sometimes it is important that we should carry forward the value of a variable from one call of a function to the next. An example of this is *seed* in the *random* function. If *seed* had been declared as a local variable, we should have lost its value by next call. On the other hand we can retain its value from call to call if it is declared in the main program. Variables declared in the main program are described as *global* variables. Although the main program has no access to local variables in the function, a function has access to any variable declared in the main program, *provided* there is not also, within the function declaration, a local variable with the same name. If there is such a local variable, the function will select it and ignore the global variable. The whole question of access to different variables is covered more fully later in this chapter.

7.4 VARIABLE PARAMETERS

An alternative, and generally better, method of preserving values of variables from one call to the next, or indeed of passing values (additional to that which is passed by the function name) from the function to the main program are by what are known as *variable* parameters, to distinguish them from the kind of parameter we have already discussed, called *value* parameters.

We could use a variable parameter *seed* in the *random* function by declaring it in the function heading thus:

```
FUNCTION random (VAR seed : INTEGER;
                 max : INTEGER) : INTEGER;
```

This new heading has two formal parameters, the variable parameter *seed* being additional to the original value parameter *max*. There is no limit to the number of parameters that a function may have, provided that, when it is called, the calling statement has the same number of actual parameters, listed in the same order and each of the same type as the corresponding formal parameter in the function heading.

To call this revised function we need a statement such as

```
number := random ( xyz, 36 )
```

where 36, as before, is the actual value parameter corresponding to *max* and *xyz* is the name of the variable that corresponds to *seed* in the main program. From what has been said above about the lack of conflict between local and global variables, there is no reason why the global variable, here represented by *xyz*, should not also be *seed* and in practice it probably would be, but it makes things easier to explain if we use *xyz* for the present.

The effect of the above call is that *max* will be assigned the value 36 at the time of call, but that *seed* will be synonymous with *xyz* for *the whole time* that the *random* function program is activated. Thus, after the statement

```
seed := seed * 2
```

has been executed, the value of *xyz* will be doubled. We have therefore achieved our objective of having a library function that may be inserted in any program and can access variables within the program, irrespective of the name given to those variables.

When a formal parameter list consists of two (as in this example) or more parameter sections separated by a semicolon, the sections may appear in any order. We could equally well have written

```
FUNCTION random (max : INTEGER;
                 VAR seed : INTEGER) : INTEGER;
```

but it is, of course, essential that the parameters of the call are also put in the revised order:

```
number := random (36, xyz)
```

One more procedure that we might use in *NewRoulette* is

```
PROCEDURE inSeed (VAR seed : INTEGER);

   (*   For initialising 'seed' from INPUT   *)
```

```
BEGIN
  WRITE
    ('What is the starting seed (1 to 10036) ? ');
  READ (seed);
  seed := (ABS (seed)) MOD 10036 + 1
END ;
```

You will see that this procedure is self-correcting if a number outside the stated range is supplied.

This short program may be thought almost too short to use as a procedure that takes up nearly twice the space of the four relevant statements. However, there are three factors that indicate the contrary. The first is that, if *random* is to be a library program, it makes sense to have the program that initialises *seed* also in the library. The second refers back to the remarks made previously, that the starting value of *seed* should be completely random, generated perhaps from the computer's internal clock. If your implementation has a method of access to this clock, then it should replace the first two statements of this function. This new method could well occupy more than two statements. The third reason is connected with overall programming strategy, which we discuss at length in Chapter 11. A long program is often more easy to follow if identifiable units of it are included as procedures or functions.

Some implementations have a convenient way of including library programs in another program, by use of the directive

EXTERNAL

This directive (which is not part of standard Pascal), appearing after a procedure or function heading, causes the compiler to search in back-up store for a library program with the same name as that given in the heading. It then loads the library program and compiles it in the same way as if it had been written out in full in the program. The following program treats all the procedures and functions that we have considered in this chapter as though they were external programs and, to save space and unnecessary repetition, we shall adopt this same approach in all future program examples that use previously defined functions or procedures:

```
PROGRAM NewRoulette (INPUT,OUTPUT);

CONST  compartments = 37;
       cyclesPerSec = 5000;

VAR number, seed, n : INTEGER;
         restart : CHAR;
```

```
FUNCTION yesNo : CHAR;

   EXTERNAL;   (* see above *)

FUNCTION random (VAR seed : INTEGER;
                        max : INTEGER) : INTEGER;

   EXTERNAL;   (* see above *)

PROCEDURE inSeed (VAR seed : INTEGER);

   EXTERNAL;   (* See above *)

PROCEDURE delay
              (outerCycles, innerCycles : INTEGER);

   EXTERNAL;   (* see above *)

BEGIN (* Main program *);
  inSeed (seed);
  REPEAT
    WRITE ('Are you ready to start?  Y or N ');
    restart := yesNo
  UNTIL restart = 'Y';
  REPEAT
    number := random (seed, 36);
    delay (4, cyclesPerSec);
    WRITELN ( 'The winning number is ', number :3);
    delay (6, cyclesPerSec);
    WRITE ('Do you want to play again?');
    restart := yesNo
  UNTIL restart = 'N'
END (* Program NewRoulette *).
```

Having now seen what procedures and functions can do, let us be rather more formal in examining the rules that govern them.

A procedure declaration consists of

$$< procedure\ heading> ; < procedure\ block>$$

A procedure heading consists of

PROCEDURE $< name > < formal\ parameter\ list >$

A function declaration consists of

$$< function\ heading> : < function\ block>$$

A function heading consists of:

FUNCTION $< name > < formal\ parameter\ list > : < type\ of\ result >$

For both procedures and functions the inclusion of a formal parameter list is optional. When included it consists of

$$(< formal\ parameter\ section\ or\ sections>)$$

If there is more than one section, then each must be separated from its successor by a semicolon.

A formal parameter section consists of either

<value parameter section>

or

<variable parameter section>

A value parameter section consists of

<identifier list> : <type>

and a variable parameter list consists of

VAR <identifier list> : <type>

Procedure blocks, function blocks and program blocks are all similar. A block consists, in the following order, of

<constant definition part>
<variable declaration part>
<procedure and function declarations>
<statement part>,

all of which have been previously defined. The one difference is that a function block must contain at least one assignment statement that assigns a value to a variable whose name corresponds with that of the function.

These definitions are necessarily lengthy. They are also very important to an understanding of the structure of the Pascal language. It may well assist you to follow them if you read them in conjunction with the syntax diagrams in Appendix II.

All the remaining rules in this chapter apply equally to functions and procedures.

The order in which procedures are defined is governed by one thing only – if one procedure calls another then the definition heading of the called procedure must appear before the part of the program that calls it.

A procedure may call itself. This is called *recursion*. As an example of a recursive program, let us examine a program to give us the prime factors of any positive integer (the prime factors of a number are those prime numbers which when all multiplied together give the number, thus the prime factors of 24 are 2, 2, 2 and 3).

The following program will give us the prime factors of any integer from 2 to MAXINT:

```
PROGRAM PrimeFactors (INPUT, OUTPUT);

VAR
   divisor, number : INTEGER;

PROCEDURE factor;
BEGIN
   IF number MOD divisor = 0 THEN
   BEGIN
      WRITE ( divisor );
      number := number DIV divisor;
      factor   (* recursive call *)
   END
END;

BEGIN
   WRITE ('Number ? ');
   READ (number);
   WHILE number > 0 DO
   BEGIN
      divisor := 2;
      WHILE divisor <= number DO
      BEGIN
         factor;
         divisor := divisor + 1
      END;
      WRITELN;
      WRITE ('Next number ? ');
      READ (number)
   END
END.
```

In this program, for each new value of *divisor*, the procedure *factor* is called. This procedure first tests whether the value is a divisor of *number*. If so, then three things happen:

(1) The value is output.
(2) *Number* is divided by the value.
(3) Procedure *factor* is called again to test whether the same value is still a factor of the new value of *number*, and the process is repeated until it is not.

Recursive procedures can often take advantage of the fact that variables declared within a procedure are in scope to that procedure only. The following program reads in a series of characters from the keyboard until the character is a space. It then writes them out in reverse order:

```
PROGRAM ReverseOrder (INPUT, OUTPUT);

PROCEDURE saveChar;
VAR
   ch : CHAR;
```

```
BEGIN
  READ (ch);
  IF ch <> ' ' THEN saveChar (* recursive call *)
       ELSE WRITELN;
  WRITE (ch)
END;

BEGIN
  WRITELN ('Enter your word');
  saveChar;
  WRITELN
END.
```

```
PASCAL ←
LACSAP
```

In this program no characters are output until the space has been read. With the word 'PASCAL' this will be on the seventh call of *saveChar*, none of the calls having so far been completed. They will then all be completed in the reverse order to that in which they were called.

Two procedures may be mutually recursive, that is to say that each may call the other. In this case they must be nested within each other in order to obey the rule that an identifier must have been declared before it appears in a statement. The following fragment shows how this is done.

```
PROCEDURE abc;

VAR....

  FUNCTION xyz : INTEGER;

  VAR ....

  BEGIN
    .....
    abc;
    .....
  END; ( Function xyz )

BEGIN (Procedure abc )
  .....
  x := xyz;
  .....
END; ( Procedure abc )
```

In this program fragment, procedure *abc* is *in scope* to function *xyz* and vice versa. All the local variables declared in *abc* are accessible to *xyz* provided that variables with the same name have not also been declared in *xyz*, but *none* of the local variables in *xyz* is accessible to *abc*. A variable that is accessible to any part of a program is said to be *in scope* to that part of the program.

This slightly complicated, but extremely useful, arrangement is best understood by considering the program as being in various *levels*, as shown in Fig. 7.1.

Level 0 is the main program, level 1 constists of all procedures declared within level 0, level 2 of those declared within level 1 and so on. At any point in the program the variables, constants and procedures in scope are those on its own particular level or those it can reach by going down steps. Those that involve climbing steps are out of scope. Thus in the main program all the constants, variables and procedures declared at level 0 are in scope, including procedures A and B and function C. But none of the variables in A, B or C is accessible to level 0. For procedure Z, however, all the following are in scope: (a) declarations within Z; (b) declarations with X including procedure Z itself; (c) declarations within A including function X; (d) declarations within the main program including procedures A, B and C but *excluding* any declarations within B and C; (e) procedure Y, provided that Y is declared before Z is defined, but excluding any declarations within Y.

An alternative way of handling mutually recursive procedures is by use of the directive FORWARD. FORWARD is a standard Pascal directive, and has some similarities to the non-standard directive EXTERNAL already mentioned. However, while EXTERNAL refers to a procedure declared externally to the program, FORWARD refers to a procedure declared at a later stage *within* the program. Using FORWARD, the above fragment could be rewritten:

```
PROCEDURE abc;

  FORWARD;

FUNCTION xyz : INTEGER;

VAR ....

BEGIN
  .....
  abc;
  .....
END;

PROCEDURE abc;

VAR ....

BEGIN
  .....
  x := xyz;
  .....
END;
```

Function *xyz* can still call procedure *abc* and vice versa but you should note that this construction has a different block structure from the pre-

Fig 7.1 levels of access: each level has access to all variables, constants, procedures and functions declared in its own block and all those that may be reached without climbing up steps vious one. Variables declared within *abc*, which were previously in scope to function *xyz*, are no longer in scope.

7.5 STANDARD FUNCTIONS

Since many functions, for example trigonometrical ratios, squares and square roots, are used in a variety of programs, Pascal defines these as *standard functions* which are presumed to have been *predefined*. (They may conveniently be thought of as having been defined at 'level −1'.) They do not have to be defined or declared within the program, but they may be called at any time. Most of them are described in Table 7.1.

Table 7.1   Standard functions

Function	TYPE of x	Effect	Result is of TYPE
ABS(x)	Real or integer	Computes the absolute value of x	Same as x
SQR(x)	Real or integer	Computes x^2	Same as x
SQRT(x)	Real or integer	Computes square root of x (provided that x is not negative)	Real
SIN(x)	Real or integer	Computes *sine x* where x is in radians	Real
COS(x)	Real or integer	Computes *cosine x* where x is in radians	Real
ARCTAN(x)	Real or integer	Computes *arctangent x*, giving the result in radians	Real
LN(x)	Real or integer	Computes the Naperian logarithm of x	Real
EXP(x)	Real or integer	Computes the exponent (Naperian antilogarithm) of x	Real
ODD(x)	Integer	Result is TRUE if x is odd, FALSE otherwise	Boolean
TRUNC(x)	Real	The integral part of x	Integer
ROUND(x)	Real	As TRUNC, but rounded up if fractional part $\geqslant 0.5$	Integer
CHR(x)	Integer	Results in the character whose value as held in the computer is x	Char

There are three additional useful standard functions, ORD(x), SUCC(x) and PRED(x), whose full definitions will be discussed more fully in Chapter 9, where we shall discuss data types other than REAL, INTEGER, CHAR and BOOLEAN.

We have already met ORD(x) in connection with types CHAR and BOOLEAN. It returns the integer value of the ordinal position of x. Thus, using the ASCII code, ORD ('3') is 51 and ORD ('A') is 65. ORD (FALSE) is zero and ORD (TRUE) is one.

The result of SUCC is the *successor* in the range. This can be clarified by some examples:

(1) If x is an integer,

$$\text{SUCC}(x) \text{ is } x + 1$$

Therefore

SUCC(77) is 78
SUCC(−2) is −1

(2) If x is CHAR,

$$\text{SUCC}(x) \text{ is the character having the value } x + 1$$

Therefore

SUCC('5') is '6'
and, in the ASCII code,

SUCC('a') is 'b'

(3) If x is Boolean,

SUCC(FALSE) is TRUE

Similarly, PRED(x) gives the predecessor to x:

PRED(x) is $x - 1$
PRED(77) is 76
PRED(−1) is −2
PRED('7') is '6'
PRED(TRUE) is FALSE

If the parameter within the brackets (often called the *argument* of the function) is itself at the end of the range, the result is undefined. For example if x has the value MAXINT, SUCC(x) will probably give an error. PRED('A'), SUCC('Z'), PRED('0') and SUCC('9') will probably all give values, but these will be implementation dependent and may not necessarily be the same values on another implementation.

In addition to these standard functions there are five standard procedures and two standard functions that are all used in the handling of input and output of data. We have already discussed three of the procedures, READ, WRITE and WRITELN, without actually describing them as 'procedures'. You will recognise that they have a syntax that is similar to other procedures, except that the number of parameters can vary. All the input/output procedures and functions are discussed more fully in Chapters 8 and 10.

CHAPTER 8

EXTERNAL FILES

So far all exchange of data between ourselves and our Pascal programs has been via the standard INPUT and OUTPUT devices of the computer. Frequently we would like to save our results for future use, to use the output of one program as the input for another one or, if our standard output device is a VDU, to obtain a printed record of our results.

Data that is stored outside the computer, in the back-up store mentioned in Chapter 1, is said to be stored in *external files*. The commonest forms of storage media in use today are magnetic tapes and magnetic discs. If you are operating on a terminal that is remote from the computer, you may not even know what file storage method is used. If you are operating a mini- or microcomputer, you are probably very familiar with it. You probably have had to use it to load your Pascal compiler.

It will help our discussion of files if, for the present, we consider them as magnetic tape files, whatever the media that are actually used. This is logical because, at the time that Pascal was first formulated, magnetic tape was the most popular form of back-up storage in use and Pascal file handling statements reflect this. Users of audio or video tape recorders will be familiar with many of the features of such machines. They will know, for example that there are two modes of operation: play and record. The equivalent modes with Pascal files are 'reading' (or 'inspection') and 'writing' (or 'generation'). They will also be aware how difficult it is, at least for an amateur, successfully to record an addition on to the end of a previously recorded tape. Pascal does not even allow us to try to do this. If we wish to extend, or alter, an existing file we must read in the data from the original file and (usually concurrently) write it out, with any additions or alterations, to a completely new file. A Pascal file may be either 'open' or 'not open'. If it is open it is either 'open for reading' or 'open for writing'.

To open a file for writing we use the standard Pascal procedure:

REWRITE (<file name>)

This does three things. It opens the file for writing, it does the computer equivalent of rewinding the tape to its starting position and it erases anything that may previously have been written in the file. The file is now defined as being 'empty'.

We can now write data to it using the WRITE or WRITELN procedures that we have already met; however, to show that we wish to write to the file and not OUTPUT, we put < file name > as the first parameter:

WRITE (< file name >, 'Length is', length, 'mm')

The use of WRITE and WRITELN in this context is not inconsistent, as it may at first appear, because OUTPUT and INPUT are both considered as Pascal files, albeit of a special kind. In fact

```
WRITE (length)
```

implies

```
WRITE (OUTPUT, length)
```

Indeed, the latter form is perfectly legitimate though unnecessary.

When we have finished writing all the data we wish to write to a file that is open for writing, it must be closed before we can read from it in the current program. The Pascal statement that closes a file for writing is the same one that opens it for reading, the standard procedure

RESET (< file name >)

RESET therefore does three things. It closes the file for writing, if it was open for that purpose, it resets the file to its start (equivalent of rewinding the tape) and it opens it for reading.

To read from a file we use the standard procedure READ:

READ (< file name > , < read list >)

or, if we assume that we have a program where *DimensionFile* has been declared as a file name (in the manner that will shortly be described) and *length*, *breadth* and *height* have been declared as three integer variables, then we can give a specific example:

```
READ (DimensionFile, length, breadth, height)
```

You should note that a file name can be any name we choose as long as it complies with the rules for naming identifiers given in Chapter 2. In particular you should note that it is no requirement of the Pascal language that the word *File* should be incorporated in the name, though you may do so for clarity if you like. It is for that purpose that it has been incorporated here.

When the above statement is executed, the next three values on the file will be assigned to the variables *length*, *breadth* and *height* respectively. No check is made to ensure that the three values read are indeed *length*, *breadth* and *height*. If, for example, a previous program had written them as *height*, *breadth* and *length*, they will be read in that order in the current program, irrespective of the names that have been given to the current variables. Certain checks are automatically made. For example, if the program calls for the reading of an integer value and the number on the file is real, this will show as an error. So it is the programmer's responsibility to ensure that his READ list always matches what is on the file and, conversely, that his files are well documented so that it will always be possible for him or someone else to write programs that read them correctly.

A file may be any length from zero to the maximum permitted by the implementation. The end of a file is the point at which there is no more data written on it. This point can be recognised, when reading a file, by the standard Boolean function, EOF (*End Of File*):

$$EOF (<\text{file name}>)$$

has the value TRUE if there is no more data on the file and FALSE otherwise. We shall demonstrate the use of EOF in an actual program shortly. Meanwhile there are two further points that must be made.

The data on a file must all be of the same type. It must, for example, be all INTEGER or all REAL, but for the present the only files we shall be discussing will be files of CHAR, which are also called *text files*. There are certain advantages in restricting our discussions to text files at this stage. For one thing a text file is not restricted to strings. It can also represent both real numbers and integers, so we have much greater flexibility. (The penalty we pay is in the amount of space we need in the file and in the speed of reading and writing, neither of which is likely to be a serious constraint at this stage.) Another reason is that the data in the text file is the easiest to depict graphically, and therefore, hopefully, easier for the reader to understand. Thirdly, a full appreciation of other types of file requires an understanding of parts of the Pascal language that are not dealt with until later in the book. To delay a discussion of files until then could restrict the things we could program on the computer.

File names must be declared in Pascal programs in two places. The first is in the program heading where they take their place after the declaration of the INPUT and/or OUTPUT files, thus

```
PROGRAM FileExample (OUTPUT, OldFile1,
                     OldFile2, NewFile);
```

If all input and output is from and to files other than INPUT and OUTPUT, the Pascal language does not require either INPUT or OUTPUT

to appear in the program heading, but some implementati...
OUTPUT to be declared in case there are any error messages t...

File names must also appear in the **VAR** declarations, togeth...
the type of file. There are two ways this can be done for text files,
equally correct. Either

```
OldFile1, OldFile2, NewFile : FILE OF CHAR;
```

or

```
OldFile1, OldFile2, NewFile : TEXT;
```

where **FILE** is a Pascal reserved word and TEXT is a standard type definer
in the same way that CHAR and REAL are. 'FILE OF CHAR' and 'TEXT'
are synonymous.

We can now introduce a program using files. It is a new version of one
that we have already met.

```
PROGRAM Payroll3 (HoursRates, WagesFile);

VAR
   hours, wageRate, weeksPay : REAL;
   num (* employee's number *) : INTEGER;
   HoursRates, WagesFile  : TEXT;

BEGIN
   RESET (HoursRates);
   REWRITE (WagesFile);
   WHILE NOT EOF (HoursRates) DO
   BEGIN
     READ (HoursRates, num, hours, wageRate);
     weeksPay := hours * wageRate;
     WRITE (WagesFile, num, hours, weeksPay)
   END;
   RESET (WagesFile)
           (*Probable implementation requirement*)
END.
```

You will note the comment alongside *RESET* (*wagesFile*). It is not a
standard Pascal requirement to close a file before the end of the program,
but many implementations require that files that have been open for
writing should be closed. On some implementations the end of the file will
not be identifiable unless it has been closed by a RESET statement.

You will see how EOF has been used in the above program to enable
us to quit the **WHILE** loop. If there were no EOF marker the program
would not have run correctly (precisely what would have happened is
implementation dependent). In fact even with the EOF the above program
is not completely secure. Suppose that, due to some error in a previous
program, the EOF marker had appeared after *num* and before *wageRate*,

the subsequent behaviour of this program would be unpredictable. Just how far a programmer should go in protecting his programs (for example by preceding the reading of each number by a test for EOF) in such cases is a matter of judgement.

The file names used in the above program are not necessarily those that are used outside the program. There is a similarity here with the parameters of a procedure. In fact the identifiers appearing in the parentheses of the program heading are known as the *program parameters*. These are the equivalent of the formal parameters of a procedure. The equivalent of an actual parameter varies considerably from implementation to implementation. Probably it will include a file name. It may also have to include the number of the tape or disc drive into which the tape or disc is loaded and sometimes a password is also included to allow access to the file. The method of passing the actual parameters to the program is also implementation dependent. In some implementations the program is 'called' in a similar way to a procedure:

```
EXECUTE PAYROLL3 (WEEK27HOURS.1, WEEK27WAGES.2)
```

while in others the actual parameters are passed within the program itself. In the author's implementation there is a predefined procedure TITLE which has two forms:

(a) TITLE (<file name>)
(b) TITLE (<file name>, '<outside file name>')

In the first the user is prompted to supply the outside file name from the keyboard and, in the second, the programmer can stipulate the name of the file before the program is compiled. These two methods between them give great flexibility. (There is a third, even more powerful form, that allows the outside name to be selected from a list according to the results of computations made during the running of the program.)

We have so far covered files in back-up store and INPUT and OUTPUT. If an implementation has a VDU as its normal output device, it will probably also have one or more printers available. A printer is treated as any other file except that, unless it is a teletypewriter with a keyboard, it will be possible to use it only in 'write' mode. The precise operations will be implementation dependent, but typically the name 'printer' is reserved for the printer and it has to be included in the program heading after OUTPUT and before other files. It may, or may not, have to be declared as a file variable. If it is, it will be of the type TEXT or **FILE OF** CHAR. Your documentation should tell you this and whether or not you have to open it for writing.

Let us now look at WRITE and READ operations with text files in more detail. The rules for writing numbers (real or integer) and string constants to any text file are the same as those for writing to OUTPUT that we discussed in Chapter 3. Field width parameters may be used, though for reasons we shall discuss shortly they should be used with caution when writing to text files.

Before we go further, let us see what a text file looks like after a WRITE operation. Assume that the file has just been opened with a REWRITE statement. It can now be represented as shown in Fig. 8.1.

Fig 8.1 *a file after REWRITE (fileName): the shaded portion represents the empty file*

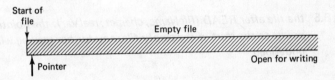

The arrow represents an imaginary pointer, pointing to the start of the file, and there is a long empty file ahead of it. Now assume that we then have a statement

```
WRITE (FileName, thousand :6, ' A', -pi :10 :5)
```

The representation will be as in Fig. 8.2.

Fig 8.2 *the file after the statement WRITE (fileName, thousand : 6, 'A', -pi : 10 : 5)*

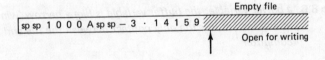

Now let us see how we read such a file. First we must close it and re-open it for reading (Fig. 8.3).

Fig 8.3 *the same file after RESET (fileName)*

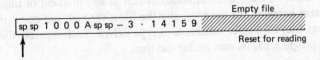

Now let us read the integer, READ (fileName, intVar) (Fig. 8.4).

Fig 8.4 *the file after READ (fileName, intVar)*

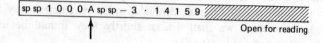

Open for reading

The action on reading is for the pointer to skip any spaces preceding the number, then to read the characters that make up the number, and to stop as soon as it encounters the first character that is not part of the number. Thus the pointer is now in a position to read the character 'A'. A further instruction, READ (fileName, charact, realVar) would give *charact* the value A and *realVar* the value −3.14159 (see Fig. 8.5).

Fig 8.5 *the file after READ (fileName, charact, realVar): the pointer now points to the start of the empty file; any further reading will be undefined*

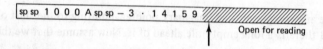

Open for reading

The imaginary pointer is now pointing to the start of the empty file and EOF is true. Any attempt now to read from this file would produce results that are 'completely undefined', which is another way of saying that anything might happen, depending on the implementation.

The correct name for the imaginary pointer is *buffer variable* and a better way of representing it would be as in Fig. 8.6.

Fig 8.6 *a buffer variable: the buffer variable is like a narrow 'window'; at any instant it is the only contact between the file and the computer*

```
sp sp 1 0 0 0 A sp sp − 3 · 1 4 1 5 9
       A
Buffer variable
```

It is called a variable because space is allocated to it in the Pascal program as a result of the file declaration. In fact at any moment of time the only contact between the program and the file is through this one variable. For a text file, the buffer variable is of type CHAR. Each separate file declared in a program has its own buffer variable.

The successive steps in a READ (fileName, charact) statement are as follows:

(1) The value in the buffer variable is transferred to the variable *charact*.

(2) The buffer variable is advanced one position along the file.

(3) The value at this new file position is copied into the buffer variable.

For a WRITE (fileName, charact) statement the steps are as follows:

(1) The value of *charact* is copied into the buffer variable.

(2) The value is transferred from the buffer variable to the file.

(3) The buffer variable is advanced one position along the file.

We have gone into this in some detail, because a full understanding of the step by step operation is necessary to an understanding of some of the problems that arise with files. (If you know a little about electronics, you will appreciate that the above is not the full story. In practice there has to be another, multicharacter, buffer between the buffer variable and the file, but this is part of the computer's operating system and does not normally concern the Pascal programmer.)

Reading numbers from a text file is an elaboration of character reading. It is convenient to describe the algorithm in the Pascal language. Assume we have a READ (fileName, intVar) instruction where *intVar* is an integer variable and that there is some way of examining the buffer variable before it is assigned to a variable:

```
WHILE bufferVariable = ' ' DO READ (charact);
intVar := 0;
sign := 1;
IF (bufferVariable = '+') OR
                    (bufferVariable = '-') THEN
BEGIN
  READ (charact);
  IF charact = '-' THEN sign := - 1
END;
WHILE (bufferVariable >= '0')
            AND (bufferVariable <= '9') DO
BEGIN
  intvar := intVar * 10 + ORD(charact) - ORD('0'))
END;
intVar := intVar * sign
```

Every Pascal implementation has an algorithm in its system, usually written in machine code, to carry out an operation along these lines. Similar algorithms exist for reading real numbers and for writing real and integer numbers.

Field width parameters can lead to unintended errors when using back-up text files. The problem can best be demonstrated using a deliberate mistake:

```
WRITE (FileName, thousand :6, pi :7 :5)
```

would give the output

$$10003.14159$$

A subsequent READ (fileName, intVar, realVar) would read 10003 for the integer and then indicate an error when it tried to read the real number, since there would be a decimal point in the buffer variable and Pascal real numbers must have at least one digit before the decimal point. This problem arises because a WRITE (fileName, number) instruction always finishes with a digit and, as we saw in Chapter 3, if the field width is not wide enough, the leading spaces are sacrificed. There are two ways round this. The first is not to use field width parameters. The default representation in the absence of such parameters is implementation dependent, but it is almost certain to include at least one leading space. The other, completely safe, way is to output a space character before each number:

```
WRITE (FileName, ' ', thousand :5, ' ', pi :7:5)
```

This adds to the programming effort and is generally only necessary if field width parameters are essential (for example, because the same file is to be used for a print-out) and there is a possibility that a value may be too great for the field.

We have previously seen how WRITELN with OUTPUT causes the subsequent display to start on a new line. WRITELN with a printer file will do the same, but the use of WRITELN with back-up text files needs special mention. The statement

WRITELN (<file name>, <write list>)

causes all the data in <write list> to be written and then it outputs an *end of line* component. The actual representation of the *end of line* component is implementation dependent. It is treated by the Pascal program as though it were a space character, except that it has one additional feature – its presence can be detected by the Boolean function EOLN. If the buffer variable contains the end of line component, then

EOLN (<file name>)

is true; otherwise it is false. Thus when reading a back-up text file that has been written with lines, it is always possible to test for the end of a line. There is one possible source of error in using this test that must be mentioned. Text files are often prepared on one program for use on another. Typically a word processor or text editor program may be used for setting up data. Let us consider a simple example.

A certain school has six forms. The number of pupils in each form varies. A program has been written to calculate, by forms, the average number of marks scored in a certain examination. The input to this program consists of six lines, prepared on a word processor. Each line lists, for each form in turn, starting with the First Form, the marks gained by each individual pupil, thus

```
27 84 56 17
98  0 44 49 27 33 21
18 54 67 83 67 83 76 91 75
22 37 84 63 19
54 79 38 45 67 21
33 52 64 38 69
```

Since each line contains the marks for one form, the following program uses EOLN to test when the last entry for each form has been read:

```
PROGRAM AverageMarks (OUTPUT, MarksFile);

VAR
   form, total, pupils, mark : INTEGER;
   MarksFile : TEXT;

BEGIN
   RESET (MarksFile);
   FOR form := 1 TO 6 DO
   BEGIN
     total := 0;  pupils := 0;
     READ (MarksFile, mark);
     WHILE NOT EOLN (MarksFile) DO
     BEGIN
       pupils := SUCC (pupils);
       total := total + mark;
       READ (MarksFile, mark)
     END;
     WRITELN ('Average for form', form :2, ' is',
                            (total / pupils) :7 :2 )

   END
END.
```

This program will fail if there are superflous spaces between the last digit and the end of line component on any line of input data or if there is no end of line component on the last line. (You should satisfy yourself that this is true). These are conditions that we are unable to check from the listing since neither spaces nor <newline> produce marks on the paper. There are several ways round this, but all involve more programming. (See Exercise 8.1 and 8.2 at the end of this chapter.)

Since Pascal treats the end-of-line component as a space, READ (<file name>, <number variable>) skips past any occurrence of this component before the number, in the same way as it skips past spaces.

There is another standard procedure, which must be introduced at this stage, READLN. The effect of

READLN (<file name> , <list>)

is exactly the same as

> READ (<file name> , <list>);
> **WHILE NOT** EOLN (<file name>) **DO**
> > READ (<file name> , <character>);
> READ (<file name> , <character>)

after which the buffer variable will contain the first character *after* the end-of-line component, as shown in Fig. 8.7.

Fig 8.7 *position of the buffer variable after a READLN operation: it is placed immediately after the end-of-line component*

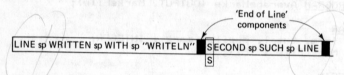

Thus, the following program fragment

```
WRITELN (File1, 'ABCD');
WRITELN (File1, 'EFGH');
RESET (File1);
READLN (File1, char1, char2);
READLN (File1, char3, char4);
WRITELN (char1, char2, char3, char4, '.')
```

would give the output

```
ABEF.
```

One more standard procedure used with files is PAGE. This procedure may be called only with output files. It has the syntax:

PAGE (<file name>)

and, as might be expected, results in advancing the text to the top of the next page. The actual effect of calling this procedure is implementation dependent and should be described in the documentation. However, when used with a printer and continuous stationery it will normally result in the output of the requisite number of <newline> characters to advance the form to the top of the next page. When used with storage files it will usually write a specific character (in the ASCII character set this is CHR (ORD(12))) representing *form feed*. With a VDU display, the effect is generally to clear the screen and to commence any subsequent writing at the top left hand corner of the screen. If PAGE is used without a parameter, then the normal OUTPUT device is assumed.

The standard files, INPUT and OUTPUT, are text files of a special kind. Their names never appear in a **VAR** list and they are assumed to be open from the start of a program until its end. (Some implementations may have their own rules for the use of RESET and REWRITE respectively with these files.) Obviously INPUT is only open for reading and OUTPUT for writing, and you cannot have statements such as WRITELN (INPUT) or READ (OUTPUT, < list >).

Apart from these points, there are few differences between these two files and any other text files. Such differences as there are all revolve around line structuring and the use of the end-of-line component and of the < newline > key.

When OUTPUT is a printer or teletypewriter, it is usually essential to ensure that the text is structured into lines containing no more characters than the maximum permitted for the equipment. Different machines respond to over-length lines in different ways. Some continue printing when they reach the right margin and the final character can rapidly develop from a nasty mess into a solid black rectangle. Others halt when they reach the margin, often sounding an alarm, and wait for human intervention. A few supply their own < newline > instruction when they reach the right margin and continue printing on the next line, but if that margin is reached in the middle of a word, then the word will be split between the two lines. VDUs almost invariably treat over-length lines in this last way.

Another point to remember with VDUs is that, once the bottom line of the screen is full, the information scrolls up the screen and the top line is lost. This will happen, of course, whether the lines are properly structured or not. If it is important that data should not be lost in this way, or if the lines are scrolling too fast for you to read them, then the best solution is to introduce a loop that halts the program after a fixed number of lines of output. If *dummy* is a CHAR variable, then the program will halt if it encounters a READ (dummy) statement until an appropriate key is pressed. What precisely is 'appropriate' depends on the way that the implementation deals with INPUT, a subject that will now be discussed.

If INPUT is a keyboard and data is being supplied during the running of the program (usually in response to prompts from a VDU or printer), this mode of operation is called 'interactive'. Interactive working introduces certain problems which are aggravated by implementation differences. Some implementors treat the keyboard itself as the INPUT file, with each keystroke going straight to the buffer variable when the key is struck. Others make a 'line input buffer' the INPUT file. A line input buffer is a specially reserved part of the computer's store that can best be regarded as a text file of restricted length (typically about 100 characters). As each key is pressed its relevant value is written into this file until the <newline> key is pressed. Pressing <newline> has the equivalent effect of RESET (INPUT). The program's buffer variable now has access to the INPUT file (access which was denied until the pressing of the <newline> key). Standard Pascal requires only that there should be an INPUT file and is not concerned with the way it is implemented, so neither approach is incorrect. The differences are important to those who are programming for interactive working. Rather than clutter the text with details, the subject is covered more fully in Appendix III. The examples given in the text, wherever possible, are 'neutral' in that they will work with either approach.

The use of READLN with interactive working can cause problems in some implementations. Figure 8.8 shows the position of the buffer variable as the result of a READLN call.

Fig 8.8 *READLN may cause a 'hang up' with unbuffered keyboard input: in some implementations the READLN operation is not complete until there is data in the first position after the EOLN component*

It is pointing to the beginning of the empty part of the file. In some implementations, execution of the program will 'hang' at this point until the buffer variable receives valid data. To put it another way, it will hang until the next character is provided from the keyboard. Thus in the following fragment

```
WRITE ('What is the length ? ');
READLN (length);
WRITE ('What is the height ? ');
READLN (height)
```

the result might be

```
What is the length ? 47←
8What is the height ?
```

After the length, 47 <newline>, had been entered the program hung until another character, 8, was entered. You should be careful how you use READLN with interactive working until you have gained some experience with your own implementation and know how it responds. If your implementation has a line buffer, then you will probably find READLN more satisfactory than READ. If it uses direct input, then you should use READLN only when you find it absolutely necessary and you should be prepared for its idiosyncracies.

A final point to remember about interactive working is that each character provided by INPUT is usually automatically 'echoed' on the OUTPUT file. This can affect the format of OUTPUT. In particular a < newline > supplied at INPUT automatically forces a new line on OUT-PUT.

EXERCISES

8.1 One way to avoid the problems that might arise with the *AverageMarks* program is to 'clean' the data file before it is used. Write a program that will read in a *MarksFile* and write out a clean or validated one. The things it must do are as follows: (a) remove the spaces (if any) between the final digit of the last number on each line and the end-of-line component; (b) ensure that there is an end-of-line component at the end of the sixth line.

[*Hint*: Remember that there must be at least one space between each pair of numbers.]

8.2 Assuming that the solution of Exercise 8.1 is not used, emend the *AverageMark* program so that it will not fail due to spurious spaces or missing end-of-line components.

8.3 A certain trader keeps a record of transactions of each of his 10 000 customers. The format of the file is as follows: (a) an integer, the customer's reference number; (b) a series of pairs of numbers described below; (c) a zero, a marker indicating the end of this customer's transactions.

The pairs of numbers consist of (a) an integer representing the item number; (b) a real number representing the quantity.

Write a program to 'validate' this file. The program is required to check the following:

(a). The customer's number must be an integer in the range from 1 to 99 999.

(b) The item number must be an integer in the range from 1 to 100.

(c) The quantity may be a real number, negative (credits) or positive (sales). Its absolute value should not be greater than 15 000. This affords some protection against absurd errors.

(d) The last number on the file must be a zero.

The program is also required to provide an output of the total number of customers who have had transactions during the period to which the file relates. (It is assumed that the file has already been sorted so that each customer's number appears once only, together with all his transactions for the period. Customers who have had no transactions do not appear on the file.)

Devise suitable error messages for output. Remember that a common error will be the omission of a relevant number or the insertion of a spurious one.

CHAPTER 9

ARRAYS

9.1 INTRODUCTION

An array is a data structure which, like a file, is composed of elements all of the same type. However, there are two important differences. First, whereas the number of components in a file is indeterminate and can change during the running of a program, the number of components in an array is predetermined and unalterable. Secondly, all the elements of an array are accessible at all times during the execution of the program, unlike a file whose elements, as we have seen, can be accessed only sequentially.

A typical application for an array is a trader's price list, which he might need *inter alia* in a program for preparing customers' invoices. In such a program it would be necessary, for each customer, to multiply the quantity of each item he had purchased by the price. The problem, you will recognise, is similar to the *payroll* program where we had to multiply hours by rate. But, whereas each employee had his own rate of pay which was needed only for calculation of *his* pay packet, several different customers may be buying the same goods, albeit in different quantities. The same data (unit price per item) may thus be required many times, for different customers, during the running of an invoicing program. It would be tedious to have to keep re-entering the price of each item for each customer that had purchased it. It would be much more convenient if the whole price list could be entered into the computer's memory, once only at the beginning of the run, and the computer itself was made to look up the price each time that particular item was to be invoiced.

An array allows us to reserve a number of store locations, all with the same name (for example, *price*) but distinguished from each other by means of a *subscript* or *index* enclosed in square brackets following the name. The index may not be of type, REAL. Let us for the present assume that it is an integer number. Thus we might have *price[1]*, *price[2]*, ... *price[100]* as the prices of the hundred items. This array would be declared thus:

```
VAR  . . .
        price : ARRAY [1..100] OF REAL
```

and the array would be said to consist of 100 *components* or *elements*, each component of which is of type REAL. Note that the two full stops together '. .' form a standard Pascal symbol with the meaning 'on my left, the lowest number in the range and on my right the highest'. This symbol must not be confused with the row of dots that is sometimes used to indicate intentional omissions from a text. On implementations where square brackets are not available, the combined symbols (. and .) may be used instead.

With this preamble, let us now look at a program for preparing customers' invoices:

```
PROGRAM InvoicePrep (OUTPUT, PriceList,
                               CustPurchases);

VAR
   grandTotal, invTotal, extension, qty : REAL;
   item, customer, numInvoices : INTEGER;
   price : ARRAY [1..100] OF REAL;
   PriceList, CustPurchases : TEXT;

BEGIN
   RESET (PriceList);  RESET (CustPurchases);
   FOR item := 1 TO 100 DO
                READ (PriceList, price [item]);
   grandTotal := 0;
   numInvoices :=0;
   WHILE NOT EOF (CustPurchases) DO
   BEGIN
      READ (CustPurchases, customer);
      WRITELN ('Customer No. ', customer);
      invTotal := 0;
      READ (CustPurchases, item);
      WHILE item <> 0 DO
      BEGIN
         READ (CustPurchases, qty);
         WRITE (item :4, qty :12 :3);
         IF (item >= 0) AND (item <= 100) THEN
         BEGIN
            extension := qty * price [item];
            WRITELN (price [item] :12 :2,
                                     extension :12 :2);
            invTotal := invTotal + extension
         END
         ELSE WRITELN ('Item no', item,
                             'not recognised');
         READ (CustPurchases, item)
      END;
      WRITELN ('------------' :40);
      WRITELN ('Total this invoice    £',
                               invTotal :12 :2);
```

```
    WRITELN ('===========' : 40);
    PAGE;
    grandTotal := grandTotal + invTotal;
    numInvoices := SUCC (numInvoices);
  END;
  PAGE;
  WRITELN ('Number of invoices', numInvoices :28);
  WRITELN ('Total sum invoiced          £',
                      grandTotal :12 :2)
END.
```

Input to this program is from two files. The first, *PriceList*, contains the current prices of the one hundred items. The format of this file is simply a series of one hundred real numbers, the first of which is the price of item number 1, the second is the price of item number 2 and so on. The **FOR** loop, near the start of the program, loads each price in turn into a successive element of the array, *price*.

The other file, *CustPurchases*, has the identical format to that of Exercise 8.3 at the end of Chapter 8, viz. (a) an integer, the customer's reference number; (b) a series of pairs of numbers described below; (c) a zero, a marker indicating the end of this customer's transactions.

The pairs of numbers consist of (a) an integer representing the item number; (b) a real number representing the quantity.

The operation of this program can now be followed through. After the array has been loaded with the prices of the items, provided that the end of the *CustPurchases* file has not been reached, the customer's number is read in and immediately output. The item number is then read in and, provided that this is not zero, the quantity is also read in and they are both output.

The item number is then tested to ensure that it lies within the range 1..100. This is done to ensure that, later, when we use this number as the index for the array, we are accessing a valid element of the array. It should not be strictly necessary to do this, because most implementations make this check automatically. However, if such an error is discovered, the execution is usually aborted. We might prefer to continue the run, simply marking the faulty invoice accordingly, rather than having to run the whole program again. In normal commercial practice, the *CustPurchases* file would probably already have been run through a validation program similar to the one described in Exercise 8.1 (Chapter 8).

After this validation the quantity is multiplied by its price which is obtained from the relevant element of the *price* array to give a value, *extension*:

```
extension := qty * price [item]
```

The remainder of this program is straightforward.

9.2 MULTIDIMENSIONAL ARRAYS

One typical use for an array is for designating the squares on a chess board. There are 64 such squares and they could thus be represented on an array

```
board : ARRAY [1..64] OF INTEGER
```

However, it is usually more convenient to think of a chess board as consisting of an 8 × 8 matrix. Pascal allows us to declare this matrix:

```
VAR
   board : ARRAY [1..8, 1..8] OF INTEGER
```

where the first dimension refers, say, to the rows and the second to the columns. The square at the top right corner would thus be designated *board [1, 8]* and that at the bottom left would be *board [8, 1]* . Such an array is described as being 'two-dimensional'.

There is no theoretical limit to the number of dimensions in an array (though there are sometimes implementation limitations). For example, a chess-playing program may wish to consider and record possible future moves, up to, say, 100 ahead. This could be done on an array:

```
board : ARRAY [1..8, 1..8, 0..100] OF INTEGER
```

where *board [r, c, 0]* represents the present position and *board [r, c, 27]* shows the board after 27 more moves. This could be further extended; for example, if the program is designed to play simultaneously against up to 50 players

```
board : ARRAY [1..8, 1..8, 0..100, 1..50]
                                    OF INTEGER
```

but such an array would have 320 000 components and would need quite a large computer.

9.3 SYNTAX OF ARRAYS

An array declaration consists of

        < variable identifier > : **ARRAY** [< range or ranges >]
                               OF < component type >

< range > takes the form

                < low bound > . . < high bound >

For the present, we shall assumed that <low bound> and <high bound> are both integers. The declaration is only valid if

$$\text{<high bound>} \geqslant \text{<low bound>}$$

The number of components of the array is given by

$$\text{<high bound>} - \text{<low bound>} + 1$$

If there is more than one < range > within the square brackets, then each must be separated from its predecessor by a comma.

The syntax for a component of an array is

$$\text{<array variable identifier>} [\text{<index or indices>}]$$

where <index> is an expression having a value that falls within the <range> for the particular array. There must be the same number of indices as there are index types in the array declaration and if there is more than one index, each must be separated from its predecessor by a comma.

Arrays of identical type (that is, having identical ranges and components that are assignment compatible) can be assigned in an assignment statement. Thus with

```
VAR
    arrayA, arrayB : ARRAY [1 .. 50] OF INTEGER;
    arrayC : ARRAY [1 .. 25] OF INTEGER;
    arrayD : ARRAY [1 .. 50] OF REAL;
```

the following are all legitimate assignments:

```
    arrayA := arrayB;
    arrayB := arrayA;
    arrayD := arrayA;
    arrayD := arrayB
```

but no other assignments are permissible. In particular note that *arrayA := arrayC* is not allowed even though *arrayA* is big enough to receive the contents of *arrayC*. Transfer of data in this case would have to be done component by component, using, for example, a **FOR** statement. None of the arithmetical operators or relational operators may be used with arrays, with the exception of *string arrays* (see below).

9.4 PACKED ARRAYS

By their nature, arrays sometimes occupy quite a lot of space in the computer's memory. There will be times, either with large programs or with small computers, or both, when it is important to save space, even at the expense of slower execution of the program. The programmer can declare his wish to save space by declaring an array as *packed*. This is done at the same time as the structure is defined, by use of the reserved word **PACKED**. Thus

<variable> : **PACKED ARRAY** [<index type>]
OF <type>

The use of **PACKED** does no more than express the desire of the programmer to save space. The way in which the compiler responds to this request, if at all, is implementation dependent. There are, however, two important points for the programmer to remember. A packed array can *never* be compatible with an unpacked one and the component of a packed array may not be used as a *variable* parameter of a function or procedure.

It is sometimes necessary to convert a packed array into a normal one or vice versa. The following fragments show one way in which this can be done:

```
VAR
    normalArray : ARRAY [nLow .. nHigh] OF xType;
    packedArray : PACKED ARRAY [pLow .. pHigh]
                                    OF xType;
    n, start : INTEGER;
```

In the above declarations it is assumed that the index range of *normalArray* is equal to or greater than the index range of *packedArray*, that is

$$(nHigh - nLow) >= (pHigh - pLow)$$

If the ranges are not equal, then we have the option of packing only part of the total range of *packedArray* starting at *start* provided that in this case

$$(nHigh - start) \geqslant (pHigh - pLow)$$

If the ranges are equal, then *start* = *nLow*;

We can now pack the appropriate components of *normalArray* into *packedArray* by the statement

```
FOR n := pLow TO pHigh DO
    packedArray [n] := normalArray [n - pLow + start]
```

and we can unpack the components of *packedArray* back into the appropriate part of *normalArray* by

```
FOR n := pLow TO pHigh DO
    normalArray [n - pLow + start] := packedArray [n]
```

Pascal has two standard procedures which can replace the above statements:

```
PACK (normalArray, start, packedArray)
```

and

```
UNPACK (packedArray, normalArray, start).
```

Your should take care, when using these procedures, to ensure that the indices stay within range.

9.5 STRINGS

We have already encountered strings as constants in programs, where they must be enclosed in single quotes. We have seen them as parameters of WRITE and WRITELN procedures. They may also be declared as string constants. For example:

```
CONST  knockOff = 'Time to go home!';
       . . .

       WRITELN (knockOff)
```

would produce the same result as

```
WRITELN ('Time to go home!')
```

Strings do not, however, have to be constants. They can also be variables. A packed array of type CHAR whose lowest index has the value 1 and whose highest index is greater than 1, is a varibale of *string type*. Such an array may be altered or manipulated in much the same way as any other array.

You may try the following program, which demonstrates this. We declare a string variable

```
string : PACKED ARRAY [1..10] OF CHAR
```

into which we can read up to 10 characters from the keyboard and then, to demonstrate that they have been held in the array, we write out the contents of the array, first as entered and then in reverse order.

```
PROGRAM ReadTest (INPUT, OUTPUT);
VAR  n : INTEGER;
     string : PACKED ARRAY [1..10] OF CHAR;
BEGIN
   FOR n := 1 TO 10 DO READ (string [n]);
   FOR n := 1 TO 10 DO WRITE (string [n]);
   WRITELN;
```

```
      FOR n := 10 DOWNTO 1 DO WRITE (string [n]);
      WRITELN
   END.
```

In practice, it is comparatively seldom that we want to handle strings of a fixed predetermined number of characters. Names, addresses, sentences, etc., all have a varying number of characters and the handling of such strings can introduce problems for which the programmer needs to be on the look-out. The first can be fairly easily demonstrated:

```
PROGRAM StringTest (INPUT, OUTPUT);

VAR
   string : ARRAY [1 .. 10] OF CHAR;
   n : 0 .. 10;

PROCEDURE readString;
BEGIN
   n := 0;
   REPEAT
      n := SUCC (n);
      READ (string [n])
   UNTIL string [n] = ' '
END;

PROCEDURE writeString;
BEGIN
   WRITELN;
   FOR n := 1 TO 10 DO
      WRITE (string [n]);
   WRITELN
END;

BEGIN
   WRITELN ('Write ''Mastering<space>''');
   readString;
   writeString;
   WRITELN ('Write ''Pascal<space>''');
   readString;
   writeString
END.
```

If the prompts are correctly obeyed, the input/output of this program will be (subject to implementation differences on line spacing)

```
Write 'Mastering<space>'
Mastering ←
Mastering

Write 'Pascal<space>'
Pascal ←
Pascal ng
```

The spurious 'ng' (and a space which follows it) after the output of 'Pascal ' have been left over from the first call of *readString*.

There are various ways of avoiding this. One would have been to alter the *writeString* procedure so that output ceased on encountering the first space. Another is to use 'padding' characters. Padding characters are usually, but not invariably, non-printing characters (typically a space or the ASCII 'null' or 'erase' characters). There are two common ways of inserting such characters into a string variable. They can be exemplified by the following modifications to the *readString* procedure: either before reading the input

```
FOR n := 1 TO 10 DO string [n] := ' ';
n := 0;
REPEAT
   <read in characters until a space is
                              encountered>
```

or after reading the input

```
<read in successive characters>
UNTIL string [n] = ' ';
FOR n:= SUCC (n) TO 10 DO string [n] := ' '
```

Earlier we stated that the Boolean operators may not be used with arrays as operands. There is one exception to this rule. When the arrays are compatible string types (that is, they both have the same number of components and they are both packed arrays of type **CHAR**) the Boolean operators

$$= \quad < > \quad < \quad > \quad <= \quad >=$$

may be used. The rules for comparison are that the characters are compared in turn starting with *index : = 1* until a value of the index is found where the characters are not equal. The comparative values of the two strings is then decided by the comparative values of the two characters. Thus

'produce' < 'product'   and   'one' < 'zero'

would both be true because 'e' is less than 't' and 'o' is less than 'z', but the relationship between 'eight' and 'eighteen' would depend on the value of the padding character that followed the 't' in 'eight'. From this it will be seen that the choice of padding characters is important when strings are being compared, especially for equality.

Relational comparisons of strings have an important part to play in sorting lists of names or other words and in searching though such lists, subjects that will be discussed in the next chapter. Meanwhile you might

116

like to consider the implications of the fact that in the ASCII character set
the ordinal value of < space > is lower than that of any printing character.

EXERCISES

9.1 Write a program that, having read from the keyboard a word of up to
seven characters, will then output a list of all the possible permutations of
those characters. Use the program to list all the anagrams (including
meaningless ones) of the word 'SEAT'.

9.2 In the *InvoicePrep* program in this chapter, assume that the item
numbers may be any integer from 1 to MAXINT. It would be quite
impractical to have an array with MAXINT elements for only 100 items.
One solution to this problem would be to have two arrays:

```
itemNum : ARRAY [1..100] OF INTEGER;
price   : ARRAY [1..100] OF REAL;
```

To use this solution, it would be necessary, after reading each item number, to search through the array *itemNum* to find the subscript that
corresponded to that number and to use that subscript for access to the
price array.

Instead of using two arrays, it would be possible to use one multidimensional array

```
itemPrice : ARRAY [1..2, 1..100] OF INTEGER;
```

provided that the price was always held in pence or cents (assume there
are no fractions of a penny or cent).

Write the programs for these two approaches.

[*Note*: If you have difficulty in programming the search through the
array, you might like to defer this part of the problem until you have read
the next chapter.]

CHAPTER 10

APPLICATIONS 2: SORTING, SEARCHING AND MERGING

□ This chapter deals with the application of the Pascal language to the sorting and merging of arrays and files and searching for elements of an array. It is addressed principally to new computer users. No new aspects of the Pascal language are introduced and, as with all these chapters on applications, it may be skipped by those who seek only a knowledge of the language. □

10.1 SORTING

Suppose that we have an array, *list*, of, say, 100 components, each containing an integer in the range 1..1000. Assume that the integers are in random order in the list and that we know that no number appears in the list more than once, then the simplest and quickest way to sort the numbers would be to take each number in turn from the list and place it in its correct position in another array, *order*, whose index type is 1..1000. Having done that, we can return the numbers to the array *list* in the same order that they appear in the *order* array. The following fragment would do this:

```
FOR m := 1 TO 1000 DO order [m] := 0;
FOR n := 1 TO 100 DO order [list [n]] := list [n];
n := 1;
FOR m := 1 TO 1000 DO
IF order [m] <> 0 THEN
BEGIN
   list [n] := order [m];
   n := SUCC (n)
END
```

In ideal conditions, which must not depart too far from the above, this is by far the fastest method of sorting. Unfortunately such ideal conditions seldom exist. For example, it is only rarely that we know for certain that no number will appear more than once in the list. More importantly, the range of the numbers may be so great that the resulting array is too big for the computer's store. Finally, the items to be sorted may be real numbers or strings which cannot be used as index types for arrays. So we usually have to look for other methods.

There are several such methods commonly in use. Many of them rely on comparing successive pairs of values, and then reversing each pair if it is not in the required order. Probably the easiest to understand, but unfortunately usually the slowest in execution, is the 'bubble sort'.

Suppose, for simplicity, that we wish to sort the following five numbers into ascending order, left to right:

    7 1 4 9 3

We compare each pair in turn from the left, exchanging them if the one to the left is greater than the one to the right

    1 7
      4 7
        7 9
          3 9

giving us a new order:

    1 4 7 3 9

From the logic of what we have done, rather than looking at the figures, we can at this stage be sure of one thing. The rightmost number is the highest of all. We do not have to look at it again, but must now repeat the process again for the remainder:

    1 4
      4 7
        3 7

giving

    1 4 3 7 9

We then repeat the process again with one less pair:

    1 4
      3 4

giving

    1 3 4 7 9

and lastly we have only the left hand pair left to compare:

    1 3

giving

  1 3 4 7 9

To us, who could see at a glance that the numbers were properly ordered at the penultimate stage, the final stage may seem superfluous. But the computer cannot 'see at a glance'. It can only respond to simple logical instructions and must be programmed to complete the paired comparison, even when no changes are necessary. You can obtain a better idea of the way a computer sorts numbers by laying half a dozen or so playing cards in a row face down and carrying out the above operation, exposing only one pair at a time.

The Pascal statement for doing a bubble sort is

```
FOR n := (last - 1) DOWNTO 1 DO
FOR m := 1 TO n DO
IF list [m] > list [m+1] THEN
BEGIN
   temp := list [m];
   list [m] := list [m+1];
   list [m+1] := temp
END
```

Note that, to exchange two values in a computer, it is always necessary to store one of them temporarily in a third variable (in this case *temp*).

Other 'paired comparison' sorts in common use are as follows:

(a) *Selection sort* Instead of comparing adjacent pairs, each element is compared in turn with a temporary value which starts at a low value, −MAXINT for example. Whenever the value of an array element is found that is higher than the temporary value, then the new value is placed in the temporary store and the subscript of the element is noted. When the whole array has thus been scanned, the highest value is removed from its place on the array and placed at the end, the remaining elements being 'closed up' to fill the gap. The process is repeated, each time, stopping just short of the last sorted element until the whole array is sorted.

(b) *Insertion sort* After the first pair have been compared and exchanged if necessary, the third component is compared with each of those two and inserted in its correct place, shifting those already sorted if necessary. The process is then repeated for the fourth and each subsequent component.

These last two sorts have approximately the same speeds and both are usually marginally faster than a bubble sort. All three suffer from the fact that the time taken to sort a list is approximately proportional to the square of the number of components to be sorted. They have, however, the advantage that their programs are short and simple. In fact it is a feature of sorting programs that the penalty for speed is length and complexity of program.

A method that is considerably faster than any of the above, but still approximately proportional to the square of the number, is the *Shell sort*, which has similarities with the bubble sort. Instead of always comparing adjacent components, a 'rough cut' is taken in the first scan by comparing, and exchanging if necessary, components that are located *n* spaces apart. For each succeeding scan, *n* is halved until *n* is equal to 1. There are several variants on the method, all with substantially the same speed. They differ in the way the first value of *n* is arbitrarily chosen and what is done when $n = 1$. Probably the simplest is the one that starts with

$$n : = total \ \mathbf{DIV} \ 2$$

and finishes by repeatedly scanning the whole list, comparing and exchanging adjacent pairs, until the final scan is identified as one in which no exchanges have been necessary.

The Shell sort is usually adequately fast for lists of a few thousand components, but where speed is more important than program length, then the *Quicksort* should be used.

To demonstrate Quicksort we need to have rather more elements than we had for the bubble sort:

$$5 \quad 7 \quad 3 \quad 9 \quad 6 \quad 8 \quad 2 \quad 1 \quad 9 \quad 4 \quad 8$$

the first step is to take the leftmost number, 5, and put it in suspense. This is the *datum* value. We then have

$$(5) \quad 7 \quad 3 \quad 9 \quad 6 \quad 8 \quad 2 \quad 1 \quad 9 \quad 4 \quad 8 \quad Datum \ \underline{5}$$

(The number just moved is shown underlined. The position it has vacated is shown in parenthesis.) The aim now is to put the datum number in its final position, at the same time so adjusting the position of the other numbers so that those to the left are lower than or equal to the datum and those to the right are higher or equal. The following describes how this is done.

First the array is scanned *from the right* to locate the first number that is *lower* than the datum. This number is placed in the vacant position:

$$\underline{4} \quad 7 \quad 3 \quad 9 \quad 6 \quad 8 \quad 2 \quad 1 \quad 9 \quad (4) \quad 8 \quad Datum \ 5$$

Next, the array is scanned *from the left* to find the first number that is *higher* than the datum. Again it is placed in the vacant position:

$$4 \quad (7) \quad 3 \quad 9 \quad 6 \quad 8 \quad 2 \quad 1 \quad 9 \quad \underline{7} \quad 8 \quad Datum \ 5$$

This scanning should be continued alternatively from the right and from the left, until the two scans meet:

```
4   1   3   9   6   8   2  (1)  9   7   8   Datum 5
4   1   3  (9)  6   8   2   9   9   7   8   Datum 5
4   1   3   2   6   8  (2)  9   9   7   8   Datum 5
4   1   3   2  (6)  8   6   9   9   7   8   Datum 5
```

The two scans having met, the datum value is placed in the vacant position:

```
4   1   3   2   5   8   6   9   9   7   8   Datum (5)
```

The array is now considered in two parts – the part to the left of the old datum ($\leqslant 5$) and the part to the right ($\geqslant 5$). Each part is dealt with in the same way as above:

```
(4)  1   3   2                            Datum 4
 2   1   3  (2)                           Datum 4
 2   1   3   4                            Datum (4)


(2)  1   3                                Datum 2
 1  (1)  3                                Datum 2
 1   2   3                                Datum (2)


         (8)  6   9   9   7   8           Datum 8
          7   6   9   9  (7)  8           Datum 8
          7   6  (9)  9   9   8           Datum 8
          7   6   8   9   9   8           Datum (8)

         (7)  6                           Datum 7
          6  (6)                          Datum 7
          6   7                           Datum (7)

                     (9)  9   8           Datum 9
                      8   9  (8)          Datum 9
                      8   9   9           Datum (9)
```

giving the final order

```
1   2   3   4   5   6   7   8   8   9   9
```

Paradoxically, although Quicksort is far faster than the other methods when large quantities of components are to be sorted, it is often slower (depending on both the implementation and the starting order) with less than about a dozen. For this reason Quicksort programs sometimes include a switch to another method (for example a Shell sort) whenever the number remaining to be sorted drops below some arbitrary figure.

You will realise that a Quicksort procedure is quite an involved program. We shall therefore be using it as an example in Chapter 11, when we discuss the development and writing of longer programs. Meanwhile you may be interested in Fig. 10.1 which shows the relative speeds for sorting random integers, using different methods on the author's implementation.

Fig 10.1 *time taken to sort a given number of random integers by different methods on the author's implementation*

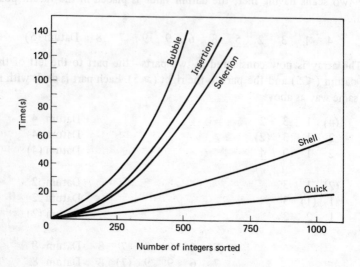

Number of integers sorted

10.2 SORTING MULTIDIMENSIONAL ARRAYS

So far we have considered the sorting of single dimensional arrays only, although it is comparatively rarely that we want to do this. For example, if we had a price list we should probably have two arrays, one with the catalogue number and one with the price. (If the price array is REAL, we are not strictly discussing multidimensional arrays, but the argument is the same for two arrays or one two-dimensional array.) When we have two such arrays, it is convenient to refer to the one that contains the data on which searching takes place as the *key* array and the one that has the associated information as the *information* array. In our example the key array has the catalogue numbers and the information array has the prices. When we are sorting, it is essential, each time components of the key array are moved into a new position, that the corresponding component of the information array is moved as well. This slows down the speed of the sort, but cannot be avoided.

When there is more than one array containing information, it is usually advisable to adopt a slightly different approach. In this case, the information arrays are static during the whole sorting process and we have another array, the *directory* array, which contains the index or 'address' at which the associated information will be found. During sorting, only the components of the key and directory arrays are moved. After sorting, the key array is in order and each key's associated directory component holds the address of the relevant information. The key and its associated information could, for example, be output by the following statement:

```
FOR n := 1 TO 100 DO
   BEGIN
      d := directory [n];
      WRITELN (partNum [n], price [d], stock [d],
                         discount [d], vatRate [d])
   END
```

10.3 SEARCHING

The simplest way to find a particular entry in an array is to start at one end and successively compare each entry in turn with the 'reference' value. This method is known as a *linear search*.

A disadvantage of a linear search is that it can be slow. On average, and assuming the distribution to be random, half the components of the array have to be compared before a match is discovered. There is a faster method, called a *binary search* that can be used, *provided* that all the components of the array are known to be in order (alphabetical or numerical).

The principle of the binary search is simple. The reference value is compared with the component in the middle of the array. If it is equal to that component, then the search is finished. If it is greater than that component, then the required component must be in the upper half of the array. Otherwise it must be in the lower half. This process is then repeated for the relevant half, which is then halved again if necessary, and so on, until we finally 'home in' on to the component that matches the reference. For 100 components, a maximum of seven comparisons will be needed, for 1000 it will be 10 and, the more components there are, the greater the advantage of a binary search over a linear search.

10.4 MERGING

Another problem that often arises is where we have two lists (named, say, A and B) already sorted into order and we want to merge them into a third list, C, that will also be in order. This operation is comparatively simple. Suppose A and B are arrays of numbers and we want to merge them into C (with as many or more components as the sum of the components of A and B). Imagine A and B as two piles with the lowest numbers on top of each pile. All we have to do is to compare the number on the top of each pile and transfer the lesser one to the next vacant position in

C. This is repeated until either A or B is empty, whereupon the remaining numbers from the non-empty pile are transferred to C.

It is very frequently necessary to merge two files. The process is similar to merging arrays except that it is never necessary to hold more than two lots of data in the computer's store at one time. Suppose it is necessary to merge file A with file B. The first requirement is that A and B must both be already sorted into similar orders (that is, sorted on the same key item and either both in ascending order or both in descending order). Let us assume they are in ascending order. The first item is read from A and B and the lesser one is then written to file C. If the lesser one was, say, from file A, then it is replaced by the next item from the same file and the process repeated until one of the input files is empty. The remainder of the other one is then written to file C.

'Updating' of files is similar to merging, but with some important differences. Suppose we have a file of employees' rates of pay that we wish to update with amendments which are held on another file. The amendments might fall into any one of three categories: (a) employees who have joined since the last update; (b) employees who have left; (c) employees whose rates of pay have been changed.

Again we must assume that both files have already been sorted. This time, in addition to merging the new employees, we shall also have to deal with the case when the two key items (employees' clock numbers) are equal. When this happens we will have to take one of two actions depending whether we are dealing with a change of rate (only the new rate goes forward) or a leaver (neither goes forward).

10.5 SORTING OF FILES

Short files can usually be sorted by loading the data into an array, sorting the array and writing the revised order to a new file. However, files often contain more data than can be loaded into the computer's store at one time. The solution here is to form an array that is as large as possible. Then, assuming that the file to be sorted is file A, to read as many items as possible from A, sort them and write the sorted results to a small file, A1. The next block of data is read from A, sorted and written to A2. The process is then repeated until the whole file A has been so dealt with. Then A1 is merged with A2, the result merged with A3 and so on.

10.6 STACKS AND QUEUES

The need often arises to store data temporarily while some other work is being carried out. Provided the data is all of the same type, an array can conveniently be used for this storage. The simplest type of such storage works on the principle of 'last in first out' (LIFO) and is called a *stack*. A variable, called a *pointer*, is given the value of the index of the first vacant component of the array. After each item of data has been added to the stack (often called 'pushing'), the pointer is *incremented* (increased by one). When an item is removed ('popped' or 'pulled') from the stack the pointer is decremented *beforehand*. There is an example of the use of a stack in the next chapter.

A *queue* works on the principle of 'first in first out' (FIFO). For this, two pointers are required: one pointing to the next vacant space (the 'tail' of the queue) and the other to the oldest inhabitant or 'head' of the queue. These pointers are incremented as items are entered or removed respectively. With a long queue the 'tail' pointer may overstep the last element in the array. Therefore the array may be considered to be a ring with its first component following immediately after its last. The programming of this in Pascal is simple. Provided the dimensions of the array are [0.. < array size − 1 >], each increment can be programmed as

$$< pointer > : = SUCC (< pointer >) \textbf{ MOD} < array size >$$

Arrays for both stacks and queues must be large enough to accommodate the maximum number of components expected, often a matter of guess-work. Therefore a stack pointer should be tested for overflow after each increment. Similar tests should be made in ring queues, but here an overflow is indicated when the tail pointer catches up with the head pointer. The reverse, head pointer catching tail pointer, is not an error but indicates that the queue is empty.

EXERCISES

10.1 An integer array of 100 components holds a series of random numbers in the range 0 .. MAXINT. They have already been sorted into ascending order of value. Write a program which reads in a number and then writes out the index of the component in the array that has the same value.

Modify your program to allow for the fact that the value you input might not be present in the array. In this case the program is required to output two indices, the neighbours, immediately above and below, of the reference.

10.2 Write **PROCEDURES** for each of the following: (a) a bubble sort; (b) a selection sort; (c) an insertion sort. Assume that for each there is integer array of 1000 components.

CHAPTER 11

PROGRAMMING STRATEGY

□ This chapter examines program strategy with reference to a particular Pascal application. No new aspects of the language are introduced and the chapter may be omitted by those who are familiar with 'top-down' programming. □

Good programming requires knowledge and skill. Knowledge of the whole of the Pascal language can be obtained from this book and the part of the language so far covered enables many useful programs to be written. Skill needs to be developed. Like all skills, programming needs practice, guidance and the avoidance of bad habits.

Practice is up to you. Write programs to solve any problem you can think of. You must have had some ideas about the sort of problems you wanted to solve when you started to read this book but, if you cannot think of new problems, then do not be above re-solving old ones that others have solved before – after all it is the practice you are after. The popular monthly computer magazines have reference, in the text or in advertisements, to dozens of programs that others have thought it worth while to write. If you try to tackle such problems yourself, at least you have the satisfaction of knowing that they can be solved because others have done it before you!

The rest of this chapter is devoted to giving you guidance on programming strategy and good habits to adopt.

A program strategy must start with a clear and complete statement of the problem. So here it is:

THE GREAT GLOBALVISION SONG CONTEST

One of the highlights of the broadcasting calender is the annual world-wide song contest. The rules have been based on those of its successful predecessor, the Eurovision Song Contest. The main differences are the following: the competition is now open worldwide, not only to all member countries of the United Nations but also to 'approved' sub-divisions, so that, for example, every state of the USA, every republic of the USSR and each of the four countries of the UK provides a competitor. In all some 400 competitors take part. Each competing organisation provides a panel of 100 judges, each of whom can cast one vote, only, for one competitor. In order to ensure that the voting is completely impartial, each competitor is given a number and the judges only know them as 'Competitor No. 1', 'Competitor No. 2', etc., though viewers at home are also told the state or nation that they come from. After some 70 hours of non-stop, world-class singing, the great moment arrives when the judges have to give their verdicts. Each panel of judges, in an order that has been predecided by lot, delivers its verdict in turn in a way similar to that used in the Eurovision contest except that the competitor's number is used instead of his nationality. After the last mark has been read out, the senior judge of the panel then solemnly states 'and that concludes the voting of the judges from *such-and-such*'. This last is necessary because the imperialist countries, in an arrogant fit of chauvinism, managed to impose a rule that if the marks of any panel do not add up to a total of exactly 100 then the marks of the whole panel are void. This was decided on the illogical basis that, if judges cannot add up, they are not qualified to judge a song contest!

The organisers of the song contest have asked us to write a program that will enable the following:

(1) The competitor's number and the points awarded by the panel to be keyed into a computer on receipt.

(2) The total points awarded by the panel to be added up immediately on receipt of the 'and that concludes. . . ' message.

(3) If the total is not equal to 100, a message to be displayed on the 'telecomp' to the effect that the panel's marks are not accepted. ('Telecomp' is a sort of combined high quality VDU coupled to a TV camera and thus able to inject computer output on to the TV screens of viewers at home. To the computer it is just another output file.)

(4) Provided this total is 100, the relevant points are to be added to the relevant competitors' totals; the list of competitors is to be sorted into descending order of points received; and the position in the list (together with '=' if tied with other competitors), the competitor's number, his nationality and the number of points awarded to him are to be sent to the telecomp. In order to maintain the feverish heat of breathtaking excitement, it is essential that this should be done as quickly as possible, so that the cameras can switch to the next panel of judges.

(5) As soon as one competitor gets an unassailable lead, this is to be indicated on the telecomp by an asterisk alongside his score. Thus the name of the winner may immediately be flashed to the waiting press of the world.

You must now decide whether the above is a clear and complete statement of the problem. Your decision will largely depend on whether or not you are familiar with the Eurovision Song Contest and the method of announcing the points used by the judges. Also you would be right in asking what constituted an 'unassailable lead' and how competitors' nationalities are to be reconciled with their numbers. Presumably a competitor gets an unassailable lead when his lead over his nearest rival is greater than the votes left to be cast and presumably there is a file which correlates competitors' numbers and nationalities. But it should never be assumed that the programmer knows this.

Even if you are both the person posing the problem and the programmer who is going to solve it, it is always wise to state the problem clearly and completely. Few things are more frustrating than suddenly discovering, at the end of a long piece of programming, that it is all wasted anyway because the problem was stated ambiguously.

Let us assume that these points have been satisfactorily settled and that we are now ready to go on to the next step. The next step is *not* to go straight to the keyboard of your computer or terminal. That should be the *very last* thing you do. Now is the time for a lot of thought and careful planning. The complete solution of the problem should be clear in your mind and on paper before you write the first line of Pascal code.

It is now generally agreed that the best approach to computer programming is the so-called 'top down' approach. This sometimes misleading term means, in effect, that we first look at the total solution to the problem without any thought to the programming language to be used. Top-down programming is often thought of in terms of *levels*. Thus the plan for tackling the *overall* problem can be called 'level 1'. It is usually first written in plain language thus:

Level 1 (version 1)

Step 1 Preliminaries and initialisation.

Step 2 Input (*competitor's number, points scored*) repeatedly until 'end of list' marker.

Step 3 Summate all points in the list. If equal to 100 proceed to next step. Otherwise reject and output message.

Step 4 Add points gained by each competitor to his current total of points.

Step 5 Sort the competitors list (comprising competitor's number, name and score) into descending order of score.

Step 6 Compare the leader's lead with the number of votes yet to be cast.

Step 7 Output ('position in order of scores adjusted for ties, competitor's number, name of state or country, score with leader marked with asterisk if outright winner') repeatedly for all competitors in descending order of total score.

Step 8 Repeat steps 2–7 until all panels of judges have reported.

Initialisation of variables and other preliminary work must often be left until the rest of the program is clear, but we can see at this stage one preliminary action that must be taken before we can properly define some of the other steps. How many competitors are there? Presumably this will change from year to year. Therefore probably the best way will be to ask for this number and to input it from the keyboard right at the start.

Bearing this point in mind, it is now possible to formalise level 1 as follows:

Level 1 (version 2) (formal)

Step 1 Initialise and preliminaries including inputting number of competitors.

REPEAT

Step 2 Repeatedly Input (*competitor's number, points*) until 'end of list' marker.

Step 3 Summate all points in the list.

If equal to 100 THEN

BEGIN

Step 4 Add points gained by each competitor to his current total of points.

Step 5 Sort the competitors list (comprising competitor's number, name and score) into descending order of score.

Step 6 Compare the leader's lead with the number of votes yet to be cast. Set flag if outright winner.

END ELSE

BEGIN reject this verdict.

Output message and delay.

END

Step 7 Repeatedly output ('position in order of scores adjusted for ties, competitor's number, name of state or country, score, with asterisk if flag is set') until number of iterations equals number of competitors.

UNTIL number of iterations equals number of competitors.

You will note that this formal set out begins to look more like the shape of a computer program. You may even think that it begins to look more like a *Pascal* program. But do not be misled by the REPEATs, IFs, ELSEs, etc. Other languages use them too. What it *does* start to look like is a *structured program* and Pascal is one of several structured languages.

One result of this more formal approach is that we have highlighted a point that was not clear before. When a verdict becomes void because the points do not add up to 100, we know from the original specification of the problem that a message has to be sent to telecomp. But do we then want to retransmit the current scorecard? This will have to be cleared up with the organisers, but for the time being let us assume that we do want to do so, in order that the commentators can remind their audience how exciting it all is before they switch to the next judges. This introduces a problem that was not envisaged by the organisers. (This is not unusual. The client *never* envisages all the problems!) It is necessary to introduce a delay immediately after the 'void' message is displayed, otherwise there would not be time for the audience to read it before the message of step 7 is flashed up. After consultation with the organisers it was decided that if a 'void' message appeared, it should stay on screen until the producer signalled to the computer operator that it should be replaced by the 'step 7' message.

Now that the 'bugs' at this level have been resolved it is possible to finalise it. In the final version we try to identify all global variables and constants. We can also start to firm up on the level 1 syntax. Since all steps are clearly defined in version 2, we can abbreviate them in this final version. Thus we get

Level 1 (version 3)

Global constants.
  NumberOfJudges = 100
  Maximum Competitors = 500
Global variables.
  NumberOfCompetitors, Count : INTEGER
  Flag : BOOLEAN
  Numbers, Scores : INTEGER ARRAY [1..MaximumCompetitors]
  Names : STRING ARRAY [1..MaximumCompetitors]
BEGIN
  Initialise
  FOR count := 1 TO NumberOfCompetitors DO
  BEGIN
    Input scores
    Check scores
    IF scores = NumberOfJudges THEN

```
      BEGIN
            Add scores
            Sort
            Check winner
      END ELSE Void message.
            Scores message
   END
END.
```

It is always good policy to declare and give names to all constants used in the program, particularly if there is a chance that they may change later. For instance the rules may be changed and the number of judges on each panel altered. When *NumberOfJudges* is declared, there is only one, easily identified, point in the program where the number, 100, has to be changed.

This level, as now written, has eight easily identifiable subunits (Initialise, Input scores, Check scores, Add scores, Sort, Check winner, Void message and Scores message). The fact that some eventually prove to be quite long and others very short, does not matter. They enable us to see the total solution within the syntax construction of the program at level 1. Some of them may eventually be separate *procedures* or *functions*; others may be just one or two simple statements. Some programmers like to make all such subunits into procedures, so that the final main program looks almost exactly as shown in level 1 (version 3). Other prefer to use procedures only for such subunits that are called more than once in this program or are *library programs* which have been, or might be, used in other programs. The choice is a personal one, though the author prefers the latter approach, with the rider that very long subunits, even if appearing only once in the program, can often be more easily handled as procedures.

Now that level 1 is finalised as far as possible at present, level 2 can be treated in the same way. For the purpose of this book, it is proposed to deal with only one subunit in any detail: the fifth in the list ('Sort'), which we shall identify as level 2.5.

Since it has already been specified that speed is essential in computing the results, the sorting method we shall use will be a Quicksort until each 'span' is reduced to below a predetermined 'switchPoint' when a Shell sort will be used. These two methods have been described in Chapter 7. What has been written there constitutes the 'statement of the problem'.

What follows now is the author's own development of the *Sort* program taken straight from his notes made at the time. Some major blunders were made at various stages. These are unashamedly reproduced here. One of the great advantages of the top-down approach is that errors made in the early stages can be easily corrected. Another advantage is that the action of putting the outline down on paper and thinking about the following stage highlights errors and problem areas very rapidly. Had an attempt been made to write the program in Pascal from the start, the errors would still have been there, would have been much harder to find and, in their correction, would almost certainly have introduced all sorts of other errors in their wake.

So here 'warts and all' is a first attempt at a solution:

Level 2.5 (version 1)

Step 1   Initialise. SwitchPoint : = 16.

Step 2   Select *datum* (the value at the lower bound) and put it in its final location with values less or equal in the lower subspan and values greater or equal in the higher subspan.

Step 3   Save the higher subspan to be used later. Repeat step 2 using the lower subspan.

Step 4   Repeat steps 2 and 3 until the lower subspan has less than *switchPoint* components.

Step 5   Carry out Shell sort on this span.

Step 6   Pick up the last subspan saved and repeat steps 4 and 5 until there are no more subspans saved.

Although step 6 was thought to be clear at the time it was written, it does not really describe what is to happen. In the first place, the intention was that step 6 should have been repeated until there are no more subspans saved. This is not stated. Furthermore, picking up 'the last subspan saved' could lead us into one of the most frustrating of all programming errors, the closed loop. The time will arise when step 3 ceases to save subspans. The last it saves will always be the 'last' which step 6, without further clarification, will continue to pick up. It is evident that what we really want here is a LIFO stack, step 3 putting subspans on to the stack and step 6 repeatedly removing them until there are no more.

We need to have a better definition of a 'subspan' in this context. What we are going to save on the stack is not the value in the span or subspan, but its lower and upper bounds defined by the respective subscripts to the array that we are sorting. We must also decide arbitrarily on the sequence in which they will be placed on the stack, to ensure that they are properly allocated when they are subsequently removed. We shall therefore stipulate that the *low bound* will be placed on the stack first, followed by the *high bound*. This means, of course that the high bound will be *removed* first.

We can be rather more precise about step 1. Things that need initialising in addition to *switchPoint* are the quantity of values to be sorted, or the bounds of the array in which they are to be found, and the stack pointer.

We can now try again:

Level 2.5 (version 2)

Step 1   Initialise. SwitchPoint : = 16
                Set upper and lower bounds.
                Pointer : = 1

Step 2   Select *datum* (the value at the lower bound) and put it in its final location with values less or equal in the lower subspan and values greater or equal in the higher subspan.

Step 3   Put lower and higher bounds of the higher subspan on to the stack. Repeat step 2 using the lower subspan.

Step 4   Repeat steps 2 and 3 until the lower subspan has less than *switchPoint* components.

Step 5   Carry out Shell sort on this span.

Step 6   Recover higher and lower bounds from stack. Repeat steps 4 and 5.

Step 7   Repeat step 6 until stack empty.

Closer examination shows that there is still one error in this version. The test to see whether the switch should be made to Shell sort is made in step 4. What happens if the total number of values to be sorted at the start is less than *switchPoint*? Obviously this test should be made right at the beginning, before any sorting is attempted.

Correcting this point, and after some juggling to discover the best way of carrying the high and low bounds forward from iteration to iteration, we can now be more formal:

Level 2.5 (version 3)

Sorting Procedure (parameters. High, Low)
Constants   SwitchPoint = 16
               StackSize = 20 (see note below)
Variables   Pointer
               Stack : Array [1..StackSize]
BEGIN
    Pointer : = 1
    Put Low and High on stack
    REPEAT
        Take High and Low off Stack
        If (High − Low) > SwitchPoint THEN
        BEGIN
            Place datum, put bounds of (a) higher subspan and (b) lower subspan on Stack
        END

ELSE Shell sort
   UNTIL Stack is empty
END

Stack overflow checking is unnecessary since the maximum size can be calculated in advance. The size of 20 is adequate for 512 components, but would have to be increased for more components. The rule for calculating stack size can be given as

$$2 \times (\text{TRUNC}(\log(\text{base } 2)\ \text{NumberOfComponents})) + 2.$$

The logarithm to base 2 of a number can be obtained, accurately enough for this formula, by multiplying the Naperian logarithm by 1.45.

Apart from the straightforward operations of taking values off the stack, there are two sections that need fuller consideration at the next lower level: 'Place datum' and 'Shell sort'. We shall call these Level 3.5.1 and Level 3.5.2 respectively.

Level 3.5.1, 'Place datum', can be attempted as

Level 3.5.1 (version 1)

Step 1 Initialise

Step 2 Take the value at the lowest bound. Call it *Datum*.

Step 3 Progressively test the values in the array, in descending order starting from the high bound, until a value is found that is less than Datum. Put it in the space vacated by step 2.

Step 4 Do the same as step 3, this time ascending from the low bound until a value greater than Datum is found. Put it in the space vacated by step 3.

Step 5 Repeat steps 3 and 4, each time starting at the point previously reached, until the left and right scans meet.

Step 6 Put *Datum* in the empty space

Step 7 Save on stack the low and high bounds of the high and low subspans which are respectively:

       the 'location' of step 6, plus 1,

       High (as it was at start),

       Low (as it was at start) and

       the 'location' of step 6, less 1.

Examination of the above reveals a flaw. It is quite possible for the two scans to overlap after *either* step 3 *or* step 4. Therefore the test of step 5 must be made after both steps 3 and 4.

Another point which this attempt highlights is the necessity for two more variables. Since we need to preserve the initial values of *Low* and *High* until the end of the opeation for step 7, we need two more variables (which we shall call *Lo* and *Hi*) to act as pointers in the intermediate steps.

We can now attempt a more formal version:

Level 3.5.1 (version 2)

```
BEGIN
    Lo  : = Low
    Hi  : = High
    Datum  : = Store [Low]
    REPEAT
          WHILE (store [Hi] > Datum) AND (Hi > Lo) DO
              Hi  : = Hi − 1
          IF  Hi > Lo THEN
          BEGIN
              Store [Lo]  : = Store [Hi]
              WHILE  (Store  [Lo] < datum) AND (Lo  < Hi) DO
                  Lo  : = Lo + 1
                  IF Lo < Hi THEN
                      Store [Hi]  : = Store [Lo]
          END
    UNTIL Lo = Hi
    Store [Lo]  : = Datum
      (or Store [Hi]  : = Datum, they are the same)
    Save on stack:  Hi + 1, high
    Save on stack:  Lo − 1, Low
END
```

It will be seen that, as frequently happens at the lower levels when using the top-down approach, we have now reached a stage where what has been written can be transliterated straight into a Pascal program. This is the stage at which we should test out the program with a pencil, paper and real data. This is a very necessary but rather tedious chore. There are often ways in which this can be speeded up. For example, although the above program is intended to operate on more than 16 components, a preliminary check can be made using half a dozen or less. Furthermore, the first check should always be done on what is called 'worst case' data. What actually constitutes 'worst case' depends very much on what the program is intended to do and no hard and fast rules can be laid down. An experienced programmer subconsciously identifies the parts of a program that might cause problems and the type of data that could cause them. For example he will usually test to see what happens the first and last time round a **FOR. . .TO** loop. Particularly, if the starting or finishing value of the control variable is itself a variable, what happens if the finishing value is equal to or less than the starting value? Is the finishing condition of a **WHILE** or **REPEAT** loop always going to be achieved?

In the above program the worst case for data is likely to be either (or both) of two conditions: the components are already in the right order at the start or they are completely in the reverse order. If we examine either of these in the above program we shall see a serious flaw. Let us assume the latter case and that we are sorting four values, 4, 3, 2 and 1, in that order. The result, using the format that we used in Chapter 7, will be

$$
\begin{array}{llll}
(4) & 3 & 2 & 1 \qquad \text{Datum } \underline{4} \\
\underline{1} & 3 & 2 & (1) \qquad \text{Datum } 4 \\
1 & 3 & 2 & \underline{4} \qquad \text{Datum } (4)
\end{array}
$$

Lo and Hi would both be equal to High, and when it came to saving the low and high bounds on the stack they would be High and High+1 respectively. This would never do because the low bound would be greater than the high bound, leading to complete confusion and possible subscript overflows when the numbers were picked off the stack later. If you now test the program with the numbers starting in the correct order, you will find a similar flaw at the other end. The high bound will be saved as Low − 1.

If we think about it, there is no need to save the bounds of a subspan that consists of no components. Therefore, we should go back to level 2.5 (version 3) and alter

Save on stack: Hi + 1, High
Save on stack: Lo − 1, Low

to

IF Hi < High THEN save on stack: Hi + 1, High
IF Lo > Low THEN save on stack: Lo − 1, Low

Actually a little reflection shows that if Hi is equal to (High − 1), there will only be one component in the subspan, and the same applies if Lo equals (Low + 1), so there is no need to save them in that case. The final, Pascal, version given below does not save spans of less than two components.

The Shell sort program can be developed in the same way as the Place Datum program:

Level 3.5.2 (version 1)

Step 1 Initialise.

Step 2 Halve the span.

Step 3 Compare the lowest component with the one that is a span away.

Step 4 If the value of the 'higher' component is less than that of the 'lower', then exchange them.

Step 5 Repeat steps 3 and 4 progressing up the array until the 'higher' component is the highest in the array.

Step 6   If the span is greater than 1, halve the span.

Step 7   Repeat steps 5 and 6 until all are in correct order.

When we come to formalising this program there are two points that will need special consideration. The first is that, as was noted in Chapter 7, the exchanging of two values necessitates the introduction of a third. We shall therefore need an extra variable, *temp*, as we had in the bubble sort. Secondly, the expedient that has to be used for step 7 needs some explanation. We declare a Boolean variable *Done* which is initialised as TRUE at the start of each iteration. If, during the iteration, any exchanges take place, then this variable is set to FALSE. We then repeat until *Done* is TRUE at the end of an iteration.

We can now formalise Shell sorting as a procedure:

Level 3.5.2 (version 2)

```
PROCEDURE shellSort (low, high) : integer;

(*    Sorts integers in a global array "store"      *
 *       in ascending order by Shell's method.      *
 *    "low" and "high" are lower and upper bounds   *)

VAR  span, Lo : INTEGER;
     temp, done : BOOLEAN;

BEGIN
  span := high + 1 - low;
  WHILE span > 1 DO;
  BEGIN
    span := span DIV 2;
    REPEAT
      done := TRUE;
      FOR Lo := low TO (high - span) DO
        IF store [Lo] > store [Lo + span] THEN
        BEGIN
          temp := store [Lo];
          store [Lo] := store [Lo + span];
          store [Lo + span] := temp;
          done := FALSE
        END
    UNTIL done
  END
END;
```

We can now write the whole of level 2.5 as a Pascal procedure:

```
PROCEDURE quickSort (low, high : INTEGER);

(*    This procedure sorts the components of an     *
 *       array 'store' into ascending order.        *
 *    'low' and 'high' are the lower and upper      *
 *       bounds of the components to be sorted.     *
```

```
*          'StackSize' should be set according        *
*                      to needs.                      *
*      'SwitchPoint' is the point at which Shell      *
*        sort is undertaken instead of quickSort.   *)

CONST  switchPoint = 16; (* Change to Shell sort *)
       stackSize = 22; (* Enough for 1028 compnts *)

VAR  pointer : INTEGER;
        stack : ARRAY [1..stackSize] OF INTEGER;


PROCEDURE shellSort (low, high : INTEGER);

EXTERNAL (* see above *);


PROCEDURE push (first, second : INTEGER);

(*  Puts two values, 'first' and 'second',     *
*        on the stack in that order.            *)

BEGIN
  stack [pointer] := first;
  pointer := SUCC (pointer);
  stack [pointer] := second;
  pointer := SUCC (pointer)
END; (* push *)


PROCEDURE placeDatum;

(*  Puts value from 'low' component of an array,   *
*      'store [low..high]', into final position    *
*     with values below being less or equal and    *
*       those above being greater than or equal.  *)

VAR  datum, Lo, Hi : INTEGER;

BEGIN

  Lo := low;
  Hi := high;
  datum := store [Lo];
  REPEAT
    WHILE (store [Hi] > datum) AND (Hi > Lo) DO
      Hi := PRED (Hi);
      IF Hi > Lo THEN
      BEGIN
        store [Lo] := store [Hi];
        WHILE (store [Lo] < datum) AND (Lo < Hi) DO
          Lo := SUCC (Lo);
        IF Lo < Hi THEN
            store [Hi] := store [Lo]
      END
  UNTIL Lo = Hi;
  store [Lo] := datum;
```

```
    IF (Hi + 1) < high THEN push (SUCC (Hi), high);
    IF (Lo - 1) > low THEN push (low, PRED (Lo));
END; (* placeDatum *)


BEGIN  (* quickSort *)

  pointer := 1;
  push (low, high);
  REPEAT
  (*      Pull bounds off stack         *)
    pointer := PRED (pointer);
    high  := stack [pointer];
    pointer := PRED (pointer);
    low := stack [pointer];

    IF (high - low) > switchPoint
          THEN placeDatum
          ELSE shellSort (low, high)
  UNTIL pointer = 1
END;
```

This procedure has been written as a library procedure to sort a single integer array.† In the song contest program there are three such arrays, one for the scores (on which the sorting takes place), one for the song number and one for the name. The last two should be moved each time the first is. However, all such movements take time and movement of a string array can take a comparatively long time since each character has to be moved separately. Thus the sorting of string arrays should be avoided where possible. The following shows how this can be done in this program.

Of the three arrays (score, number and name) the first starts empty and the second and third start in competitor number order thus:

number [1]   = 1   name [1]   = UTOPIA
number [2]   = 2   name [2]   = EREHWON
number [3]   = 3   name [3]   = RURITANIA
  .   .   .   .   .   .
number [327] = 327 name [327]   = BARATARIA
          .   .   .   .

If the *number* array is always sorted in step with the *score* array, the *name* array can be left unaltered. When the time comes for writing the information to the telecomp, an instruction such as the following will ensure that the correct name appears against each score:

†*Shellsort* can also be used as a library procedure

```
FOR n := 1 TO numsongs DO
   WRITELN (Telecomp, n, number [n],
                   name [number [n]], score [n] )
```

In the days when it cost more to hire a computer by the hour than it now costs to buy a computer of the same power, programming efficiency was almost entirely concerned with saving time during the execution of the program. Although this can still be important, especially in 'real time' applications where the computer is required to produce results before the next activity can proceed (as in the control of industrial processes or for a Globalvision Song Contest), it is now generally realised that the greatest savings in time and cost can be made by good programming strategy.

The approach advocated in this chapter may appear long winded. It would be possible to code the *quicksort* program straight into Pascal without the preliminary stages. But the proof of the pudding is in the eating. The above program worked correctly the first time it was put on the computer. It would have been a good programmer indeed who could have coded even a comparatively simple program such as this straight into Pascal and made the same claim. If a program does not work correctly the first time, its 'debugging' can take hours or days. The result is then often a patchwork which is difficult for anyone to understand or follow. It is important that a program should be easy to understand because it may have to be modified or extended. Commercial and industrial firms often find it more economical to start again rather than try to modify poorly written or poorly documented programs. This must be wrong. The whole story of evolution indicates that we ought to try to improve on the past, not to scrap it and start again.

Nowhere, perhaps, are the opportunities for developing and evolving good software as great as they are in schools, colleges and universities. Each new generation (and there is a new 'generation' every year) has the chance of developing and improving on the work of previous generations. Never before, in any branch of education or learning, has there been such an opportunity, but it can only be grasped if the 'legacy' programs are clear, well written and well documented.

Compared with some other languages, Pascal has a flying start. Its structure imposes certain disciplines and programs are comparatively easy to follow. But if a program is to be modified or improved, the underlying reasoning and logic (whether good or bad) behind it must be on record. Program documentation that does not include this is seldom worth the paper it is written on.

This chapter has only scratched the surface of a large and important subject. For further reading you could do much worse than Ledgard *et al.* (1979).

EXERCISES

Note: All your programs from now on will, of course, be developed top-down with full documentation. This does not prevent your incorporating, in your programs, procedures or fragments that you have already developed or that you have culled from this book or elsewhere.

11.1 Write a program that will enable you to prepare a chart for your implementation similar to that in Fig. 10.1 (Chapter 10). Fill an array with 1000 random integers in the range from 0 to 10 000 and then sort them by each of the methods. The actual sort should start when the <newline> key is pressed. As soon as the sort is complete send a short message to OUTPUT. Time this part of the program for various quantities of random numbers and prepare the chart.

11.2 Write the full program required by the organisers of the Globalvision Song Contest. No competitor's name exceeds 12 characters in length.

CHAPTER 12

APPLICATIONS 3: SIMULATION

□ This chapter discusses the application of Pascal to simulation problems. No new features are introduced and the chapter may be skipped by those to whom the subject is of no interest. □

12.1 INTRODUCTION

Many statistical problems can be solved by the use of well known formulae, but problems involving a large number of variables, interacting on each other, can often be more easily solved by simulating on a computer what happens in real life. A typical example occurs in road traffic engineering, where the arrival of vehicles and pedestrians at a busy road junction can be simulated. It is then possible to try out the effect of different traffic control arrangements, traffic light sequence and timings, etc., without the risk of snarling up a whole neighbourhood.

Such a program may be long, but the principles it employs are quite straightforward, almost always involving the generation of pseudo-random numbers. We have already seen a very simple example with only one variable, in the *Roulette* programs. As an introduction to more complicated programs, let us look at a slightly more complicated game of chance, with two random variables. The following *TwoDice* program simulates the result of repeatedly rolling a pair of dice and adding their scores together:

```
PROGRAM TwoDice (OUTPUT);

CONST
    width = 64;    (* Characters per line *)

VAR
    seed, n, m : INTEGER;
    done : BOOLEAN;
    total : ARRAY [2 .. 12] OF INTEGER;
```

```
PROCEDURE inSeed (VAR seed : INTEGER);

EXTERNAL;  (* Chapter 7 *)


FUNCTION random (VAR seed : INTEGER;
                      max : INTEGER) : INTEGER;

EXTERNAL;  (* Chapter 7 *)


PROCEDURE display;

BEGIN
  PAGE;
  FOR n := 2 TO 12 DO
  BEGIN
    WRITE (n :8, ' ');
    FOR m:= 1 TO total [n] DO WRITE ('*');
    WRITELN
  END
END;

BEGIN
  inSeed(seed);
  FOR n := 2 TO 12 DO total [n] := 0;
  done := FALSE;
  REPEAT
    n := random (seed, 5) + random (seed, 5) + 2;
    total [n] := SUCC (total [n]);
    IF total [n] >= width - 10 THEN done := TRUE;
    display  (* if VDU output *)
  UNTIL done;
  display   (* if teletypewriter output *)
END.
```

This program has alternative forms. The *display* procedure is called within the loop if a VDU is used. This allows you to see the histogram being developed. If you have teletypewriter output, it should be called after completion of the loop, thereby saving several hundred pages of paper!

In this simulation the random numbers (1 .. 6) in each case are required to be evenly distributed, each number having an even chance of showing up. Despite this, the result is heavily weighted towards the value 7, as shown in Fig. 12.1. Very frequently, it is a *weighted* random number that we need. To demonstrate this, let us imagine that we wanted to develop a game which simulated a football tournament. As we are inventing the game we can make our own rules. We can say, for example, that no team will be allowed to score more than nine goals in any one match, because

Fig 12.1 *example of a computer simulation: pairs of pseudo-random numbers in the range 1–6 have been added together to simulate the rolling of a pair of dice; each asterisk represents one occurrence of the relevant score; computing time for the 315 'throws' was 13 seconds*

```
 2 **************
 3 *************
 4 *********************
 5 ********************************
 6 ***************************************************
 7 *****************************************************************
 8 ********************************************************
 9 *********************************************
10 ****************************
11 **********************
12 **********
```

experience tells us that this very seldom happens. But it would hardly be satisfactory to use a statement such as

$$teamScore := random (seed, 9)$$

to generate the scores of the teams in our game because this would imply that a team would have just as much chance of scoring nine goals as it would have of scoring, say, two. Experience tells us that this is most unlikely. In fact in 59 games played in the English and Scottish football leagues on a recent Saturday

> 30 teams did not score,
> 36 scored 1 goal,
> 35 scored 2 goals,
> 13 scored 3 goals,
> 4 scored 4 goals.

Thus 118 teams scored a total of 161 goals.

For our tournament, we would need to develop a method such that random numbers are generated in approximately the same frequency as the above results. One, somewhat cumbersome, way to do this would be to form an array of 118 integer components and to give each component in turn a value equal to the goals scored by each of the 118 teams. A statement such as the following would then, at each call, give us a score that had the same weighting as on this particular Saturday:

$$score := list [random (seed, 117) + 1]$$

A neater way would be to start by preparing a cumulative sum list:

> 30 teams scored zero
> 66 teams scored 1 or zero
> 101 teams scored 2 or less
> 114 teams scored 3 or less
> 118 teams scored 4 or less.

We could then load a much smaller array *cumList[0. .4]* **OF** INTEGER as follows:

```
cumList [0] := 30;
cumList [1] := 66;
cumList [2] := 101;
cumList [3] := 114;
cumList [4] := 118;
```

The following fragment will then return a weighted score:

```
number := random (seed, 117) + 1;
n := 0;
WHILE number <= cumList [n] DO n := SUCC (n);
score := PRED (n)
```

Although this is less cumbersome than the previous suggestion, we still have two problems. The first is that we still have to count up the number of teams scoring 0, 1, 2, etc., goals, and the second is that we do not know if the pattern of scores on this particular Saturday was typical. Fortunately the science of statistics can come to our aid to solve the latter problem, and it certainly reduces the amount of work involved in the former.

A study of statistics is beyond the scope of this book and there are several popular books on the subject, for example Moroney (1951). However, there are two types of elementary distribution curve, an understanding of which will open up many opportunities for writing simulation or games programs. The rest of this chapter will deal with these briefly.

12.2 POISSON DISTRIBUTION

Statistics can predict the number of teams that will score 0, 1, 2, etc., goals provided that we know the total number of teams and the total number of goals. This will give us the mean (average) number of goals per team. If we call this mean z, then the *probability* that any one particular team will score 0, 1, 2, 3, etc., goals is given by the successive terms of the following series:

$$e^{-z} \times (1 + z + z^2/2! + z^3/3! + z^4/4! + z^5/5! + \ldots).$$

When 118 teams score a total of 161 goals, the mean is 1.3644 goals per team and the successive terms are as shown in Table 12.1. This is known as the *Poisson distribution*.

Table 12.1

Number of goals	Probability of scoring the stated number of goals	Cumulative probability
0	0.255 534	0.255 534
1	0.348 651	0.604 185
2	0.237 849	0.842 034
3	0.108 174	0.950 208
4	0.036 898	0.987 106
5	0.010 069	0.997 175
6	0.002 290	0.999 464
7	0.000 446	0.999 911
8	0.000 076	0.999 987
9	0.000 012	0.999 998
10	0.000 002	1.000 000
11	0.000 000	1.000 000

A word about probability for those who do not know. Probability in statistics is always expressed as a fraction of unity. A probability of 1.0 is therefore an absolute certainty. A probability of 0.1 is equivalent to one chance in 10 or 10 chances in 100 or 10%.

Since the above gives the probability of *one* team scoring the stated number of goals, the *number of teams* expected to score the stated number of goals can be obtained by multiplying each term by the total number of teams. If you multiply them by 118, you will note that the predicted results are quite close to those actually scored. If we had taken the results over a whole football season instead of a single Saturday, then we would expect to get even closer correspondence between the actual figures and those predicted.

Since the standard Pascal function, EXP($-z$), will give us e^{-z} and the successive terms of the series are those that we have already met in Chapter 5, it is quite easy to prepare a theoretical cumulative list similar to the actual one above. We must know the theoretical number of teams (this is the same as the number of different random numbers we propose to generate) and the mean number of goals scored.

The following program was used to obtain the above table:

```
PROGRAM Poisson (INPUT, OUTPUT, printer);

VAR
  prob, cumProb, z (* Average *) : REAL;
  n: INTEGER;
  printer : TEXTFILE;
```

```
BEGIN
  write ('z= ?');
  read (z);
  WRITELN (printer,
    'Number       Probability of        Cumulative');
  WRITELN (printer,
    ' of       scoring the stated       Probability');
  WRITELN (printer,
    ' goals      number of goals');
  WRITELN (printer);
  prob := EXP (-z);
  cumProb := prob;
  n := 0;
  WHILE prob > 0.0000005 DO
  BEGIN
    WRITELN (printer, n : 4, prob :17 :6,
                              cumProb :22 :6);
    n := SUCC (n);
    prob := prob * z / n;
    cumProb := cumProb + prob
  END
END.
```

Exit from the loop occurs when *prob* reaches a very small value, rather than when *cumProb* reaches 1.0. This is because, owing to rounding errors, *cumProd* may never reach 1.0. Another effect of this is discussed in the next paragraph.

In order to use this Poisson distribution program in a simulation of a football tournament, or for any other simulation, the random numbers we use must be in the range from 0 to 1.0. Numbers in this range can be directly obtained from the random number generator of Chapter 7 by the following statement:

```
ran := (random (seed, 10000)) / 10000
```

In actual practice, for the reason given in the last paragraph, it is better to restrict the largest value of *ran* to 0.9999 by generating random integers in the range from 0 to 9999, as is done in the following program, which simulates the probable scores of 118 teams for any mean score.

```
PROGRAM Football (INPUT, OUTPUT);

CONST
  numTeams = 118;

VAR
  prob, cumProb, z (* Goal mean *), ran : REAL;
  seed, n, m : INTEGER;

FUNCTION random (VAR seed : INTEGER;
                     max : INTEGER) : INTEGER;
```

```
EXTERNAL;  (* see chapter 7 *)


PROCEDURE inSeed (VAR seed : INTEGER);

EXTERNAL;  (* see chapter 7 *)

BEGIN
  inSeed (seed);
  write ('z= ?');
  read (z);
  FOR m := 1 TO numTeams DO
  BEGIN
    ran := (random (seed, 9999)) / 10000;
    prob := EXP (-z);
    cumProb := prob;
    n := 0;
    WHILE cumProb < ran DO
    BEGIN
      n := SUCC(n);
      prob := prob * z / n;
      cumProb := cumProb + prob
    END;
    WRITE (n :4);
    IF m MOD 16 (* Sixteen teams per line *) = 0
             THEN WRITELN
  END
END.
```

If you run the above program, using a goal mean of 1.3644, you are unlikely to get the same distribution as the actual scores given above. You will also find that repeated running of the program with different seeds will also give slightly differing results. It is in the nature of statistics that small samples seldom match theory exactly.

A Poisson distribution can be represented as a *histogram* or *bar chart* as in Fig. 12.2.

Fig 12.2 *histogram showing the probability of a team scoring the stated number of goals*

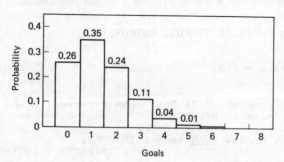

12.3 NORMAL DISTRIBUTION

Let us suppose that someone is cutting up lengths of timber. For simplicity let us suppose that he has cut 64 lengths and that he was trying to cut each length so that it measured 100 mm exactly. When he had finished cutting he might measure his results. Depending on his expertise, the state of his saw, the accuracy with which he was able to measure and other factors, his results will probably vary slightly from the ideal at which he was aiming. Figure 12.3 gives a typical histogram of the results he might get. You will see that, although he has succeeded in getting more into the range 99.5 to 100.5 than into any other range, there are a lot that are shorter than he intended and about the same number that are longer. This type of distribution is known as a 'normal' or 'Gaussian' distribution.

Fig 12.3 *histogram indicating the lengths of a number of pieces of wood, all of the same nominal length; each cell extends from 0.5 mm below to 0.5 mm above the stated length*

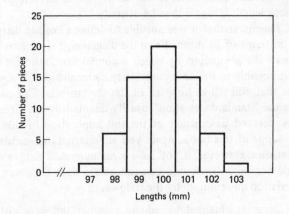

Not only is it the distribution that is often achieved when people are endeavouring to achieve a norm, but it is also the sort of distribution often found in nature. For example, the heights of people of the same age, sex and race usually have a normal distribution. So do the IQs of the whole population.

Reverting to the wood-cutting example. If the same exercise had been undertaken by a skilled craftsman, his results might have been similar to those shown by curve A in Fig. 12.4, while those of an inept amateur might have been more like those of curve B. In both cases the distribution is symmetrical and similar in shape to that in Fig. 12.3, but the expert's is tall and narrow, while the amateur's is broad and flat. The amateur's

Fig 12.4   *possible results obtained by an expert (curve A; mean = 100;*
standard deviation ≃ 0.7) and an amateur (curve B; mean = 103;
standard deviation ≃ 1.5)

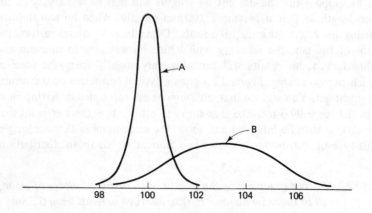

also displays another difference. In his desire not to cut the pieces too
short, his mean length is longer than he desired.

You will remember that it was possible to define a Poisson distribution
completely in terms of its mean. From the diagrams, it is obvious that the
mean is one of the parameters by which a normal distribution is defined.
But it is not possible to define it completely by mean alone. We need also
a parameter that will tell us how tall or flat the curve is. This parameter
is known as the 'standard deviation', usually denoted by the Greek letter
sigma, σ. A detailed description of the full implication of this term is
beyond the scope of this book. Again you are referred to a standard text-
book on statistics. However, if you have some numerical data which you
believe to be normally distributed you can obtain both the mean and the
standard deviation quite simply by the following:

(1) The mean is obtained by adding together the values of all the
entries and dividing the total by the number of entries.

(2) The standard deviation is obtained by adding together the *squares*
of all the entries and dividing the total by the number of entries. From this
result the *square of the mean* must be subtracted. The square root of this
last result is the standard deviation.

It is quite easy to write a Pascal program that will do this (see the front
cover of this book). However, for simulation purposes we wish to reverse
this process. Given the mean and standard deviation, we wish to generate
a series of random numbers that are weighted accordingly. There is a
mathematical formula for the normal distribution curve, and from it we
could generate a curve of probabilities that we could use in a way similar

to that which we used for the Poisson distribution. The mathematics becomes rather complicated and, anyway, in a book on Pascal programming there are sentimental reasons for using another approach, as we shall shortly see.

If we look again at Fig. 12.3 and evaluate the height of each of the bars, we shall see that they are 1, 6, 15, 20, 15, 6 and 1 respectively. If you are familiar with binomial expansion in algebra, you will recognise these as the coefficients of the successive terms of the expansion of $(a + b)^6$. The coefficients for other expansions of $(a + b)^n$ with different values of n are given in Table 12.2.

Table 12.2

n	Coefficients in the expansion of $(a + b)^n$										
1	1	1									
2	1	2	1								
3	1	3	3	1							
4	1	4	6	4	1						
5	1	5	10	10	5	1					
6	1	6	15	20	15	6	1				
7	1	7	21	35	35	21	7	1			
8	1	8	28	56	70	56	28	8	1		
9	1	9	36	84	126	126	84	36	9	1	
10	1	10	45	120	210	252	210	120	45	10	1
11	1	11	55	165	330	462	462	330	165	55	11	1

.
.
.

There are certain features of Table 12.2 that should be noted. The first is that each row has $(n + 1)$ terms. The second is that, if you add up all the terms in any row, you will find that the total comes to 2^n. Furthermore, Blaise Pascal pointed out that, assuming that the blank ends of each row are zeros, you can derive any term in any row except the first simply by adding the term immediately above it to the term on that one's left. For this reason this construction is generally called 'Pascal's triangle'. In computing we can write a simple algorithm to do the necessary addition and to develop the expansion of any number of terms. It is fitting that, three and a half centuries later, we can make good use of Pascal's discovery in the language which now bears his name.

We are going to develop the expansion for the case where n is 16. We need the following declarations:

```
VAR
  n, m : INTEGER;
  cell : ARRAY [0..17] OF REAL
```

and we start by clearing *cell[0]* and initialising the first two terms for the case where $n = 1$:

```
cell [1] := 1;
cell [2] := 1
```

Then, with two **FOR** loops we carry out Pascal's additions:

```
FOR n := 2 TO 16 DO
  FOR m:= n + 1 DOWNTO 1 DO
    cell [m] := cell [m] + cell [m - 1]
```

Since we shall be wanting cumulative values, we now add the cells:

```
FOR m:=2 TO 17 DO
    cell [m]:= cell [m] + cell [m-1]
```

Since it is cumulative probabilities that we are aiming for and the value in *cell[17]* is now n^{16} or 65 536, the values in all cells must be scaled down by dividing them by 65 536:

```
FOR m:= 1 TO 17 DO
    cell [m] := cell [m] / 65536
```

We can now use the same method as we used for generating a Poisson distribution – generating random numbers in the range from 0 to 1 and identifying the cell in which the random number occurred. The following fragment would generate 1000 cell numbers in the range from 1 to 17 and the frequency with which each was generated would be weighted according to the normal distribution:

```
FOR n := 1 TO 1000 DO
BEGIN
  m := 1;
  ran := random (seed, 10000) / 10000;
  WHILE cell [m] < ran DO m := SUCC(m);
  WRITELN (m)
END
```

If we were to take the mean and standard deviation of these numbers we should find that the mean was very close to 9 and that the standard deviation closely approximated 2. These close approximations will always arise when taking samples and are quite acceptable in simulation work. Of course, we shall seldom require weighted numbers in the range from 1 to 17 with a mean of 9 and a standard deviation (*sigma*) of 2. We shall wish to stimulate our own mean and sigma. Assuming that these values have been supplied earlier in the program, we could replace the above WRITELN(m) instruction with

```
WRITELN (0.5 * sigma * (m-9) + mean)
```

to give us the weighted random numbers we need.

We can now assemble all these fragments together to give us the following program which will generate 50 random numbers weighted in accordance with a normal distribution:

```
PROGRAM NormalDistribution (INPUT, OUTPUT);

VAR
  seed, number, n : INTEGER;
  cell : ARRAY[0..17] OF REAL;
  mean, sigma, ran : REAL;

FUNCTION random (VAR seed : INTEGER;
                 max : INTEGER ) : INTEGER;

EXTERNAL; (* see chapter 7 *)


PROCEDURE inSeed (VAR seed : INTEGER;

EXTERNAL;  (* see chapter 7 *)


BEGIN
  inSeed (seed);
  WRITE ('Mean and Standard Deviation ?');
  READ (mean, sigma);
  FOR n := 0 TO 17 DO cell [n] := 0;
  cell [1] := 1;
  cell [2] := 1;
  FOR number := 2 TO 16 DO
    FOR n:= number + 1 DOWNTO 1 DO
        cell [n] := cell [n] + cell [n-1];
  FOR n := 2 TO 17 DO
        cell [n] := cell [n] + cell [n-1];
  FOR n := 1 TO 17 DO
        cell [n] := cell [n] / 65536;
  FOR n := 1 TO 100  DO
  BEGIN
    number := 1;
    ran := random (seed, 10000) /10000;
```

```
    WHILE cell [number] < ran DO
            number := SUCC (number);
    WRITE
        ((0.5 * sigma * (number - 9) + mean) :8 :2)
    END
    END.
```

It gives the following output with a seed of 1, a mean of 100 and a standard deviation of 6.7:

86.60	96.65	106.70	93.30	93.30	96.65
103.35	96.65	83.25	120.10	96.65	100.00
89.95	103.35	96.65	100.00	106.70	96.65
106.70	103.35	110.05	103.35	93.30	100.00
96.65	93.30	106.70	113.40	110.05	100.00
96.65	106.70	93.30	103.35	103.35	113.40
103.35	96.65	93.30	103.35	96.65	100.00
103.35	96.65	96.65	113.40	93.30	89.95
89.95	113.40	110.05	96.65	89.95	100.00
100.00	100.00	103.35	93.30	89.95	93.30
93.30	100.00	103.35	96.65	103.35	100.00
110.05	93.30	100.00	103.35	106.70	86.60
96.65	100.00	93.30	106.70	106.70	96.65
93.30	93.30	106.70	93.30	106.70	103.35
103.35	93.30	89.95	103.35	110.05	86.60
103.35	103.35	100.00	93.30	93.30	96.65
100.00	106.70	100.00	100.00		

The above two distributions, and some others of a similar type, play a large part in most simulations used in games and in business and, indeed, they form the basis of many 'business games'.

12.4 A SIMULATION PROBLEM

You might like to try to build a simulation model to solve the following problem, based on an actual case.

A certain seaport has a large grain terminal. Grain comes in by ship and is stored in a silo from which customers collect it by lorry. Ships arrive at irregular intervals from many parts of the world (Poisson distribution). The ships are all approximately the same size (Gaussian distribution). Grain is removed from the silo by customers' lorries. The daily call-off closely follows a Gaussian distribution. Ships are unloaded as soon as they arrive, whatever the day of the week. Customers, however, do not collect grain on Saturdays or Sundays. (To simplify the problem you may ignore public holidays. Alternatively you may complicate the model by making your own rules about them.)

The mean amount of grain removed each day is 11 000 tonnes with a standard deviation of 1900 tonnes. The mean size of cargo in the ships is 23 000 tonnes with a standard deviation of 2500 tonnes. From this it is possible to calculate that the mean period between ship arrivals is 2.93 days.

You should have little difficulty in programming a model of this operation. It could be used, for example, to decide the appropriate size of the silo. A major difference between a model of this type and actual practice is that there is no harm in having negative stock in the silo during a simulation run. At the end of the simulated period the required size of silo is the difference between the maximum stock and the minimum stock during the period. The trace of Fig. 12.5 was produced by such a program. It simulates the activity at the silo over a period of 50 years. One additional feature has been added to this program. The amount in the silo would fluctuate between wide limits without some form of control. Control is usually

Fig 12.5 *simulation of a silo operation: each bar represents the highest and lowest points in one month and the total trace represents 50 years of operation; it was produced in two hours on a microcomputer*

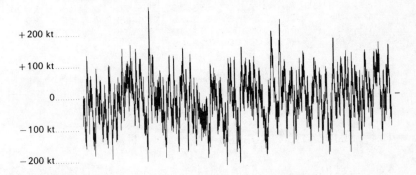

exercised by the silo manager by scheduling the deliveries. Because many of his deliveries will already be on the high seas when he gives his instructions, there may well be a delay of several weeks before they have any effect. The trace of Fig. 12.5 has a crude control. Each quarter the deliveries for the next quarter but one are rescheduled on the basis of what is currently in the silo and what is due for delivery in the coming quarter.

According to your interests and inclinations you can develop and modify this model in a variety of ways. For example:

(a) You can formulate and develop improved control strategies for the silo manager to use to minimise the size of the silo.

(b) You can put your own price tags on such things as the cost of extra silo capacity, the demurrage that has to be paid when a ship is kept waiting, and the loss of profit when a customer's order cannot be met because of the absence of grain. You can then modify the model and run it to develop a policy for maximising the profit.

(c) You can use it to see the effect on the size of the silo when new 150 000 tonne bulk carriers replace the 25 000 tonners now in use.

(d) Above all you can use the *principles* of this model to develop models or games that are more appropriate to your own needs.

CHAPTER 13

APPLICATIONS 4: GRAPHICS

□ This chapter discusses the use of standard Pascal in the preparation of computer graphics in mathematics, for business charts and in games. It may be omitted by readers to whom the subject is of no interest. □

Pascal can be used to obtain somewhat crude graphics using standard output devices. The following program produces the curve of Fig. 13.1.

```
PROGRAM DampedOscillation (printer);

(*   This program charts a damped oscillation   *
 *            using the formula                  *
 *     exp ( -x * d ) * sin ( 2 * pi * x )       *
 *          where d is a damping factor.         *
 *    The abscissa is vertical and the loci      *
 *         are indicated by asterisks          *)

CONST   width = 80; (* Characters per print line *)
  linesPerCycle = 20;
  numCycles = 3; (* Number of full cycles *)
  dampingFactor = 1;
  pi = 3.14159;

VAR   x, y : REAL;
  spaces,   (* Count of spaces before asterisk *)
    line : INTEGER; (* line count *)

BEGIN
  FOR line := 0 TO numCycles * linesPerCycle DO
  BEGIN
    x := line / linesPerCycle;
    y := EXP ( -x * dampingFactor)
                  * SIN ( 2 * pi * x );
    spaces := width DIV 2
                  + ROUND ( width DIV 2 * y);
    WRITELN (printer, '*' : spaces)
  END
END.
```

Fig 13.1 *damped oscillation:* $y = e^{-dx} \sin 2\pi x$

Using a standard printer or visual display, we are controlled by the character spacing and the line spacing of the printer or display screen. These are usually measured in characters per inch (typically from six to 12) and lines per inch (typically from three to eight). A VDU screen has usually between about 1000 character positions (16 lines of 64 characters) and 2000 character positions (24 lines of 80 characters). Printer line lengths typically vary between 40 and 150 characters, but printers have the advantage that the length in the other direction is limited only by the length of paper. This is one of the reasons that for printed graphics the traditional positions of the x and y axes are reversed.

Another sound reason for reversing the position of the axes is that, since y is usually dependent on x and not vice versa, the programming is easier. To program the above with the x-axis horizontal would have required setting up a CHAR array of 80 × 75 elements. They would first have had to be set to set to <space> and then, as the position of each point was determined, it would be replaced by an asterisk. Finally the whole would be printed out as a series of line strings.

There are times when this approach is the most convenient. The following program generates the spiral of Fig. 13.2:

```
PROGRAM Spiral (printer);

CONST
  lineWidth = 80;
  numLines = 48;
  aspectRatio = 1.66667;
  constant = 2;
  revs = 2;
  pi = 3.14159;

VAR
  radius, angle : REAL;
  n, x, y : INTEGER;
  grid : ARRAY [-39 .. 40, -23 .. 24 ] OF CHAR;

BEGIN
  FOR x := -39 TO 40 DO
    FOR y := -23 TO 24 DO
      grid [x,y] := ' ';
  FOR n := 0 TO revs * 64 DO
  BEGIN
    angle := n * pi / 32;
    radius := constant * angle;
    x := ROUND (radius * COS(angle) * aspectRatio);
    y := ROUND (radius * SIN(angle));
    grid [x, y] := '*'
  END;
  FOR y := -23 TO 24 DO
  BEGIN
    FOR x := -39 TO 40 DO
      WRITE (printer, grid [x,y]);
    WRITELN (printer)
  END;
END.
```

Fig 13.2 *the spiral generated from the expression r = kφ*

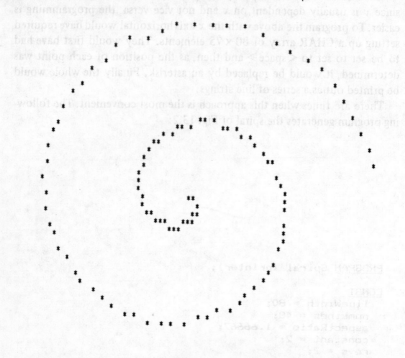

Sometimes a single, one line, array is all that is required. The following program is a modification of the *DampedOscillation* program above:

```
PROGRAM Damped2 (printer);


CONST  width = 78; (* Characters per print line *)
  linesPerCycle = 20;
  numCycles = 3; (* Number of full cycles *)
  dampingFactor = 1;
  pi = 3.14159;

VAR  x, y : REAL;
  n, spaces, line : INTEGER;
  buffer : ARRAY [-39 .. 39] OF CHAR;

BEGIN
  FOR line := 0 TO numCycles * linesPerCycle DO
  BEGIN
    x := line / linesPerCycle;
    y := EXP ( -x * dampingFactor)
                   * SIN ( 2 * pi * x );
    spaces := width DIV 2
                   + ROUND ( width DIV 2 * y );
```

```
        FOR n := -39 TO 39 DO buffer [n] := ' ';
        buffer [0] := ':';
        buffer [-39 + spaces] := '*';
        buffer [ 39 - spaces] := '*';
        FOR n := -39 TO 39 DO
                            WRITE (printer, buffer [n]);
        WRITELN (printer)
    END
END.
```

Its output is shown in Fig. 13.3.

Fig 13.3 *combination of two damped oscillations of the type shown in
            Fig 13.1*

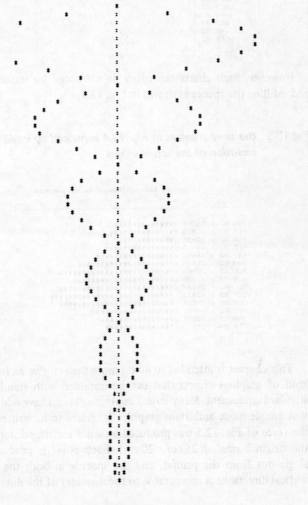

Business charts can often be produced as a by-product of other computing operations. Figure 13.4 gives the gross sales of a hypothetical company.

Fig 13.4 *a typical business graph*

```
          Gross sales (thousands of pounds)
        0        10        20        30        40
        ----------------------------------------------
        :
JAN 82  :           *
FEB 82  :            *
MAR 82  :           *
APR 82  :             *
MAY 82  :              *
JUN 82  :                 *
JUL 82  :                    *
AUG 82  :                  *
SEP 82  :                    *
OCT 82  :                      *
NOV 82  :                    *
DEC 82  :               *
JAN 83  :             *
FEB 83  :            *
```

However, such charts can often be enhanced by including the values and infilling the spaces as shown in Fig. 13.5.

Fig 13.5 *the same graph as in Fig. 13.4 enhanced by infilling and the inclusion of the actual values*

```
          Gross sales (thousands of pounds)
        0        10        20        30        40
        ----------------------------------------------
        :
JAN 82  : 13257 :*************
FEB 82  : 13928 :**************
MAR 82  : 13413 :*************
APR 82  : 14823 :**************
MAY 82  : 16606 :*****************
JUN 82  : 21415 :**********************
JUL 82  : 25003 :****************************
AUG 82  : 22928 :************************
SEP 82  : 24867 :**************************
OCT 82  : 27417 :*****************************
NOV 82  : 25213 :**************************
DEC 82  : 18401 :*******************
JAN 83  : 15557 :****************
FEB 83  : 15451 :****************
```

This chapter is intended to do no more than to give an indication of the kind of graphics effects that can be obtained with standard Pascal and standard equipment. Many Pascal implementations have additional facilities that enable more ambitious graphics programs to be written. For example the trace of Fig. 12.5 was produced on a dot matrix printer (reduced from the original size of 25 cm × 20 cm). Each point is produced by using a single dot from the printer, and the spacing in both the horizontal and vertical directions is comparable to the diameter of the dot.

CHAPTER 14

DATA TYPES

☐ We have now reached a stage in our study of the Pascal language where, if a problem can be programmed in Pascal at all, it can probably be programmed using no more of the language than has been so far discussed. The next four chapters cover some enhancements to the language, enhancements that increase considerably the 'power' of the language. Unfortunately they introduce concepts that you may find difficult to understand until you have a lot of programming experience. Newcomers are therefore strongly advised to skip them and go to Chapter 19. Later, when you are programming confidently in Pascal, you may come back to these four chapters to see how you may program even more effectively. ☐

14.1 INTRODUCTION

In addition to the four 'required' data types, INTEGER, REAL, CHAR and BOOLEAN, which we have already met, the Pascal language gives a programmer considerable latitude to declare his own types. Such types are known as 'user types'. The following program demonstrates the use of such user types:

```
PROGRAM PackOfCards (OUTPUT);

TYPE
   suit = (club, diamond, heart, spade);
   cardValue = (ace, two, three, four, five, six,
         seven, eight, nine, ten, knave, queen, king);

VAR
   suitDealt : suit;
   cardDealt : cardValue;
```

```
BEGIN
  PAGE (OUTPUT);
  FOR suitDealt := club TO spade DO
    FOR cardDealt := ace TO king DO
    BEGIN
      CASE cardDealt OF
        ace    : WRITE ('Ace');
        two    : WRITE ('Two');
        three  : WRITE ('Three');
        four   : WRITE ('Four');
        five   : WRITE ('Five');
        six    : WRITE ('Six');
        seven  : WRITE ('Seven');
        eight  : WRITE ('Eight');
        nine   : WRITE ('Nine');
        ten    : WRITE ('Ten');
        knave  : WRITE ('Knave');
        queen  : WRITE ('Queen');
        king   : WRITE ('King')
      END;
      WRITE (' of ');
      CASE suitDealt OF
        club    : WRITELN ('Clubs');
        diamond : WRITELN ('Diamonds');
        heart   : WRITELN ('Hearts');
        spade   : WRITELN ('Spades')
      END  (* CASE *)
    END
END.
```

The output from this program would be 52 lines from Ace of Clubs to King of Spades.

Newcomers to Pascal often find difficulty in understanding user types because, on their own, they seldom appear to be an aid to programming. There are, for example, more elegant ways than the above to achieve the same results. However, you are asked at this stage to accept the fact that such understanding is essential to what follows in this and subsequent chapters and not to reason 'why?' if, at present, the objective seems rather obscure.

In the above *PackOfCards* program, the reserved word **TYPE** defines two user types, *suit* and *cardValue*. The *suit* definition indicates that any variable (such as *suitDealt*) that is later declared as being of type *suit* can take any one of only four values, *club*, *diamond*, *heart* or *spade*. Any attempt to assign any other value than these to a variable of type *suit* would result in an error. By the same token, any variable (such as *cardDealt*) that is defined as being of type *cardValue* can take any one of the 13 values shown and no other.

You will recognise the similarity of this to the standard type BOOLEAN, which can take only the values FALSE and TRUE. In fact, if you imagine that outside every Pascal program there is a block with, *inter alia*, a definition

```
TYPE
  BOOLEAN = (FALSE, TRUE)
```

then you will have an exact parallel with a user type definition. Just as FALSE and TRUE are allocated the ordinal numbers 0 and 1 inside the computer, so in this example are *club*, *diamond*, *heart* and *spade* allocated the ordinal numbers 0, 1, 2 and 3 respectively. Similarly *ace*, *two*, etc., are allocated the numbers 0, 1, etc., up to *king* which is 12. Thus SUCC (*club*) is *diamond* and PRED (*queen*) is *knave*. Because their indentifiers appear in the list in a given order and each is associated with an ordinal number, types such as *suit*, *cardValue* and BOOLEAN are called *ordinal* types. In fact all the types that we have so far met, with the exception of REAL, are ordinal types (although INTEGER is a special case with the ordinal numbering of its internal representation commencing at −MAXINT and not zero).

Just as we may declare a variable as being of type BOOLEAN, so were we also able to declare the variable *suitDealt* as being of type *suit*. This enabled us to write statements such as

```
FOR suitDealt := spade DOWNTO club DO
```

etc., and

```
CASE suitDealt OF
  club : WRITELN ('Clubs')
```

etc. This last example is possible because *club*, and the other identifiers in the type definition list, are, in fact, constant identifiers.

The standard function ORD can be used to return the value by which any one of these identifiers is held in the computer. For example,

$$ORD \ (queen)$$

would return the value 11, and

```
FOR suitDealt := club TO spade DO
  FOR cardDealt := ace TO king DO
    WRITELN (ORD (suitDealt), ORD (cardDealt))
```

would give 52 lines of output:

0	0
0	1
0	2
.	.
.	.
.	.
3	11
3	12

Unfortunately we are not permitted a statement such as WRITE (*cardDealt, 'of', suitDealt*), outputting the names of user-type variables as strings. This is because WRITE operates only on the four "required" data types (REAL, INTEGER, CHAR and BOOLEAN). Such a facility would have greatly simplified the PackOfCards program.

In any case, this program is somewhat artificial. It has been written to demonstrate the use of user types, but not necessarily their *efficient* use. If we had omitted the **TYPE** definitions completely, shown all the variables in the **VAR** declaration as INTEGER, and replaced each occurrence of each type constant by its ordinal value, then the program would have been slightly shorter and would have produced the same results. It might also have been slightly less readable. Although not an important factor in this case, program readability is often considerably improved by the inclusion of user types.

Just as we cannot have a statement, WRITE (spade), where *spade* is a variable of the type *suit*, so also the response 'spade' to the statement READ (suitDealt) would be unacceptable in most implementations. An integer, corresponding to the ordinal position of the value, would generally be the correct response.

The Boolean operators, $=$, $<>$, $>$, $<$, $>=$ and $<=$ can be used with ordinal types. If used with the actual identifiers of an ordinal type list, their use is somewhat irrelevant, since, for example

$$club < spade$$
$$king > knave$$
$$six <> seven$$

are always true and

$$ace = two$$
$$three > eight$$
$$five <> five$$

are always false. However, the following, highly simplified, fragment (which might be, say, from a game of bridge) demonstrates a slightly more practical use of relational operators:

```
TYPE
   suit = (club, diamond, heart, spade);
   cardValue = (ace, two, three, four, five, six,
      seven, eight, nine, ten, knave, queen, king);

VAR
   bidNorth, bidEast, bidSouth, bidWest : suit;
   cardPlayed, cardLastPlayed, discard : cardValue;

   .  .  .  .  .  .
```

```
IF (bidEast > bidNorth) OR (bidNorth < bidWest)
   THEN bidSouth :=  etc
```

It is important to note that only variables of the same type may be compared by the Boolean operators. Thus, with the above definitions.

$$bidEast > heart$$
$$bidEast = bidNorth$$
$$heart < spade$$

are all valid expressions, but *(bidEast > Ace)*, *(CardPlayed = club)* and *(discard < bidEast)* are all invalid because in each case the comparands are of different types. However, an expression such as

```
IF ORD (discard) = ORD (bidSouth) THEN
```

is quite valid because, since ORD returns an integer value, the comparison is between two comparands of type INTEGER. The fact that expressions of mixed type are not usually accepted can be a great help to the programmer. Such invalid comparisons, which generally result from a programming error, will be identified as an error by most implementations and this introduces an element of automatic checking. In all implementations, any attempt to evaluate a non-existent value (for example PRED(*ace*) or SUCC *(king)* with the above definitions) should show a run-time error. Such automatic checking can help to avoid erroneous results from programs.

The natural corollary of the necessity to avoid mixing types is that each identifier must be defined as being of one type *and one type only*. For example, in

```
TYPE
   weekday = (mon, tues, wed, thur, fri, sat);
   weekend = (sat, sun);
   heavenlyBody = INTEGER;

VAR
   sun, moon : heavenlyBody;
```

sat has been defined as being of type *weekday* and of type *weekend*, and *sun* as *weekend* and INTEGER. Such duplication within the same block is not permitted.

All the user types so far discussed are known as *enumerated types*. The syntax definition of such enumerated types has the general form

$$<enumerated type> = (<identifier list>)$$

where <identifier list> consists of one or more identifiers. With more than one identifier, each must be separated from its successor by a comma. All type definitions must appear after the reserved word **TYPE** which itself must appear immediately after all the **CONST** definitions at the start of the relevant block. Thus all type definitions appear before any **VAR** declarations in the same block.

It is not always imperative to have a separative **TYPE** definition. The following are quite valid declarations:

```
VAR
   restDay : (sat, sun);
   bidEast, bidWest
              : (club, diamond, heart, spade);
```

and have the same effect as the equivalents that we have already met. It is often a matter of individual preference which form of syntax is used.

One type may be defined as being identical with another one, in which case the definition would be

$$<\text{type}> = <\text{type identifier}>$$

where $<$type identifier$>$ is the identifier of a type that has previously been defined.

14.2 SUBRANGE TYPES

A subrange type can be exemplified by the following type definitions (from a program written for northern temperate zones):

```
TYPE
   year = (jan, feb, mar, apr, may, jun, jul,
                         aug, sep, oct, nov, dec);
   summer = may .. aug;
```

The second definition indicates that *may*, *jun*, *jul* and *aug*, besides being of type *year*, are also members of a subrange type *summer*. The injunction given earlier that no identifier may appear in two or more type definitions does not apply here because *summer* is a *subrange type* of the *base type*, *year*.

In the above example, *summer* is a subrange of a *user-defined* type. In practice, the subranges that are probably most frequently used are those of the two *predefined* ordinal types, INTEGER and CHAR:

```
TYPE
   posInt = 0 .. MAXINT;
   player = 1 .. 11;
   upperCase = 'A' .. 'Z';
   lowerCase = 'a' .. 'z';
```

```
VAR
  number : posInt;
  scorer : player;
  initial : upperCase;
  smallLetter : lowerCase;
```

The use of subrange types greatly extends the automatic checking capabilities already discussed. With the above definitions, any attempt to assign a negative value to *number* should result in an error message together with an indication of the point in the program at which the error arose. The same would happen if any of the other variables are assigned a value that is outside the stated range. It may be argued that such an error would cause the final result to be incorrect and that this should be obvious anyway, but in practice such errors are not always obvious. Even when they are recognised, it is often difficult to locate the source of the trouble. The use of subranges can be of great assistance when debugging a program. For this reason, future program examples in this book have defined subrange types where applicable.

As before, the type definition and the variable declaration can be combined:

```
VAR
  number : 0 .. MAXINT;
  scorer : 1 .. 11;
  initial : 'A' .. 'Z';
  smallLetter : 'a' .. 'z';
```

The syntax for the definition of a subrange type is

$$\text{<subrange type>} = \text{<constant \#1>} .. \text{<constant \#2>}$$

where <constant #1> must not be greater than <constant #2>. Definitions of subrange types may be interspersed with those of enumerated types in the same **TYPE** definition of a block with the proviso that no subrange type may be defined until the base type of which it forms a subrange has already been defined. Remember that INTEGER and CHAR are predefined and do not need to be defined again. Thus the following is a valid **TYPE** definition part:

```
TYPE
  year = (jan, feb, mar, apr, may, jun, jul,
                        aug, sep, oct, nov, dec);
  posInt = 0 .. MAXINT;
  summer = may .. aug;
  upperCase = 'A' .. 'Z';
  spring = apr .. may;
```

but it would not have been valid if *spring* or *summer* had been defined before *year*. Note also that *may* appears in two subranges. This is quite permissible. You may have as many subranges of one base range as you like.

14.3 TYPE COMPATIBILITY AND ASSIGNMENT COMPATIBILITY

We can now deal more formally with a subject that we discussed in the earlier chapters of this book when we were dealing with assignment statements and relational operators. Using relational operators, what types can we compare with what? And what types may appear in the same assignment statement?

Two types are described as being *compatible* if they are the same type or if one is a subrange of the other or if both are subranges of the same base type. This means that, given the definitions

```
TYPE
    posInt = 0 .. MAXINT;
    partNum = posInt;
    negInt = -MAXINT .. -1;
    upCase = 'A' .. 'Z';
    ucVowel = (ucA, ucE, ucI, ucO, ucU);
    lowCase = 'a' .. 'z';
    weekDay = (mon, tues, wed, thur, fri);
    weekEnd = (sat, sun);
```

we have the following:

(a) *posInt* and *partNum* are the same.

(b) *posInt* and *negInt* are compatible, even though they have no values in common, because they are both subranges of INTEGER.

(c) *upCase* and *lowCase* are compatible because they are both subranges of CHAR, but *ucVowel* is not compatible with either because it is not a subrange type.

(d) *weekDay* and *weekEnd* are similarly not compatible.

However, if there had been the definitions

```
week = (sat, sun, mon, tues, wed, thurs, fri);
weekDay = mon .. fri;
weekEnd = sat .. sun;
```

then *weekDay*, *weekEnd* and *week* would all have been compatible with each other.

The types compared by relational operators must either be compatible or, if one is REAL, the other may be (though not necessarily) INTEGER.

For assignment statements the rules are rather stricter. A value of *type2* is *assignment compatible* with a value of *type1* if any of the following is true:

(a) *type1* and *type2* are the same type.

(b) *type 1* is REAL and *type2* is INTEGER (but not vice versa).

(c) Both types are compatible ordinal types and the actual value of *type2* is in the range specified for *type1*.

For the most part, assignment compatibility is a matter of common sense. A list of examples of valid assignment statements would not be particularly helpful, because the actual value of the variable of *type2* at the time of execution of the statement can decide whether the assignment is valid. For example, if *ucLetter* is a variable in the range 'A' .. 'Z', then

```
ucLetter := CHR (n)
```

is a valid assignment so long as the value of *n* is in the appropriate range. Similarly,

```
VAR
   lowRange : 0 .. 20;
   highRange : 10 .. 100;
BEGIN
   READ (lowRange);
   highRange := lowRange
```

would give an error if the value of *lowRange* is less than 10.

The above compatibility definitions will suffice for the present. We shall be adding to them later in the book as new types and topics are introduced.

14.4 STRUCTURED TYPES

The types we have so far been considering in this chapter have either been ordinal types or REAL. These are known as *simple* types. In contrast a *data structure* is a formalised combination of elements. These elements or components may be simple types or they may themselves be structured types. We have already encountered two structured types: files and arrays. We shall be having more to say about files in later chapters and for the present we shall discuss some of the implications of our newly acquired knowledge as it affects arrays, though much that we will discuss is equally applicable to other structures.

In the program *InvoicePrep* in Chapter 9 we gave an example of an array declaration:

```
VAR   . . .
  price : ARRAY [1..100] OF REAL
```

The following would have been equally acceptable:

```
TYPE
  catNos = 1 .. 100;

VAR
  price : ARRAY [catNos] OF REAL;
```

or again

```
TYPE
  catNos = 1 .. 100;
  list = ARRAY [catNos] OF REAL;

VAR
  price : list;
```

The syntax for an array declaration given in Chapter 9, although adequate at the time, now needs bringing up to date in the light of what we have learnt in this chapter:

<component identifier> : **ARRAY** [<index type or types>]

OF <component type>

<index type> may be any ordinal type as defined in the last chapter. If there is more than one <index type>, then each must be separated from its predecessor by a comma. <component type> may be any type, including those yet to be discussed.

The syntax for a component of an array is

<array variable identifier> [<index or indices>]

where <index> is an expression of the index type. There must be the same number of indices as there are index types in the array declaration and if there is more than one index, each must be separated from its predecessor by a comma.

Since the component of an array may be any type, the following variable declarations are legitimate:

```
row : ARRAY [1 .. 8] OF chessMen;
board : ARRAY [1 .. 8] OF row;
```

board is, in fact, the multidimensional array we met in Chapter 9:

```
board : ARRAY [1 .. 8, 1 .. 8] OF chessMen;
```

Arrays may be used as the variable and value parameters of functions and procedures provided that the formal and actual parameters are of identical type.

When an array component is of a simple type it can, with one exception, be treated in the same way as any variable of a simple type. It may appear, for example, on either side of an assignment statement. Its value may be used as a parameter in a READ or WRITE procedure or as a value parameter in any procedure or function. The one exception is the one already mentioned in Chapter 9 – a component of a packed array may not be used as a variable parameter of a procedure or function.

14.5 SUMMARY

Data typing is one of the strengths of the Pascal language. First, it can make programs much easier to read and to follow. Secondly, since the assignment or comparison of incompatible types should result in a compile-time error, it helps to guard against careless mistakes. Thirdly, by declaring a range of values, an error will be indicated at run-time if the value is ever outside the range. Finally, depending on the implementation, it can sometimes save storage space and speed execution.

CHAPTER 15

RECORDS

15.1 INTRODUCTION

The *InvoicePrep* program of Chapter 9 was somewhat artificial, since the output did not include the customer's name and address. These were omitted largely because string handling methods had not been discussed at the time the program was introduced. With the knowledge we now have, we can see at least two different ways in which we can arrange for this information to be output. The first involves having a file, *CustName*, which has a series of entries comprising: (a) the serial number by which the customer is identified; (b) the name and address of the customer; (c) a marker character. This last must be a character (for example, '↑') that will never appear in an address. Two successive entries on this file might then be

```
126<newline>
Jones Computing Company Ltd<newline>
334 High St<newline>
BASINGHALL<newline>
Herts WD27 8QT <newline>
↑ <newline>
129 <newline>
Mr John Smith <newline>
The Little House <newline>
POPCORN-IN-THE-MARSH <newline>
Somerset BL31 6WW <newline>
↑ <newline>
etc.
```

The program fragment to find and print the relevant customer's name and address might be

```
WHILE NOT EOF (CustName) DO
BEGIN
   READ (CustName, num);
   (* Search for customer's number *)
```

```
WHILE num <> custNum DO
BEGIN
  READ (CustName, ch);
  WHILE ch <> '↑' DO
    READ (CustName, ch)
  END;
  READ (CustName, num)
END;
(* Print out customer's name and address *)
READ (CustName, ch);
WHILE ch <> '↑' DO
BEGIN
  IF EOLN (CustName) THEN WRITELN (printer)
  ELSE WRITE (printer, ch);
  READ (CustName, ch)
END;

<output rest of invoice>

END;
WRITE ('Customer No', num, ' not in file')
```

Each of the entries in the file, starting with the first digit of the customer's number and finishing with the <newline> after the ↑ is known as a 'record'. In this case the record is described as being in *free* format, because the length of the character string is not specified. A *fixed* format record, on the other hand, comprises a string or a number of strings, of predefined length. In the following records we are assuming that the length of the alphanumerical string is exactly 120 characters. Each of the asterisks represents CHR (0), used as a padding character to bring the total string length up to 120.

```
126<newline>
Jones Computing Company Ltd<newline>
334 High Street<newline>
BASINGHALL<newline>
Herts WD27 8QT<newline>
****************************************************
129<newline>
Mr John Smith<newline>
The Little House<newline>
POPCORN-IN-THE-MARSH<newline>
Somerset BL31 6WW<newline>
****************************************************
```
etc.

Before discussing the relative merits of free and fixed format records, let us look at a possible program fragment for finding and printing out a fixed format record.

```
WHILE NOT EOF (CustName) DO
BEGIN
  READ (CustName, num);
```

```
(* Search for customer's number *)
WHILE num <> custNum DO
BEGIN
   FOR n := 1 TO 150 DO READ (CustName, ch);
   READ (CustName, num)
END;

(* Print out customer's name and address *)
FOR n := 1 TO 150 DO
BEGIN
   READ (CustName, ch);
   IF EOLN (CustName) THEN WRITELN (printer)
   ELSE IF ch <> 0 THEN WRITE (printer, ch)
END;

<output rest of invoice>

END;
WRITE ('Customer No', num, ' not in file')
```

You will see that the fixed format has enabled us to simplify the program a little. If you now try to imagine that you wish to sort a number of such records using arrays, you will probably recognise quite rapidly that the fixed format considerably simplifies the problem. The disadvantage is that the alphanumerical string in the records must each contain precisely 120 characters and counting these characters as we input the data from the keyboard would be tedious indeed and would be liable to error. However, where there are programming advantages in using fixed format, it should always be possible to write a program that translates free format into fixed format.

There is a standard Pascal data structure, **RECORD**, that enables us further to simplify programs to handle fixed format records. The following program which inputs 250 records from a file, sorts them according to customers' numbers and outputs them to a new file, illustrates one application of this structure:

```
PROGRAM CustSort (InFile, OutFile);

CONST
  max = 250

TYPE
  entry =
  RECORD
     num : 1 .. MAXINT;
     nameAddr : PACKED ARRAY [1 .. 120] OF CHAR
  END;

VAR
  temp : entry;
  list : ARRAY [1 .. max] OF entry;
```

```
      InFile, OutFile : FILE OF entry;
      n, m : 1 .. max;

BEGIN
    RESET (InFile);

    (* Load Array *)
    FOR n := 1 to max DO READ (InFile, list [n]);

    (* Bubble Sort *)
    FOR n := max-1 DOWNTO 1 DO
      FOR m := 1 TO n DO
        IF list [m].num < list [m+1].num THEN
        BEGIN
            temp := list [m];
            list [m] := list [m+1];
            list [m+1] := temp
        END;

    (* Output to OutFile *)
    REWRITE (OutFile);
    FOR n := 1 TO max DO WRITE (OutFile, list [n]);
    RESET (OutFile)
END.
```

A record in Pascal is a data structure whose components may be of any type. The exact structure of the record must be defined in a **TYPE** definition. In the above program the type, *entry*, is defined as consisting of *num* (a positive integer) and *nameAddr* (a 120-character packed array) The components of a record are usually called its *fields*. Having thus defined *entry*, we can now declare variables of type *entry* (*temp* is such a variable) and we can also define the components of the array, *list*, and of the two files as being of the type *entry*. The rest of the program shows how record variables of the same type may be read, assigned and written. No other operators may be used with them.

When we discussed files in Chapter 8, we mentioned that all the components of a file must be the same type and, until now, we have restricted ourselves to text files of type CHAR. You will see that in this case we have declared both files as being of type *entry* which is a **RECORD** type. A **FILE OF RECORD** is a powerful Pascal data structure which allows considerable program economy.

The only new syntax in the statement part of this program is the method used to access a field of a record. The syntax for this is

$$< \text{record variable} > . < \text{field variable} >$$

where the full stop or point performs a similar role to the square brackets with arrays. Thus *temp . nameAddr* would refer to the string of the record currently located in the variable *temp*. Similarly, *list[17] . num* refers to the *num* field of the seventeenth record in the array, *list*. Although records themselves may not be used with arithmetical or Boolean operators, any field of a record may undergo an operation that is permitted for a variable of similar type. Thus the expression

$$\text{list}[m].\text{num} < \text{list}[m+1].\text{num}$$

is comparing two positive integers.

An alternative method of identifying the individual fields of a record is by means of the **WITH** statement, which takes the form

$$\textbf{WITH} < \text{record identifier(s)} > \textbf{DO} < \text{statement} >$$

Thus, with suitable **TYPE** definitions and **VAR** declarations,

```
WITH recordA DO
BEGIN
  field1 := 1;
  field2 := 2;
  field3 := 3;
  field4 := 4
END
```

is the equivalent of

```
recordA . field1 := 1;
recordA . field2 := 2;
recordA . field3 := 3;
recordA . field4 := 4
```

As an example of the use of the **WITH** statement, let us consider a typical use for record types – the personnel records that an employer might keep for each of his employees. The following are the particular fields of such a record, together with the size of each field (in parenthesis) when in a fixed field format:

> Name and forenames (alphabetical string, 60 characters)
> Address (alphanumeric string, 120 characters)
> Date of birth (see below)
> Grade (integer, 1 .. 16)
> Position or trade (alphanumerical string, 30 characters)
> Rate of pay (real)
> Date joined company (see below)

The dates each consist of three separate fields:

> Day   (integer, 1 .. 31)
> Month (integer, 1 .. 12)
> Year (integer, 0 .. 99)

Let us assume that, for convenience, the records are orginally in a free

format **TEXT** file with the entry for each field ending with a marke~~
As there is a fixed number of fields (eight) in each record, it is not ne
sary to mark the end of a record. The following program will translate
from free format to fixed (**RECORD**) format.

```pascal
PROGRAM PersonnelRecords (InFile, OutFile);

TYPE
  dateType =
    RECORD
      day : 1 .. 31;
      month : 1 .. 12;
      year : 0 .. 99
    END;

  empRec =   (* Employee's record *)
    RECORD
      name : PACKED ARRAY [1 .. 60] OF CHAR;
      address : PACKED ARRAY [1 .. 120] OF CHAR;
      birth : dateType;
      grade : 1 .. 16;
      position : PACKED ARRAY [1 .. 30] OF CHAR;
      pay : REAL;
      joined : dateType
    END;

VAR
  n : 1 .. 121;
  ch : CHAR;
  buffer : empRec;
  InFile : TEXT;
  OutFile : FILE OF empRec;

PROCEDURE findMarker;
BEGIN
  WHILE ch <> '↑' DO READ (InFile,ch)
END;

PROCEDURE newline;
BEGIN
  READLN (InFile);
  n := SUCC (n);
  ch := CHR (13)
END;
BEGIN (* main program *)
  RESET (InFile);
  REWRITE (OutFile);
  WHILE NOT EOF (InFile) DO
  BEGIN
    WITH buffer DO
    BEGIN

      (* Infill with padding characters *)
      FOR n := 1 TO  60 DO name [n] := ' ';
      FOR n := 1 TO 120 DO address [n] := ' ';
      FOR n := 1 TO  30 DO position [n] := ' ';
```

```
(* Input name *)
READ (InFile, ch);
n := 1;
WHILE (ch <> '↑') AND n <= 60 DO
BEGIN
  IF EOLN (InFile) THEN
  BEGIN
    name [n] := ch;
    newline
  END;
  name [n] := ch;
  READ (InFile, ch);
  n := SUCC (n)
END;
IF (n > 60) AND (ch <> '↑') THEN findMarker;
READ (InFile, ch);


(* Input address *)
n := 1;
WHILE (ch <> '↑') AND n <= 120 DO
BEGIN
  IF EOLN (InFile) THEN
  BEGIN
    address [n] := ch;
    newline
  END;
  address [n] := ch;
  READ (InFile, ch);
  n := SUCC (n)
END;
IF (n>120) AND (ch<>'↑') THEN findMarker;
(* Input birthday *)
WITH birth DO
            READ (InFile, day, month, year);
READ (Infile, ch);  findMarker;


(* Input grade *)
READ (InFile, grade);
READ (InFile, ch);  findMarker;
READ (InFile, ch);


(* Input position *)
n := 1;
WHILE (ch <> '↑') AND n <= 30 DO
BEGIN
  IF EOLN (InFile) THEN
  BEGIN
    position [n] := ch;
    newline
  END;
  position [n] := ch;
  READ (InFile, ch);
  n := SUCC (n)
END;
IF (n > 30) AND (ch <> '↑') THEN findMarker;
```

```
      (* Input pay *)
      READ (InFile, rate);
      READ (InFile, ch);  findMarker;

      (* Input date joined *)
      WITH joined DO
                      READ (InFile, day, month, year);
      READ (Infile, ch);  findMarker;
      READLN (InFile)
   END;

   (* Output the record *)
   WRITE (OutFile, buffer)
  END;
  RESET (OutFile)
END.
```

The main points to note in this program are as follows:

(a) How the use of the **WITH** statement (seventh line of main program)
avoids the repeated use of the word *'buffer .'* before each reference to a
field.

(b) The **RECORD** *date* is a field of the **RECORD** *buffer*. This results in
the nested **WITH** statements

```
WITH buffer DO
   . . . .
   WITH date DO
      READ (day, month, year)
```

which are equivalent to

```
READ (buffer.date.day,
              buffer.date.month, buffer.date.year)
```

Although, as this program shows, the effort needed to convert from
free to fixed format is not small, the pay off comes next time it is necessary to input this record:

```
READ (filename, buffer)
```

is all that is needed.

15.2 **VARIANTS**

There are occasions when the number of fields in a record may vary
according to the actual data that are held in the record. For example,
visitors to computing exhibitions are frequently asked to fill in questionnaires. The actual details requested vary but the following could be typical:

visitor's name, company name and company address, visitor's position in company and then a question such as, 'Which type of computer do you regularly use – mainframe, mini, micro, remote terminal or none?' Then there is often a supplementary request, 'Unless the answer is "none" please fill in the appropriate section'. There then follow four separate sections under the headings 'mainframe', 'mini', etc., each with several questions appropriate to the particular kind of installation.

From what has already been written it is clear that the natural data structure to use when processing the answers to such questionnaires is the record. Separate fields will be needed on each record for the answers to each of the half-dozen personal questions and for the (often many more) questions about the installation. However, even in these enlightened days, a large number of the responders will not be a regular computer user. It could be an extravagant use of computer storage space to reserve fields for information about all the different types of installation when at most, one will be pertinent. The following construction avoids such profligacy:

```
1  TYPE
2    string25 = PACKED ARRAY [1 .. 25] OF CHAR;
3    string80 = PACKED ARRAY [1 .. 80] OF CHAR;
4    posInt = 0 .. MAXINT;
5    installationType = (mainframe, mini, micro,
                         terminal, none);
6    response =
7      RECORD
8        name : string25;
9        companyName : string25;
10       address : string80;
11       position : string25;
12       computer : installationType;
13       CASE installationType OF
14         mainframe:
15           (maker : string25;
16            makersRef : string25;
17            coreSize : posInt (* kilobytes *);
18            numTapeHndlrs, numMultiDiscHndlrs,
19              numHardDiscHndlrs, numFloppyHndlrs,
20              numRemoteTerms : posInt;
21              totalCompStaff, numProgrammers,
22              numSystAnalysts, numOptrs : posint;
23            hoursUsedPerDay : 0 .. 24;
24            daysPerWeek : 0 .. 7;
25            languagesUsed : (pascal, fortran,
26              machine, assembly, basic, cobol));
27         mini, micro :  ( <field list
                 appropriate to minis and micros> );
28         terminal : ( <field list appropriate
                 to terminals> );
29         none : ()
30     END  (* of RECORD *);
```

In the above fragment, lines 27 and 28 have been abbreviated in order to save space. The field lists would, in fact, be slightly shorter and slightly different versions of the *mainframe* field list.

The whole of the above declaration starting with line 13 through to line 29 is known as the *variant part* of the declaration as opposed to the *fixed part* (lines 8-12 inclusive). We discuss the formal syntax of records later in this chapter. For the present we shall restrict discussion to this example. The fixed part will appear in every record of type *response*, but the fields on lines 14-26 will be used ('activated') only if the type of *computer* is *mainframe*. If the type is *mini*, *micro* or *terminal*, then the field lists appropriate to those types of computer will be activated. If the type is *none* then no variant field is required. This is indicated by the empty brackets ( ) in line 29. The brackets must always appear even if no field is required.

The case label, *mainframe*, the colon, and the associated field list constitutes one *variant*. Similarly lines 27, 28 and 29 constitute three more variants.

The similarity between the variant part and the **CASE** statements which we met in Chapter 6 is so marked that it is important to highlight two important differences. Firstly, the CASE selector (*installationType*) must be a type, not a variable. Secondly the CASE in a variant part does not have an **END**. This is because the variant part must always follow the fixed part and the **END** of the record also acts as the terminator of the variant part.

There are some other important points that are not immediately apparent from the above example. The same field name may not be used twice in the same record declaration, even if it appears in different variants or in one variant and the fixed part. Therefore, if a field were required for *mini*, *micro* denoting hours used per day, then an identifier other than *hoursUsedPerDay* would have to be chosen.

The field declared immediately before the CASE clause

```
computer : installationType;
```

is known as the *tag* field. It may be any ordinal type. The tag field declaration may be combined with the CASE selector. Thus

```
CASE computer : installationType OF
```

is an acceptable abbreviation for

```
computer : installationType;
CASE installationType OF
```

The formal syntax for a record declaration is

$$<\text{identifier}> = \textbf{RECORD} <\text{field list}> \textbf{END}$$

or, since records may be packed

$$<\text{identifier}> = \textbf{PACKED RECORD} <\text{field list}> \textbf{END}$$

$<\text{field list}>$ is defined as

$$<\text{fixed part}> ; <\text{variant part}>$$

Either the fixed part or the variant part may be omitted, in which case the semicolon is also omitted. Although it is permissible to omit the tag fields (see Chapter 17), inexperienced programmers are advised always to include it, either at the end of the fixed part of after the **CASE** of the variant part.

The formal syntax of the variant part is

$$\textbf{CASE} <\text{variant selector}> \textbf{OF} <\text{variant or variants}>$$

$<\text{variant selector}>$ is defined as

$$<\text{tag field identifier}> : <\text{tag type identifier}>$$

The $<\text{tag field identifier}>$ and the colon may be omitted if the tag field has already been declared in the fixed part.

Variant is defined as

$$<\text{one or more case constants}> : (<\text{field list}>)$$

Case constants are the value that the $<\text{tag field}>$ may have at run-time. If there is more than one in the variant, then they must be separated by commas.

Since the definition of $<\text{field list}>$ already given permits a variant part, it follows that there can be variants of variants. In the above example it would have been possible, for instance, to have had a further variant within the *mainframe* variant that gave different fields according, say, to the type of multidisc handlers being used.

Remember that each and every field in one record declaration must have a different identifier.

Since the main use of variants is to save storage space in the memory, it is pertinent to examine how much space actually is saved. When a record with variants is declared, the compiler examines the space required for each variant and then reserves enough space for the largest, on the basis that any other variant will fit into the same space with room to spare. Thus if there are two variants, one very large and the other very small, in a record that forms part, say, of a larger array, space will be reserved for the large variant in every component of the array, even though it may be needed for only a few of them. Where space is at the premium, it may be necessary to employ other tactics, one of which is discussed later in this chapter.

15.3 LINKED LISTS

Consider the following problem. There is a textfile containing a single serial number (positive integer) followed by approximately 10 000 words and certainly not more than 12 000. It is desired to read in each word in turn and then to place it in one of 26 different groups according to the word's initial letter (thus all words beginning with 'A' or 'a' will be in the first group, those beginning with 'B' or 'b' in the second, etc.) Coupled with each word will be a serial number. The first serial number (the one read from the beginning of the file) will be applied to the first word. Thereafter this number will be increased by 1 as each word is read in. Finally we wish to output each group separately in alphabetical order of groups but with the words and serial numbers in that group in serial number order. (This problem is not quite so artificial as it may at first appear. It is a simplified version of the problem of preparing monthly statements for customers which we shall discuss later.)

The obvious structure for the word and serial number is a record, since we have two different types of data (string and positive integer). But how do we structure the 26 groups? We could set up 26 different arrays, but how large are we to make each array? We know that there are 12 000 words, but from the information given we will not know, until we have run the program, how many begin with each letter. We could make an intelligent estimate, based on the frequency with which each letter occurs in the language, but we are not even told the language! So the only safe size for each of the 26 arrays would be for it to contain 12 000 records. However, since there are only 12 000 words altogether, this array structure will be 26 times larger than we need and may well be too large for our computer. The technique known as *linked lists* enables us to store, with only a modest amount of additional memory, all the groups in a single array of 12 000 components. The following program shows how this can be done:

```
1   PROGRAM Words1 (OUTPUT, WordText);

2   CONST
3     wordMax = 12000;
4     wordLength = 20;

5   TYPE
6     string = PACKED ARRAY [1 .. wordLength]
                              OF CHAR;
7     secondIndex = (first,last);
```

```
 8    indicator = 0 .. wordMax;
 9    wordRecord =
10      RECORD
11        word : string;
12        serialNo : 1 .. MAXINT;
13        link  : indicator
14      END;
15
16  VAR
17    n : INTEGER;
18    serialNum : 1 .. MAXINT;
19    letter : 'A' .. 'Z';
20    follower, lastThisGroup : indicator;
21    wordBuffer : string;
22    directory : ARRAY ['A' .. 'Z', secondIndex]
                                     OF indicator;
23    groupList : ARRAY [1 .. wordMax]
                                     OF wordRecord;
24    WordText : TEXT;
25
26  PROCEDURE inWord;
27      (* This procedure, which is not detailed, *
       *      reads in the next word from the     *
       *   WordText file, converts lower case     *
       *   to upper case and assigns it to the    *
       *       global variable, wordBuffer.       *
       *     Unused character positions filled     *
       *             with spaces.                 *)
28
29  BEGIN

    (*  Initialise   *)
30    RESET (WordText);
31    READ (WordText, serialNum);
                     (* initial value from file *)
32    follower := 0;
33    FOR letter := 'A' TO 'Z' DO
         directory [letter, first] := 0;
34  (*  Read words and allocate to groups  *)
35    inWord;
36    REPEAT
37      serialNum := SUCC (serialNum);
38      follower := SUCC (follower);
39      letter := wordBuffer [1];
40      IF directory [letter, first] = 0 THEN
41         directory [letter, first] := follower;
42      ELSE
43        BEGIN
44          lastThisGroup := directory
                                  [letter, last];
45          groupList [lastThisGroup] . link :=
                  follower
46        END;
47      directory [letter, last] := follower;
48      WITH groupList [follower] DO
49      BEGIN
50        word := wordBuffer;
```

```
51            serialNo := serialNum;
52            link := 0
53        END;
54      inWord
54    UNTIL EOF (WordText);

     (* Output in groups *)
55    FOR letter := 'A' TO 'Z' DO
56    BEGIN
57      WRITELN (letter); WRITELN;
58      IF directory [letter, first] > 0 THEN
59      BEGIN
60        follower := directory [letter, first];
61        REPEAT
62          WITH groupList [follower] DO
63          BEGIN
64            FOR n := 1 TO wordLength DO
65                WRITE (word [n]);
66            WRITELN (serialNo :5);
67            follower := link
68          END
69        UNTIL follower = 0;
70        WRITELN; WRITELN
71      END
72    END
73 END.
```

Let us follow through the salient points of this program. In line 8, a type *indicator* has been defined as having any value in the range $0 ..$ *wordMax*. This is the full range of the values that the index of the array *groupLists* may take on (see line 23) plus an additional value, zero. There are five variables in the program that are declared as being of type *indicator*. These are *link* in the record *wordRecord* (line 13), the global variables *follower* and *lastThisGroup* (line 20) and all elements of the array *directory* (line 22). Each time that one of these variables is used in the program, it will be for the purpose of holding either the value of the index of the array *wordList* or zero. Thus, any use of a variable of type *indicator* can be said to 'indicate' or 'point to' a specific activation of the record *wordRecord* or, if zero, to nothing at all. Let us examine in detail how these are used in this program.

As part of the initialisation stage, *follower* and all the *first* elements of the array *directory* are set to zero (lines 32, 33). As each word is read it is placed in the *wordBuffer* (line 35). In lines 37 and 38 *serialNum* and *follower* are incremented. The indicator *follower* now points to the next vacant space in array *groupList*. The initial letter of the word is taken from *wordBuffer[1]* and is used as follows.

If this is the first word beginning with this letter to have been received, then *directory [letter, first]* is zero. In this case the zero must be replaced by the value of *follower* (line 41). Otherwise, if this is not the first word commencing with this letter, *directory [letter, last]* points to the position in the *groupList* array that holds the last occurrence of this letter. The temporary indicator, *lastThisGroup*, is given this value (line 44) so that the *link* field in the appropriate *wordRecord* may be made to point to the next entry in this group (line 45). The indicator, *directory [letter, last]* is also made to point to this entry (line 47). The word and its serial number are transferred to this entry (lines 50, 51) and the *link* field is set to zero, to indicate that this is the latest entry for this group (line 52).

A simple example may help to clarify this. Suppose the WordText contained

> 535 'The time has come,' the Walrus said,
> 'To talk of many things:
> Of shoes – and ships – and sealing wax –
> Of cabbages – and kings –
> Of why the sea is boiling hot –
> And whether pigs have wings.'

Figure 15.1 shows how this would be stored in the two arrays. By way of example the linking entries for letter 'S' have been marked.

The last part of this program outputs the groups in turn. The location of the first entry in each group is obtained from *directory [letter, first]*

Fig 15.1   *a linked list: the links for the letter 'S' have been indicated*

letter	first	last	follower	word	serial	link
A	17	31	1	THE	535	2
B	29	29	2	TIME	536	5
C	4	21	3	HAS	537	30
D	0		4	COME	538	21
E	0		5	THE	539	8
F	0		6	WALRUS	540	19
G	0		7	SAID	541	14
H	3	34	8	TO	542	9
I	28	28	9	TALK	543	12
J	0		10	OF	544	13
K	23	23	11	MANY	545	0
L	0		12	THINGS	546	26
M	11	11	13	OF	547	24
N	0		14	SHOES	548	16
O	10	24	15	AND	549	17
P	33	33	16	SHIPS	550	18
Q	0		17	AND	551	22
R	0		18	SEALING	552	27
S	7	27	19	WAX	553	25
T	1	26	20	OF	554	24
U	0		21	CABBAGES	555	0
V	0		22	AND	556	31
W	6	35	23	KINGS	557	0
X	0		24	OF	558	0
Y	0		25	WHY	559	32
Z	0		26	THE	560	0
			27	SEA	561	0
			28	IS	562	0
			29	BOILING	563	0
			30	HOT	564	34
			31	AND	565	0
			32	WHETHER	566	35
			33	PIGS	567	0
			34	HAVE	568	0
			35	WINGS	569	0

(line 60) and each succeeding entry is found from the *link* field of the current entry (line 67). A zero in this field indicates the end of the chain for this current value of *letter* (line 69).

This program has been considered in some detail because linked lists are a powerful and frequently used way of handling data in computers.

One disadvantage of the above program is the necessity to know in advance the maximum number of words that the file contains and therefore the size needed for the array *groupList*. If the number were to exceed *wordMax*, this program would fail, even if there had still been some spare store in the computer. However, Pascal has a set of constructions that enable variables to be created as required during the running of a program. Although in theory such variables, known as *dynamic variables*, may be of any type, almost always in practice they are record variables and our discussion will be limited to records.

15.4 POINTER TYPES

Any variable that is to be used in a program needs two things. It needs space allocated for it in the computer's store and it needs some means of identification. The declaration

```
VAR
    number : INTEGER;
```

meets both these needs. It says, in effect, 'reserve storage space for an integer variable and call this variable *number*'.

Another way to reserve storage is by means of a *pointer* type. A pointer type is defined as follows:

```
TYPE
    indicator = ↑ wordRecord;
```

which can be pronounced as 'the type *indicator* is a pointer type, pointing to a type *wordRecord*'. (In implementations that have no ↑ symbol, the 'commercial at' symbol, @, may be used instead.)

With this definition, *indicator* is given precisely the same role as was implied, though not explicitly stated, in the above program. Any variable of type *indicator* can take on a value that points to a specific activation of a *wordRecord* or to nothing at all. In the latter case it is assigned the value **NIL**, a Pascal reserved word.

There is a major difference between the use of *indicator* in the above program and its use as a pointer type. In the former, all the possible activations of variables of the type *wordRecord* were declared in the **VAR** declaration (line 23). It is this declaration which distinguishes a *static* *variable*. A dynamic variable, on the other hand, must not appear in a **VAR** declaration. It is created when it is needed by means of the standard procedure, NEW. The statement

```
NEW (follower)
```

where *follower* is a pointer variable of type *indicator*, creates a structure of type *wordRecord*. Until some other value is assigned to *follower* (for example by an assignment statement or by another call of NEW with *follower* as its parameter), it has a value that points to the newly created record. (The actual value is usually the 'address' in the computer store where the new structure is held. This value is not normally accessible to the programmer, nor does he need to know it.) If it is necessary to preserve this value because, for example, we anticipate further calls of *NEW (follower)*, then we may assign its value to another pointer variable; for example

```
directory [letter, first] := follower
```

as in line 41 of the above program. The only values that may be assigned to a pointer variable in an assignment statement are *either* the value held by another pointer variable *or* the value **NIL**.

When we wish to identify the variable to which a pointer is pointing, the syntax for this is

$$< \text{pointer variable} > \uparrow$$

Thus, after a statement *NEW (follower)*, the statement

```
follower ↑ . serialNo := 999
```

would assign the value 999 to the *serialNo* field of the newly created record, *follower ↑*.

As an example of the use of pointer types and pointer variables, the above *Words1* program may be rewritten as *Words2*:

```
1   PROGRAM Words2 (OUTPUT, WordText);

2   CONST
3      wordMax = 12000;
4      wordLength = 20;

5   TYPE
6      string = PACKED ARRAY
                        [1 .. wordLength] OF CHAR;
7      secondIndex = (first,last);
8      indicator = ↑ wordRecord;
9      wordRecord =
```

```
10      RECORD
11        word : string;
12        serialNo : 1 .. MAXINT;
13        link  : indicator
14      END;
15
16  VAR
17    n : INTEGER;
18    serialNum : 1 .. MAXINT;
19    letter : 'A' .. 'Z';
20    follower, lastThisGroup : indicator;
21    wordBuffer : string;
22    directory : ARRAY ['A' .. 'Z', secondIndex]
                                    OF indicator;
24    WordText : TEXT;
25
26  PROCEDURE inWord;
27    (* As before *)
28
29  BEGIN

      (* Initialise *)
30    RESET (WordText);
31    READ (WordText, serialNum);
                        (* initial value from file *)
32    follower := NIL;
33    FOR letter := 'A' TO 'Z' DO
        directory [letter, first] := NIL;
34  (* Read words and allocate to groups *)
35    inWord;
36    REPEAT
37      serialNum := SUCC (serialNum);
38      NEW (follower);
39      letter := wordBuffer [1];
40      IF directory [letter, first] = NIL THEN
41        directory [letter, first] := follower;
42      ELSE
43        BEGIN
44          lastThisGroup :=
                          directory [letter, last];
45          lastThisGroup ↑ . link := follower
46        END;
47      directory [letter, last] := follower;
48      WITH follower ↑ DO
49      BEGIN
50        word := wordBuffer;
51        serialNo := serialNum;
52        link := NIL
53      END;
54      inWord
54    UNTIL EOF (WordText);

      (* Output in groups *)
55    FOR letter := 'A' TO 'Z' DO
56    BEGIN
57      WRITELN (letter); WRITELN;
58      IF directory [letter, first] <> NIL THEN
```

```
59        BEGIN
60          follower := directory [letter, first];
61          REPEAT
62            WITH follower ↑ DO
63            BEGIN
64              FOR n := 1 TO wordLength DO
65                WRITE (word [n]);
66              WRITELN (serialNo :5);
67              follower := link
68            END
69          UNTIL follower = NIL;
70          WRITELN; WRITELN
71        END
72      END
73    END.
```

The changes in this program are the following:

(a) In line 8, *indicator* is defined as a pointer type.

(b) Line 23 has been deleted.

(c) In line 38, a new *wordRecord* is created.

(d) In lines 45, 48, and 62, the variables have been identified by means of a pointer.

(e) In lines 32, 33, 40, 52, 58 and 68, zero has been replaced by *NIL*.

In particular you should notice line 8. Here it has been necessary to define *indicator* as a pointer to *wordRecord* before *wordRecord* itself has been defined. This is because *indicator* is used in a field declaration in the record *wordRecord*. Defining a pointer type before defining the type to which it points is the only occasion in the Pascal language where it is permissible to refer to a type identifier before it is defined.

Note also that there is one additional change in line 58. In the original program we had

```
IF directory [letter, first] > 0 THEN
```

Since *indicator* had been defined as having only positive values, it was safe and correct to use the relational operator >. But in the second program this line has been changed to

```
IF directory [letter, first] <> NIL THEN
```

Since the orginal relationship of values of pointer variables is not defined in standard Pascal, the relational operator < > should always be used.

The overall strategy of the second program is the same as the first. The way it has been carried out is different. No structures of type *wordRecord* exist until the first is created by NEW. Once such structures are created, the method of linking them is exactly parallel to the method previously used. If you followed the first version through, you should have no difficulty with the second.

15.5 MORE ON LINKED LISTS

Used in the correct context, linked lists can be useful programming tools. They are flexible but access is essentially sequential, along the chain. The examples we have given work on the 'first in, first out' (FIFO) principle (also known as a *queue*). For many applications in computing, as in real life, the 'last in, first out' (LIFO or stack) principle is appropriate. This is easily achieved in linked lists by making the *link* field point to the previous entry instead of the following one. Two-way linking is sometimes needed, using two such fields, one pointing forward and the other backward. For certain applications the first and last components of a linked list may be linked to each other, thus forming a ring.

It is possible to insert extra components into a linked list. This is done by appropriate adjustments to the link fields of the component being inserted and of its neighbour (both neighbours if two-way linking is being used). Similarly a component may be deleted from the chain.

If such a removed component is no longer needed in the program, you may use the standard predefined Pascal procedure

DISPOSE (<pointer variable>)

which is described in the orignal report as indicating that storage occupied by the variable <pointer variable> is no longer needed. Some implementations, but not all, do react to DISPOSE by freeing the storage so that it can be used for other purposes, but the new standard only requires that the variable to which the pointer is pointing shall henceforth be inaccessible. If DISPOSE does recover the storage space in your implementation and you decide to use it you should make sure that the pointer variable that you use as a parameter is the only one that is pointing to the unwanted variable at the time that DISPOSE is called. Others may be reassigned some other value (for example, **NIL**).

15.6 A PRACTICAL EXAMPLE OF RECORDS AND LINKED LISTS

We started this chapter with a consideration of the preparation of customers' invoices. We shall finish it with a consideration of the preparation of customers' monthly statements.

A monthly statement (one for each customer) gives all the transactions for that customer during the month (invoices issued, sums paid, credit notes and the balance brought forward from the previous month). These are all listed and a balance outstanding is calculated, printed and carried forward. All these transactions are usually held on different files and the preparation of statements usually entails merging the several files. For efficient merging the files should be in 'customer number' order.

Since invoices are prepared daily, the invoice file is probably in date order and our problem is to sort that file into customer order. It is is not unusual for a trader to have several thousand customers on his books, of whom perhaps only a few hundred are invoiced during any one month. Of those, the majority receive only one or two invoices, but there are a few customers who receive, perhaps, a hundred or more invoices. It would probably be quite impracticable to declare an array to accommodate all the customers on the basis that each one of them might have a hundred or so invoices. (To do so we should be needing an immediate access memory of several million bytes.)

You will probably by now have recognised this problem as being very similar to the earlier one of sorting a text on the initial letter of each word. As an exercise you might like to write a program, on the lines of *Words2*, to sort the invoice file.

One of the original objectives of Pascal was to have the capability of being used for business and commercial purposes. By using record structures, the majority of such applications can be readily programmed. The major limitation to its wider use for smaller businesses may be the precision to which arithmetical calculations are carried out. In many microcomputer applications this is limited to four or five decimal places. There is a need, in such implementations, for an extra predefined type 'double integer' and/or 'double precision real' which would give numbers to a precision of nine decimal places, which should be ample for most small businesses.

CHAPTER 16

SETS

16.1 INTRODUCTION

A *set* is a collection of items of the same type. Typical examples are as follows: Members of Parliament; days of the week; months of the year; cards in a pack (deck) of playing cards; the primary colours (red, yellow and blue). From any set it is possible to make up a number of different subsets. For example, the Government Front Bench and the Opposition Front Bench are both subsets of the set Members of Parliament.

Set theory is a branch of mathematics and is outside the scope of this book, but certain aspects of it can be useful in computer programming. If you have no previous knowledge of sets and set theory, it may help to think of a set as being like a Boolean array, in which each of the elements is either TRUE (the set member is present) or FALSE (the member is absent). This analogy is appropriate because a set and a Boolean array are stored in the computer in similar ways.

A variable of type **SET** has a 'value' that is defined by the members present. Thus, if we had the definition and declaration

```
TYPE
   colour = (red, yellow, blue);

VAR
   hue : SET OF colour;
```

we could write any one of the following assignment statements:

```
hue := [red, yellow, green]
hue := [red, yellow]
hue := [red, green]
hue := [yellow, green]
hue := [red]
hue := [yellow]
hue := [green]
hue := []
```

The last statement assigns the empty set.

Each of the above statements assigns a different subset of *colour* to *hue*. Note that the order in which the members are assigned is immaterial. Thus

[red, blue] is identical to [blue, red].

The square brackets, [and], used in the above statements, are known as *set constructors*. As with array subscripts, the special combined symbols, (. and .), may be used where the implementation has no square brackets.

Certain operations can be carried out on sets. To demonstrate these, we should assume that the following definitions and declarations have been made:

```
CONST
  ucA = 'A';   ucE = 'E';   ucI = 'I';
  ucO = 'O';   ucU = 'U';

TYPE
  charSet = SET OF CHAR;
  upCaseSet = SET OF 'A' .. 'Z';
  vowelType = (ucA, ucE, ucI, ucO, ucU);
  vowelSet = SET OF vowelType;

VAR
  letters : upCaseSet;
  vowel   : vowelSet;
```

The first of these operations is *addition* to give the sum of two sets. This is shown in the following statements:

```
letters := ['A', 'E'];
letters := letters + ['E', 'I', 'O', 'U' .. 'Z']
```

After the last statement, *letters* would contain the following characters:

'A', 'E', 'I', 'O', 'U', 'V', 'W', 'X', 'Y', 'Z'

Note that the result of adding two sets together (mathematicians call this 'set union') is to make a new set whose members are all the elements that were in each of the two original sets. There is no implied quantity in sets or set union. For example, 'E' was in both of the constituent sets and thus appears in the new set, but it appears once only. Either an element is in a set or it is outside it. It cannot appear more than once.

The second possible operation is to obtain the *difference* between two sets by removing from one all those elements that are members of both. Thus, continuing from the last assignment statement,

```
letters := letters - ['D' .. 'M', 'V' .. 'Z']
```

will leave *letters* with the characters

'A' 'O' 'U'

Note that, in this case, there are a lot of letters between 'D' and 'M' that have had no effect on the result of this operation since they were not members of *letters* at the start.

The third operation on sets is *intersection* or *product*. Using the results of the most recent assignments,

```
letters := letters * vowel
```

will leave *letters* with the five vowels only, the only elements that were members of both sets.

After this last statement both sets would have precisely the same elements. They are thus *identical*, a fact that could be tested by relational operators. There are four relational operators for set operations in Pascal:

$$= \text{ equality} \qquad <> \text{ inequality}$$

$$<= \text{ and } >= \text{ inclusion}$$

The expressions

$$\text{setA} = \text{setB} \qquad \text{setA} <> \text{setB}$$

return the results TRUE and FALSE respectively if the two sets are identical, and the reverse otherwise; while the expressions

$$\text{setA} <= \text{setB} \qquad \text{setB} >= \text{setA}$$

will both return the result TRUE if all the elements of setB are also present in setA.

The final relational operator for Pascal sets is **IN**, a reserved word. It tests for the presence or otherwise of a single element in the set. When you did Exercise 6.2 in Chapter 6 you probably had statements

```
IF (ch >= 'a') AND (ch <= 'z') THEN etc
```

and

```
IF (ch = 'A') OR (ch = 'E') OR (ch = 'I')
        OR (ch = 'O') OR (ch = 'U') THEN etc
```

These two statements can both be shortened to

```
IF ch IN ['a' .. 'z'] THEN etc
```

and

```
IF ch IN ['A', 'E', 'I', 'O', 'U'] THEN etc
```

Before looking at another application of sets, let us look again at the definitions and declarations we used above. To get to the declaration of *hue* we had

```
TYPE
  colour = (red, yellow, blue);

VAR
  hue : SET OF colour;
```

As with previous type definitions, there are several other ways in which this may be expressed:

```
TYPE
  colour = (red, yellow, blue);
  colourSet = SET OF colour;

VAR
  hue : colourSet;
```

or

```
TYPE
  colourSet = SET OF (red, yellow, blue);

VAR
  hue : colourSet;
```

or

```
VAR
  hue : SET OF (red, yellow, blue);
```

All are acceptable. It is a matter of personal choice which is used for particular programs. Remember that future readability is the most important criterion.

Let us look at a program employing sets for its main data structures. We are going to simulate the shuffling and dealing of a pack of playing cards to four bridge players, respectively North, East, South and West. For convenience the 52 cards in the pack will be numbered from 1 through to 52 consecutively, rather than dividing them into suits at this stage. We can also combine the two stages of shuffling and dealing into one stage. This will be done by dealing a card to each player in turn until the pack is exhausted, but the card that is dealt will not necessarily be taken off the top of the pack. It will be chosen at random by the *random* function of the last chapter. One complication of doing this is that the random number selected may be one that has already been dealt to a player. Therefore we must check that the selected card is still in the pack before it is dealt to a player. If it is not, then it must be rejected and a new random number generated.

We shall use sets as the data structures of the pack and of the individual 'hands' that are dealt to the players. At the end of this program we wish each of the four hands to hold 13 cards. No card may appear twice either in the same hand or in different hands. In order to check this we will have a listing of the cards as they are dealt:

North	East	South	West
23	17	51	2
.	.	.	.
.	.	.	.
.	.	.	.

The program falls into three sections:

(1) Initialise.
(2) Deal one card to each player in turn.
(3) Repeat step (2) until the pack is exhausted.

Initialising consists of filling the pack with the numbers 1–52, emptying the players' hands, providing a starting seed for the random number generator and writing headings for the display.

The 'dealing' operation requires the following steps:

(1) Generate random number in the range 1 .. 52.
(2) Repeat step 1 if the generated number is not still in the pack.
(3) Delete the number from the pack.
(4) Include it in the appropriate player's hand.
(5) Display it.

Having thus analysed the problem, we can now write the following program:

```
PROGRAM DealPack (OUTPUT);

CONST
  packSize = 52;
              (* or maximum permitted size of set *)

TYPE
  cards = 1 .. packsize;
  cardSet = SET OF cards;

VAR
  cardPack, handN, handE, handS, handW : cardSet;
  seed : INTEGER;
```

```
PROCEDURE inSeed (VAR seed : INTEGER);

  EXTERNAL;   (* see chapter 7 *)

PROCEDURE deal (VAR hand : cardSet);

VAR
  card : 1..packSize;

  FUNCTION random (VAR seed : INTEGER;
                       max : INTEGER) : INTEGER;

    EXTERNAL;   (* see chapter 7 *)

BEGIN (* deal *)
  REPEAT
    card := random (seed, packSize - 1) + 1
  UNTIL card IN cardPack;
  cardPack := cardPack - [card];
  hand := hand + [card];
  WRITE (card : 8)
END; (* deal *)

BEGIN
  cardPack := [1 .. packSize];
  handN := []; handE := [];
                     handS := []; handW := [];
  inSeed (seed);
  WRITELN ('North' :9, 'East' :8,
                       'South' :8, 'West' :8);
  REPEAT
    deal (handN);
    deal (handE);
    deal (handS);
    deal (handW);
    WRITELN;
  UNTIL cardPack = [];
  WRITELN ('All Dealt')
END.
```

Most implementations place a limit on the maximum number of elements that a set may contain. On some microcomputers this number may be as low as 16. If your implementation has a limit that is less than 52, then you will have to redefine *packSize* accordingly. Almost certainly the number will be an exact multiple of four, but if it is not, then you should reduce it so that it is, otherwise the program would get into an infinite loop.

COMPATIBILITY OF SET TYPES

nd the compatibility definitions of Chapter 14 to include

(a) Two set types are compatible if their base types are compatible and either both are packed or both are unpacked.

(b) *setType2* is assignment compatible with *setType1* if they are compatible and all the members specified for *setType2* are also members of the range specified for *setType1*.

Thus, with the following declarations,

```
VAR
    charSet : SET OF CHAR;
    upCase : SET OF 'A' .. 'Z';
```

charSet and *upCase* are compatible. Also *upCase* is assignment compatible with *charSet*, but *charSet* is not assignment compatible with *upCase*.

As we said earlier, compatibility and assignment compatibility are largely a matter of common sense, but it is important that they should be explicitly defined since the syntax of programs must be meticulously correct.

EXERCISES

16.1 Why would the *DealPack* program above get into an infinite loop if *packSize* were not an exact multiple of four?

16.2 A certain shop sells

apples	bread	cream	damsons	eggs
flour	gammon	ham	ice cream	jam

and no other commodities at all. On a particular day it happens that no apples, bread or cream are in stock. Not knowing this, Anne and Betty arrive with their shopping lists and purchase what they can. They then meet Celia who is entering the shop with the following shopping list: gammon, ham, ice cream and jam. Anne and Betty give Celia the total quantity of all the items that they have and she wants. Diana arrives and says 'If the baskets of Anne and Betty contain identical sets of commodities, then I shall buy the same. Otherwise I shall buy whatever I can that Celia has not got'. She then goes into the shop and makes her purchases.

Write a program that, ignoring quantities, will READ (the ordinal values of) the shopping lists of Anne and Betty and output, in words, the contents of Diana's basket after she has completed her purchases.

CHAPTER 17

NOT FOR BEGINNERS

□ This chapter (the last covering the Pascal language) introduces certain advanced features which, for one reason or another, have been previously omitted. It is possible to write useful and efficient programs without ever using them. In fact, unless you are very experienced, their use is likely to lead to less efficient programs, either because of the risk of error or because of future difficulties in following the logic. Beginners are therefore advised to skip this chapter. □

17.1 MORE ABOUT FILES

The elements of a file may be of any type, except another file or a structure that contains a file, provided that they are all of the same type. So far we have considered only files of CHAR (text files) and files of record type. Since these two types of file can be used to represent or incorporate any other type, they are usually all that are needed for most purposes. However, if file size is at a premium and your program allows it, it may be to your advantage to declare a file of INTEGER or a file of REAL. The operative word here is 'may' because the exact representation of integers and real numbers is implementation dependent. If your implementation stores such numbers in files in their binary representation, there *may* be a saving, depending on the average magnitude of the numbers.

The unit of storage, both in the computer and on the file is the *byte*. The number of bytes required to store an integer on a textfile will be (<number of decimal digits in the number to be stored> + 2). The number of bytes required to store it in a file of INTEGER is usually given by

$$n = (\log MAXINT + \log 2)/\log 256.$$

It is up to you to decide whether it is worth while making the calculation and to decide whether there is any advantage in storing the integers in binary, always assuming that your implementation will do so!

Remember that the Pascal procedures READLN and WRITELN and the function EOLN apply to textfiles only.

When we discussed reading from a file in Chapter 8, we referred briefly to the *buffer variable*, the only contact between the program and the file. This buffer variable can be defined in a Pascal program as

<filename> ↑ (or <filename> @ if ↑ if not available)

If *F* is the file name, the value of the buffer variable can be assigned to a variable, *varble*, by the pair of statements

```
varble := F ↑ ;    GET (F)
```

The procedure GET has the effect of advancing the file so that the buffer variable becomes the next item on the file. You will recognise that this pair of statements is identical to the single procedure call

```
READ ( F, varble)
```

Similarly, with the pair of statements

```
F ↑ := varble ;    PUT (F)
```

the effect of PUT is to place the value of the buffer variable into the first empty space in the file and to advance the buffer variable to the next empty space. After this operation, the value of F ↑ is undefined. This pair of statements is identical to

```
WRITE ( F, varble)
```

Since GET and PUT are usually associated with an assignment statements involving the buffer variable, and since an assignment statement involving the buffer variable is usually associated with GET or PUT, and since READ and WRITE, respectively, are such convenient alternatives, the above constructions are seldom used.

17.2 MORE ABOUT PARAMETERS

When we discussed procedures and functions in Chapter 7 the only data types that we had then encountered were the standard types, INTEGER, REAL, CHAR and BOOLEAN. However, any data type, with one exception, can be used as a parameter provided that the actual parameter is assignment compatible with the formal parameter (see Chapter 14). The exception concerns the individual elements of a **PACKED** data structure. The individual elements of such a structure may not be used as *variable* parameters, although a packed structure itself may be so used, provided that both the formal and actual parameters are packed data structures.

Functions and procedures may also be used as parameters of functions and procedures. For example, in the following fragment the procedure *addfunction* will add the two functions *f1* and *f2* and output their values, at intervals of $\pi/16$ from 0 to 2π:

```
FUNCTION f1 ( a : REAL) : REAL;
    .   .   .

(* Definition of f1 *)
    .   .   .

FUNCTION f2 ( a : REAL) : REAL;
    .   .   .

(* Definition of f2 *)
    .   .   .

PROCEDURE addFunction
          (FUNCTION f1 ( a : REAL) : REAL,
               FUNCTION f2 ( a : REAL) : REAL);

CONST
  pi = 3.14159;

VAR
  x, y : REAL;
  n : 0 .. 32;

BEGIN
  FOR n := 0 TO 32 DO
  BEGIN
    x := pi * n / 16;
    y := f1 (x) + f2 (x);
    WRITELN (n :3, y :10 :4)
  END
END;
```

The above procedure would be called thus

```
addFunction ( f1 (c), f2 (c) )
```

It will be seen that the formal function parameters of the procedure exactly reflect the headings of the functions. This is a requirement of the Standard which is a deliberate change from the originally defined language, which did not require the parameters of the 'parameter' function or procedure to be included again. Unless your compiler is specifically in compliance with the Standard, you should check its requirements in this respect.

Certain implementations allow the use of what are called *conformant*

array parameters. This allows the actual parameter to be an array whose
index range is a subrange of that of the formal parameter array. The
precautions that have to be taken when using such parameters are rather
involved. Their description occupies nearly three pages in the Standard.
A compiler that allows conformant array parameters to be used is described as complying 'with the requirements of level 1'. Experienced
programmers who wish to use such parameters and have access to an
implementation that allows their use are advised to read the Standard
(clauses 6.6.3.6(e), 6.6.3.7 and 6.6.3.8). This book purports to comply
with the requirements of level 0, which does not include conformant
array parameters. They will not be discussed further, except to comment that their use in the *PersonnelRecords* program of Chapter 15
would have considerably shortened that program.

17.3 MORE ABOUT RECORDS

When we discussed variants in Chapter 15, it was explained that the
variant was chosen by the type of the tag field. It is not strictly necessary
to have a tag field, as the following example shows.

Telephone numbers in the United Kingdom fall into two classes. In
certain major cities (London, Birmingham, Edinburgh, Glasgow, Liverpool
and Manchester), the numbers are all numerical, starting with a prefix
(01-, 021-, 031-, etc., respectively). Elsewhere the exchange has a name
consisting of letters of the alphabet, spaces and hyphens. The longest such
name (Llanarmon Dyffryn-Ceiriog) has 25 characters. When keeping data
on, say, customers, it might be considered extravagant in computing time
always to have to fill a 25 element array with padding characters if the
majority of customers came from the major cities where a four-character
string is ample. The following fragment makes the necessary economy:

```
TYPE
   xchangeType = (numerical, alpha);
   xchangeRec =
      RECORD
         CASE xchangeType OF
            numerical : (prefix : ARRAY [1 .. 4]
                                         OF CHAR);
            alpha     : (name : ARRAY [1 .. 25]
                                         OF CHAR);
      END;

VAR
   exchange : xchangeRec;
   n : INTEGER;
   ch : CHAR;

   . . .
```

```
READ (ch);
IF ch = 'O' THEN
FOR n := 1 TO 4 DO
BEGIN
  exchange . prefix [n] := ch;
  read (ch)
END
ELSE
FOR n := 1 TO DO
BEGIN
  exchange . name [n] := ch;
  READ (ch)
END
```

You will see that the particular variant (and hence the size of array) is selected by the assignment statement. This type of record without a tag field is known as a *free union*. It is rarely used. You will note that when accessing any element of the *exchange* array later it will usually be necessary to test the first character again for 'O'. This would have been simplified if there had been a tag field:

```
tag : xchangeType;
```

A major disadvantage of the above program arises from the fact that the storage allocated for a record is normally made large enough to accommodate the largest variant. So although the above program would economise in computing time (possibly not enough to justify the additional programming effort), it does not help to economise in storage.

There is a way, in Pascal, to economise in storage: by the use of an alternative form of NEW. When we discussed NEW in Chapter 15 we showed it with one parameter, a pointer variable. If we have the declaration

```
VAR
  exch1, exch2 = ↑ xchangeRec;
```

we can create a new *xchangeRec* data structure by calling

```
NEW (exch1)
```

This structure will be large enough to accommodate a string of 25 characters.

However, a call of

```
NEW (exch1, numerical)
```

will give us a record structure of the size defined by the type of the variant *prefix*, that is four characters.

Great care must be exercised when using this form of NEW. For the duration of its existence *exch* ↑ will consist of only four characters. When it is disposed of, the same parameters must be used:

```
DISPOSE (exch1, numerical)
```

otherwise more of the store may be erased than was intended. It cannot be altered by re-assignment. For example

```
NEW (exch1, numerical);
NEW (exch2);
exch1 ↑ := exch2 ↑
```

is not permissible; nor is

```
exch1 . alpha := < a 25-character string array >
```

If we had a record type with nested variants, then we should have to specify each variant in turn as a parameter of NEW:

```
NEW (p, v1, v2, v3, etc)
```

where *p* is a pointer variable and *v1, v2, v3, etc.* are the variants in the order in which they are defined. Again, the parameters of DISPOSE must exactly reflect those of the NEW call:

```
DISPOSE (p, v1, v2, v3, etc)
```

17.4 THE GOTO STATEMENT

The **GOTO** statement has intentionally been left to last. It is seldom needed in Pascal and its use generally upsets the structure and reduces the clarity of a program. Although there are a few occasions when **GOTO** can reduce by one or two the number of statements in a program, it is usually good practice to confine its use to those very few occasions when there is no alternative construction.

A **GOTO** statement causes a jump to another statement somewhere else in the program. This other statement is identified by means of a *label*. A label must be an integer number in the range from 0 to 9999 and a labelled statement has the syntax

: <statement>

All labels used in a program must be declared at the start of the appropriate block immediately *before* all other declarations and definitions, thus:

LABEL <label or labels>;

If there is more than one label, then each must be separated from the next by a comma.

Although a **GOTO** statement can consist simply of the word **GOTO** followed by a label, almost invariably it should be part of a conditional statement:

IF <expression> **THEN GOTO** <label>

The relative positions of the **GOTO** statement and the label are important. Jumps may not be made *into* a block or *into* any structured statement. Jumps may be made to another statement at the same level of nesting or *out* of the block or structured statement to a statement at some outer level of nesting.

A very common justifiable use of **GOTO** is to jump to the end of a program and abort further execution when an uncorrectable error arises. For example, the following would protect a program against erroneous results from an attempt to assign a value greater than MAXINT to an integer variable:

```
PROGRAM Xyz (INPUT, OUTPUT, . . . );

LABEL 99;

    . . . .

    IF y > MAXINT - x THEN
    BEGIN
      z := MAXINT;
      WRITELN ('Integer overflow. MAXINT used');
      WRITELN
        ('Enter <newline> to continue, "Q" to quit');
      READ (ch);
      IF (ch = 'Q') OR (ch = 'q') THEN GOTO 99
    END
    ELSE
    z := x + y;

    . . . .

END;
99: END.
```

An example of a program that can be shortened by the use of **GOTO** is **FUNCTION** *location* given in the answer to Exercise 9.2. The version with **GOTO** is

```
FUNCTION location (number : INTEGER) : INTEGER;

LABEL 99;

VAR n : INTEGER;

BEGIN
  n := 1;
  REPEAT
    IF itemNum [n] = number THEN GOTO 99;
    n := SUCC (n)
  UNTIL n > 100;
  99: location := n
END;
```

The rules for the scope of a label are similar to those applying to other declared or defined identifiers. A label declared in any block is in scope to that block and to any nested function or procedure blocks, provided that this declaration has not been over-ridden by the declaration of a label with an identical identifier in an inner block. It should be obvious that two or more statements in the same block must not be labelled with the same label, otherwise the destination of a **GOTO** statement would be ambiguous. On the other hand, there is no limit to the number of **GOTO** statements that may use the same label.

One point to note in skeleton program *Xyz* is that **END** is not a statement. The label *99* is therefore assumed to be leading a dummy statement. It is for this reason that the immediately preceding **END** must be followed by a colon separator.

The introduction of labels means that we must now amend our definition of a block, last given in Chapter 3. A block is defined as

< label declaration part >
< constant definition part >
< type definition part >
< procedure and/or function definition part >
< statement >

CHAPTER 18

APPLICATIONS 5: REAL-TIME AND MULTI-PROGRAMING

□ This chapter discusses an advanced application of Pascal, with the aim of highlighting the versatility of the language. The author was greatly helped during its preparation by Texas Instruments Ltd. TI have been pioneers in the application of Pascal in real-time applications. □

Most of the program examples so far given in this book are designed to be executed in what is called 'batch mode', a term derived from the concept of sending a batch of work to the computer to be carried out as and when computer time becomes available. Thus in batch mode, computer availability dictates the time of program execution. More and more, computers are now being used for controlling processes, from traffic lights at street intersections to highly complex industrial plants. In such applications it is essential that the computer keeps pace with the process occurring in the real world. Such applications are described as operating in *real time*. Real-time working is often necessary in fields other than process control. Interactive working, of which several examples have been given, can be considered as a type of real time operation. For example, a word-processor must not delay the typist nor should a microprocessor-controlled cash register in a supermarket add to the existing delays at check-out.

A convenient analogy to highlight the difference between batch and real-time processing is to consider the difference between a factory producing pre-packaged 'convenience' foods and a chef who has to prepare a meal from raw ingredients and serve it at a set time. In fact cooking is an ideal example of process control. For many dishes, it is not possible to know in advance precisely how long it will take to cook. (A soufflé has to be removed from the oven the moment it rises, and served before it collapses. The time to cook a goose varies according to its age, which is not always known or easy to estimate. Guests have a habit of arriving earlier or later than expected.) Cooking a meal is, therefore, a typical real-time problem. It also exhibits another common feature of real-time computing. A chef cannot cook a meal sequentially. He cannot, for example, make and heat the soup, and then turn his attention to the meat and wait until that is ready before he turns his attention to the vegetables and then the sweet. He has to prepare and cook all the dishes concurrently, sharing his time between all the different tasks that have to be done on all the different dishes, to ensure that everything is ready at the right time.

In the same way, a computer working in real-time applications often has to share its time between many different tasks. In computer parlance this is called *multi-tasking*. A chef may complain that he cannot do two things at once. Nor can a computer. But a computer works so fast that, in a multi-tasking application, it often seems to be doing many things at the same time.

Pascal has notable advantages in real-time and multi-tasking applications. For one thing, its program and data structures are particularly suited to multi-tasking. Just as the chef, who has had to interrupt the preparation of the soup because the sauce for the cauliflower is about to boil over, must be able to return to the soup at the point where he left off and remember, for example, how much salt he has put in it, so also must a multi-tasked computer program be able to resume its original task at the next instruction with all the original data intact. We have already seen how a Pascal procedure may call another and return to the next statement with all its local variables unaffected by what has happened meanwhile.

Secondly, compiled Pascal programs, though generally slower than programs written directly in machine code, are fast enough in operation for very many applications. Even when Pascal is not fast enough for the final program, the ease with which a Pascal program can be written and proved make it an ideal language in which to undertake the initial modelling of the system. When the model is running, those parts of it that are too slow will be highlighted. Most implementations have facilities for jumping out of Pascal into machine code when needed, and back to Pascal when the need is past. Sometimes even machine code is not fast enough and hardware changes become necessary. In any case, the discipline and design effort that have gone into the original Pascal program usually form an excellent groundwork for the development of suitable machine code or hardware.

To give us a background against which to study real-time applications let us take an example close to home – a simple text editor or word processor. The hardware required for such an installation is shown in Fig. 18.1. It consists of the following:

(a) a computer, which we shall define as a mini- or micro-computer with an adequate amount of immediate access store.

Fig 18.1 *the hardware required for a single word processor*

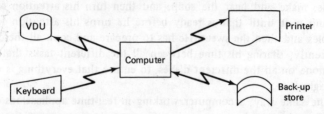

(b) a keyboard, which (in terms of the discussion of Chapter 8 and Appendix III) we shall consider as unbuffered. That is to say that the character resulting from each individual key depression is immediately available to the Pascal program.

(c) a VDU which displays a selected part of the text that is in the immediate access memory and with 'full-screen cursor control' which means that there will be facilities for steering the cursor to any part of the displayed text. Furthermore, we shall require that any attempt to steer the cursor up from the top display line or down from the bottom display line will result in scrolling of the text. The instructions to move the cursor will be given by depressing one of four cursor control keys (up, down, left and right) on the keyboard.

(d) a printer, on which we can print out the completed text, and

(e) a back-up store in which we can store our completed or partially completed texts. We shall assume that this is some form of simple disc storage.

One other parameter must be defined at this stage, the code used to represent keyboard depressions. We shall assume that all print characters are in ASCII code as given in Appendix IV. In addition there are six keys with special meanings:

Cursor up	CHR(1)
Cursor down	CHR(2)
Cursor left	CHR(3)
Cursor right	CHR(4)
\<newline\>	CHR(13)
'Escape'	CHR(27)

Depression of the 'escape' key puts the program into a mode where it expects to receive a further instruction.† These further instructions include, among others: (a) insert a character before the one at which the

---

†The term 'escape' is commonly used in telecommunications and computing to mean 'the following characters have some other meaning than those normally assigned to them'. The actual meaning is defined by the user and, in communications, must be understood by both sender and recipient.

cursor points; (b) delete the character at which the cursor points; (c) transfer the text from the computer's memory into back-up store; (d) load a file from the back-up store into memory; (e) print the text that is in memory; (f) exit from the program ('quit').

When no key is depressed, the equivalent value transmitted by the keyboard to the computer is CHR(0).

Having thus set the scene, let us consider the requirements. The basic requirement of any real-time system is very simple: to await the occurrence of an event and, when one occurs, to carry out an appropriate process. Once the process is completed, the system awaits the next event. According to the nature of the new event when it occurs, the same process will be repeated or a different one will be carried out. And so on . . .

Timing is important in such an operation. For it to be successful, one of two things must happen. Either each process must be complete before the next event occurs, or there must be some queueing arrangement whereby events that occur while a process is being undertaken can be saved for future action. For the present we shall concentrate on the former, simpler, alternative.

In the case of our text editor all the primary events are key depressions. A simple Pascal loop could be used to detect a key depression:

```
REPEAT READ (ch) UNTIL ch <> 0;
```

The process that is then to be undertaken will depend on which key is depressed. If it is a printing character or <newline>, then a procedure, *storeCharact*, will be called which first loads the character into the correct place in memory. It then calls a second procedure *echo* which transmits the necessary information to the VDU to display the character in the correct place. It then calls another procedure, *advanceCursor*, which advances the cursor to the next character position before returning to the waiting state.

If the character is one of the cursor control characters, a different procedure, *moveCursor*, would be called and if it is CHR(27) then yet a different procedure, *escape*, would be called. This procedure expects to receive further input and to take action according to the quite different interpretation that it puts on the value(s) of the character(s) it then receives. For example, it is not unusual to use the character 'Q' (quit) to indicate the desire to end the program. If we assume that the action of the procedure *escape* on receiving this character is to give the value TRUE to a global Boolean variable, *quit*, then we can write a skeleton program for our rudimentary text editor as follows:

```
PROGRAM TextEditor (INPUT, OUTPUT, Printer, File1);

CONST buffSize = ?? (* Size of text buffer *)

VAR
   .
   .

   textBuffer : PACKED ARRAY
                         [1 .. buffSize] OF CHAR;
   quit : BOOLEAN;

FUNCTION inChar : CHAR;
VAR
   ch : CHAR;
BEGIN
   REPEAT READ (ch) UNTIL ch <> 0;
   inChar := ch
END;

PROCEDURE storeCharact (ch : CHAR);

   PROCEDURE echo (ch : CHAR);
      (* As described in text *)

   PROCEDURE advanceCursor;
      (* As described in text *)

BEGIN
   (* As described in text *)
END;

PROCEDURE moveCursor (ch : CHAR);
   (* As described in text *)

PROCEDURE escape;
   (* As described in text *)

BEGIN  (* main program *)
   quit := FALSE;
   REPEAT
      ch := inChar;
      IF (ch = CHR (13)) OR
            ((ch >= CHR (32)) AND (ch <= CHR (125))
                  THEN storeCharact (ch);
      IF (ch >= CHR (1)) AND (ch <= CHR (4))
                           THEN moveCursor (ch);
      IF ch = CHR (27) THEN escape
   UNTIL quit
END.
```

The structure of this program merits some examination. It is an essential feature of real-time and multi-tasking programs that all processes should be confined to clearly defined 'packages'. The activation of each process at the correct time and the transfer of data between processes is the responsibility of a supervisory package which exercises overall control. This package is usually called an *operating system* or *executive*.

In the above, comparatively simple, program the three processes are the procedures *storeCharact*, *moveCursor* and *escape*. The executive consists of the main program together with the function *inChar* (which may also be called by *escape*). Thus it will be seen how well the Pascal block structure fulfils a major requirement of real-time and multi-task operation.

Let us now look at the timing of this program when it is being executed. An expert typist can seldom type faster than 120 words per minute. This represents an average delay between keystrokes of the order of 50 milliseconds. With the exception of printing and operations to and from the back-up store, which we shall discuss later, all the processes that the computer will have to carry out between keystrokes can be completed in the order of a couple of hundred *micro*seconds or less. Thus the computer is spending over 99 per cent of its time just waiting for another event.

Fig 18.2 *a word processor system serving two users*

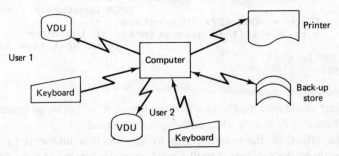

One way to utilise this extra time could be to attach an extra keyboard and VDU to the system so that two typists could share the available time (Fig. 18.2). In principle we could do this with a few modifications to the above program. There would have to be an additional text buffer for the extra typist:

```
textBuffer : PACKED ARRAY
                     [1 .. 2, 1 .. buffSize] OF CHAR;
```

there would be two separate INPUT files, *input1*, *input2* and the procedures would need the addition of a parameter, (1 .. 2), indicating which typist was being serviced.

Function *inChar* would have to be modified to read as follows:

```
FUNCTION inChar (VAR n : 1 .. 2) : CHAR;
VAR
   ch : CHAR;
BEGIN
   REPEAT
      n := (n + 1) MOD 2 + 1;
      CASE n OF
         1 : READ (Input1, ch);
         2 : READ (Input2, ch)
      END
   UNTIL ch <> 0;
   inChar := ch
END;
```

the main program would have to be modified thus

```
BEGIN  (* executive *)
   quit := FALSE;
   n := 1;  (* Start arbitarily with input 1 *)
   REPEAT
      ch := inChar (n);
      IF (ch = CHR (13)) OR
            ((ch >= CHR (32)) AND (ch <= CHR (125))
               THEN storeCharact (ch);
      IF (ch >= CHR (1)) AND (ch <= CHR (4))
                              THEN moveCursor (ch);
      IF ch =  CHR (27) THEN escape
      n := n + 1 (* To give priority to the other
                                   input next time *)
   UNTIL quit
END.
```

and *quit* would now have to be a Boolean function, within scope to *escape*, that became TRUE only when both inputs had signed off.

The effect of the modifications to the function *inChar* is to scan alternatively the two inputs until a valid character is received from one of them. The variable parameter *n* indicates to the main program which of the two inputs is active and the appropriate process is then carried out. When it is complete, the program reverts to scanning the inputs but, in the interest of even-handedness, it starts the scan with the other input in case a key has been depressed during the processing.

With the exception of printing and file transfer operations, the above program would work satisfactorily provided that one typist does not press and release a key during the period that the other typist's event is being processed. However, we cannot be sure that this will never happen. If there were half a dozen or more typists (which is quite feasible considering that each typist occupies the computer for less than 1 per cent of its time) the probability of its happening would be much greater. Therefore we need some way in which the inputs can be scanned at frequent intervals while the process is being carried out. If an event is thus detected the fact must be recorded so that it can be processed as soon as time is available. One way this might be done is shown in the following fragments which are revisions to the program *TextEditor*. We call the new program *MultiText*:

```
PROGRAM MultiText ( . . . . );

CONST
  numInputs = ??;
  queueLength = ??;

TYPE
  waiting =
    RECORD
      inputNumber : 1 .. numInputs;
      charact : CHAR
    END;

VAR
  . . .

  queuePointer, num : 1 .. queueLength;
  queue : ARRAY [1 .. queueLength] OF waiting;

PROCEDURE scan;

VAR
  n : 1 .. numInputs;
  ch : CHAR;

BEGIN
  FOR n := 1 TO numInputs DO
  BEGIN
    CASE n OF
      1 : READ (Input1, ch);
      2 : READ (Input2, ch);
      3 : READ (Input3, ch);

          etc  etc

    END; (* CASE *)
    IF ch <> 0 THEN
    BEGIN
      queuePointer := SUCC (queuePointer);
      WITH queue [queuePointer] DO
      BEGIN
        inputNumber := n;
        charact := ch
      END
    END
  END
END; (* scan *)
```

At frequent intervals in the procedures *storeCharacter, moveCursor* and *escape*, and in the procedures they call, there will be a call to the above procedure, *scan*.

The main, 'executive', program of *TextEditor* will have to be modified as follows to cater for these changes:

```
BEGIN  (* executive *)
  quit := FALSE;
  queuePointer := O;
  REPEAT
    WHILE queuePointer = O DO scan;
    WITH queue [queuePointer] DO
    BEGIN
      n := inputNumber;
      ch := charact
    END;
    FOR num := 2 TO queuePointer DO
         queue [num-1] := queue [num];
    queuePointer := PRED (queuePointer);
    IF (ch = CHR (13)) OR
           ((ch >= CHR (32)) AND (ch <= CHR (125))
           THEN storeCharact (ch);
    IF (ch >= CHR (1)) AND (ch <= CHR (4))
                               THEN moveCursor (ch);
      IF ch =  CHR (27) THEN escape
  UNTIL quit
END.
```

You will see that, instead of taking its values of *ch* and *n* directly from the inputs, the executive now takes these values from the head of the queue if the queue is not empty. It then advances the queue by one position. If the queue is empty at the beginning of the **REPEAT** loop, then the program waits until *scan* places the first input in the queue. By the time it enters the **REPEAT** loop again there is the chance that the frequent calls to *scan* in the other procedures may have put some more entries into the queue.

These frequent calls to *scan* have two distinct disadvantages. In the first place, they are imposing on the processes a task that rightly belongs to the executive, thus destroying the orderly structure of the program. Secondly, they are doing the very thing which we want to try to avoid in a real-time system – they are adding to the computing time. To be effective they must be frequent enough to ensure that no event is missed, but the more frequently they are called, the greater will be the proportion with, literally, a nil return. Each occupies a finite time, and the cumulative effect in some programs could reduce the time left for actual processing to an unacceptably low level. It is as though our chef (to return to our earlier analogy), in addition to doing the cooking, were having to make frequent visits to the front door to see if the guests had arrived. If this were done too often, the cooking might suffer. Fortunately guests can be relied on to herald their arrival by ringing the door bell. The equivalent of the door bell in most computer installations is a hardware facility known as an *interrupt*.

As part of the computer's hardware there is what is known as an 'interrupt line'. This is connected to an interrupt input terminal. All peripheral devices (keyboards, printers, process controls, process gauges, etc.) can be so wired that, whenever an event occurs at that device ('key depressed', 'printer ready for next input', etc.) a signal can be sent to this interrupt input terminal at the same time as the event is communicated in the normal way. When this signal is received, the computer halts what it is currently doing and enters an *interrupt routine*. This routine is normally in machine code and is provided by the user. In the above example, its method of working would be as follows. On receipt of the interrupt signal the computer would halt execution at the end of its current instruction and switch to the interrupt routine which, in this case, would be identical with the above *scan* procedure but written in machine code. Once the appropriate record had been placed in the queue, the computer would resume operation of the Pascal program at the point where it had left off. The procedure *scan* would only be called when an event had actually occurred, thus avoiding all unnecessary, fruitless calls to *scan*.

Successful real-time working requires a knowledge of, and access to, the available hardware facilities. Indeed, some operations may require special additional hardware to make real-time working possible. Although this is a subject that is outside the scope of this book, the following example is given to show you the sort of problem that can arise and how it can be solved with hardware.

Peripheral equipment (such as the printer and back-up store in a text editor) can be a major cause of delay in real-time and multi-tasking. It takes a few *micro*seconds to transmit one character from the main memory to the printer. It takes, typically, tens of *milli*seconds to print it mechanically. Similarly, anyone who has used one of the simpler commercial word-processing packages on a microcomputer will be aware that it is necessary to wait for a few seconds while data is transferred from memory to back-up store or vice versa. During these peripheral operations, access from the keyboard is usually denied because the computer is being used to control the data transfer. For the single user, this is an acceptable inconvenience. For users on a multi-user system it would be quite intolerable for them to have to wait every time one of the other users wished to print, load or save a file.

There is a choice of hardware solutions to this problem. One is to inter-

222

pose a *buffer* between the computer and the peripheral device. The buffer in this case is a piece of memory quite separate from the computer's memory. Its size will depend on the equipment it is serving. Typically a buffer for a printer will hold enough characters for one line of print and a buffer for a disc drive will hold 256 characters (or enough for one sector of track). Most modern printers incorporate their own line buffers whose operation is depicted in Fig. 18.3. The first stage of operation (Fig. 18.3(a)) is to transfer the data to the buffer. This typically takes a few

Fig 18.3 *the use of a buffer unit with a printer: (a) data is sent to the buffer from the computer at 'computing speed'; (b) data is sent from the buffer to the printer at printing speed, leaving the computer free for other activities*

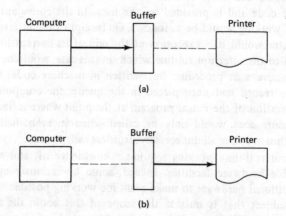

hundred microseconds. When this has been done, the printer takes over control of the buffer (Fig. 18.3(b)) and prints its contents, leaving the computer free to carry on with other work. To avoid the risk of the computer sending more data to the buffer before the printing operation is complete, the printer protects it by sending a 'printer busy' signal to the computer. This is an implementation-dependent character that is placed, by the hardware, in a specific location in the computer's memory. Once the data in the buffer has all been printed, the 'printer busy' character is replaced by a, different, 'printer ready' character.

Most Pascal implementations have a predeclared function (typically, PEEK (<location address>)) which will return the value contained in any location in memory. The Pascal programmer can thus test that the printer is ready before sending further data to the buffer. Additionally, the 'printer ready' signal can be linked by hardware to the computer's interrupt terminal, in a similar manner to that already described for the keyboards, to avoid frequent unnecessary testing of the printer status and to speed the printing operation.

All input and output devices can be buffered in this way to avoid wasting computer time during comparatively slow external mechanical processes.

An alternative to buffering is *direct memory access* which is available as hardware on many computers. This operates by giving the external device direct access to the computer's memory either by 'stealing' a few microseconds when needed or by making use of some of the nanoseconds (a nanosecond is one thousandth of a microsecond) that the computer perforce has to waste in its normal rhythm.†

We are beginning to see the important, and often complicated, role played by the executive in real-time and multi-tasking operations. The main, 'executive' program of *MultiText* has been grossly oversimplified. Even the fact that it appears to have been written in standard Pascal is deceptive. Files *Input1, Input2*, etc., have been treated as though they were normal external text files, but they are not. They are 'hardware files' and the program would have to be compiled in such a way that this fact was appreciated and the physical location of each input clearly identified. To be successful this program would have to be extended to allow for interrupts. Again, there are no facilities for this in standard Pascal. Arrangements would also have to be made for buffering the printer and the back-up store, for giving the necessary priorities when, for example, one user desired access to the back-up store while another was already using it and for dealing with a number of similar problems. Although, because of the need to interact with the hardware, executives can seldom be written in standard Pascal, the structures of Pascal and the discipline it imposes have proved it to be a highly suitable basis for a language in which to write executives and real-time programs. One such language is 'Microprocessor Pascal', described in Vincent and Gill (1981). This is a superset of standard Pascal and some of its added features will now be described.

In the program examples given so far in this chapter the process packages have all been procedures. However, the need often arises for larger, more embracing structures. Microprocessor Pascal has, effectively, five levels of block structure, as shown in Fig. 18.4, although the outermost level, the executive, is not accessible to the Pascal programmer. The outermost Pascal level is the SYSTEM. Normally only one SYSTEM can be active at any time. It can, however, contain any number of PROGRAMS which can contain any number of PROCESSES. The generic name for

†For a fuller description of the use of interrupts and direct memory access in input/output operations, see Huggins (1979, Chapters 19 and 20).

Fig 18.4 *the block structure of Texas Instruments' Microprocessor Pascal*

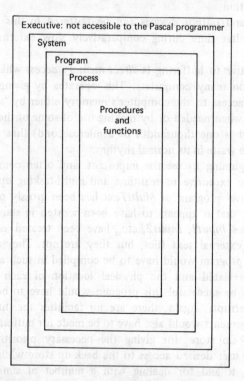

Executive: not accessible to the Pascal programmer

System

Program

Process

Procedures
and
functions

SYSTEMS, PROGRAMS and PROCESSES is 'process' (in lower case).
Any such process can contain procedures and functions. Variables can be
declared at any level and the usual Pascal rules apply regarding the scope
of identifiers.

An important feature of Microprocessor Pascal processes is that they
can be run concurrently by *multi-programming*. In the multi-tasking
operations that we have so far discussed, we switched from package to
package whenever a definitive point in a program was reached (usually
the end of a procedure or the call to a procedure). In multi-programming,
on the other hand, the executive collects all the currently active processes
under its wing, as it were, and executes short sections of each program in
rotation. Typically, this is done by allocating a finite period of time (a few
hundred microseconds or a few milliseconds) to each. When the programs
being run in this way are independent of each other (as they are, for
example, when several users are running their own programs from separate
terminals) there is no problem of interaction. But when two or more
programs need to share the same peripheral equipment, the same problems
arise in multi-programming as we have already discussed for multi-tasking.

Similar problems arise in many industrial control applications where, in addition to interactions between processes and the hardware, there frequently has to be synchronisation between the different processes themselves.

In Microprocessor Pascal this synchronisation is carried out by means of a predefined data type, SEMAPHORE, which consists of a queue (possibly empty) of processes awaiting an event. The use of semaphores and other features of Microprocessor Pascal are shown in the following example.

The example was set up as a demonstration model and is therefore a comparatively simple one, with schoolroom memories for many people. However, its principles would be equally applicable to the control of any process. Figure 18.5 shows the process to be controlled – a system of five

Fig 18.5 *the fluid system to be controlled by the DEMO program*

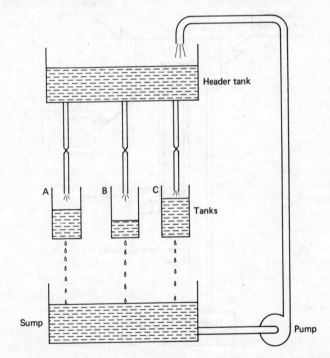

tanks. A fluid is delivered from the header tank via piping and electrically actuated valves into three tanks, A, B and C, each of which has a hole in the bottom from which the fluid discharges into a sump. The fluid can be recovered from the sump by means of a pump which returns it to the header. The problem is to maintain the levels of tanks A, B and C and of the header tank within set limits, by means of opening and closing the three valves or by altering the pump speed.

The system can operate in three different modes: *manual, automatic* or *repetitive*. In the repetitive mode, the system has the ability to 'learn' a 20-step sequence of instructions and repeat it indefinitely.

Figure 18.6 shows the configuration of the control system. The computer incorporates its own internal clock which is used to update the

Fig 18.6 *the control system for program DEMO*

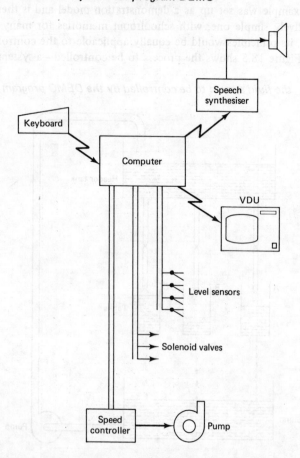

software real-time clock that is one of the processes. The keyboard is used to set the mode, to initialise the real-time clock and to set the level limits. In manual and repetitive modes, it is also used to open and close valves and to set the pump speed.

The VDU display shows the status of the valves, the pump speed and the levels. The speech synthesiser gives a running commentary of the same information.

Figure 18.7 shows the four levels of the Microprocessor Pascal program that undertakes the control of the actual model.

Fig 18.7   *the four levels of system 'demo' written in Microprocessor Pascal*

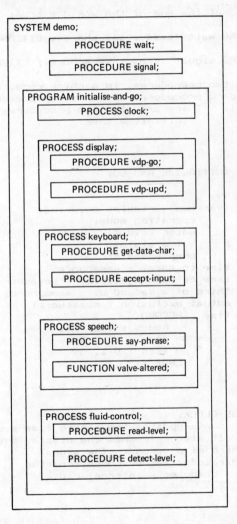

The following is the skeleton of the actual program that is used to control this model. The Microprocessor Pascal conventions for identifiers have been retained. For brevity, only those declarations and statements that demonstrate the intercommunication, process with process or process with hardware, are shown. Furthermore, some of the procedures of Fig. 18.7 have been omitted.

```
SYSTEM DEMO;

   CONST   not_the_end_of_the_world = true;

   PROCEDURE wait (sema : semaphore); EXTERNAL;

   PROCEDURE signal (sema : semaphore); EXTERNAL;

(*  These two procedures, in machine code, are    *
 *    standard procedures of TI Microprocessor     *
 *  Pascal.    There are also two procedures to    *
 *                  initialise them.              *)


   PROGRAM INITIALISE_AND_GO;

      LABEL 99;
      VAR   <Various variables covering:
                   operating mode,
                   water levels,
                   valve status,
                   pump speed etc >
            time_to_speak : semaphore;
            time_to_update_display : semaphore;
            third_of_a_second_up : semaphore;
            mutual_exclusion : semaphore;
            time : RECORD
                     hours : 0 .. 23;
                     mins : 0 .. 59;
                     secs : 0 .. 59
                   END;


   PROCESS CLOCK;
(*  This process updates the record time every   *
 *  second. It also refreshes the display every  *
 *      third of a second.  The signal           *
 *      third_of_a_second comes from the         *
 *          computer's internal clock            *)


   BEGIN
      WHILE not_the_end_of_the_world DO
      BEGIN
         FOR ticks := 1 TO 3 DO
(*  Note: the FOR control variable is implicit   *
 *    to the FOR loop in Microprocessor Pascal   *)
```

```
      BEGIN
        signal (time_to_update_display);
        wait (third_of_a_second_up)
      END;
      < Update the record time >
    END
  END;

PROCESS DISPLAY;
(*    This process refreshes the VDU display.    *
 *        It waits for two semaphores:           *
 *            time_to_update_display and         *
 *                mutual_exclusion.              *
 *  The latter is necessary since neither the    *
 *  VDU nor the audio output is buffered. Thus   *
 *    they may not be processed concurrently.    *)
  BEGIN
    WHILE not_the_end_of_the_world DO
    BEGIN
      wait (time_to_update_display);
      wait (mutual_exclusion);
      < update display >
      signal (mutual_exclusion)
    END
  END;

PROCESS KEYBOARD;
  (* This process controls the input of  *
   *        data from the keyboard.       *)
VAR word : PACKED ARRAY [1 .. 4] OF char;
BEGIN
  wait (character_received);
  < Action taken according to data input >
  IF word = 'quit' THEN GOTO 99
END;

PROCESS SPEECH;

  PROCEDURE sayphrase;
    (* This procedure outputs a phrase *
     *    to the audio output          *)
    BEGIN
      wait (mutual_exclusion);
      < output the phrase >
      signal (mutual_exclusion)
    END
  END;

  BEGIN (* speech *)
  WHILE not_the_end_of_the_world DO
  BEGIN
    wait (time_to_speak);
    < assemble the phrase appropriate to the
                   message to be delivered >
    sayphrase
  END
  END; (* speech *)
```

```
      PROCESS FLUIDCONTROL;
(*    This process scans the levels. It adjusts   *
*  the pump speed and opens and closes valves in  *
*    accordance with the levels and the current   *
*    operating mode.  By updating the variables   *
*    declared in the program INITIALISE_AND_GO    *
*  it supplies the data needed for updating the   *
*  VDU display and for the running commentary     *
*           from the audio output.               *)
      BEGIN
        < read levels and take the necessary action >
        signal (time_to_speak)
      END;

   BEGIN (INITIALISE_AND_GO)
      < initialise all variables >
      start DISPLAY;
      start KEYBOARD;
      start SPEECH;
      start CLOCK;
      start FLUIDCONTROL;
99 : END;   (* INITIALISE_AND_GO *)


BEGIN  (* DEMO *)
   start INITIALISE_AND_GO
END.   (* DEMO *)
```

The points particularly to note in this program are as follows:

(a) The method of activating each process by means of the Microprocessor Pascal reserved word 'start'.

(b) The method of ensuring that an event has occurred by means of a

$$\text{wait} (<\text{semaphore}>)$$

statement. If the event has occurred, execution of the process continues. If it has not, the executive holds the process in suspense, in a queue if necessary, until the appropriate signal has been received. This signal may be initiated by another software process by the statement

$$\text{signal} (<\text{semaphore}>)$$

or by hardware (e.g. *third-of-a-second-up, character-received*) in which case the executive will provide a similar signal. The words 'wait' and 'signal' are Microprocessor Pascal reserved words.

(c) The legitimate use of GOTO in the process KEYBOARD as a method of exit from the continuous loops of *WHILE not-the-end-of-the-world*.

Once the processes have been activated, the Microprocessor Pascal executive will run them concurrently (until 'quit'), pausing as required for events to occur.

This example shows how each process can stand on its own, sharing common variables if required, and yet be easily synchronised with events occurring in other processes or in the hardware.

Microprocessor Pascal is currently implemented on the equipment of one particular manufacturer, though similar facilities are available on version 4 of UCSD Pascal. Process control represents an area where the considerable potentials of Pascal have yet to be generally realised.

CHAPTER 19

MAINLY FOR BEGINNERS

This chapter covers many small points which in total could help you to program more effectively. Although many of the points are obvious, experience has shown that they are often overlooked.

First some hints on program speed. Even when speed is not a vital or expensive factor in a program's effectiveness, common sense indicates that features that unnecessarily lengthen the time of operation should be avoided.

The place to look for wasted time is in those parts of the program that are often repeated – procedures, functions and loops. Savings in parts of the program that are performed once only will be measured in milliseconds or less. Conversely, when the same calculations are performed within a loop that is repeated thousands of times, we may have to measure its time in seconds. And if that loop is nested within another loop ... ! So the lesson is clear. Do not put calculations within a loop if they could be performed once only outside. Remember that evaluation of the *conditions* for the repetition of a **WHILE** or **REPEAT** loop has to be done on each iteration. If speed is important, avoid complicated Boolean evaluations, where possible, in **REPEAT** and **WHILE** statements.

It usually takes the run-time system more than twice as long to locate a component of a single dimension array as it does to find a simple variable. For multidimensional arrays, each additional dimension adds an even greater time penalty. If speed is important, use them only when the program demands them (for instance, for strings).

FOR loops are usually faster than **WHILE** and **REPEAT** loops.

SUCC(n) and PRED(n) are usually faster than the equivalent $n := n + 1$ and $n := n - 1$.

Integer arithmetic, as we have seen, is much faster than floating point. So use integer arithmetic wherever possible. For example, if **MAXINT** on your implementation is large enough, it is usually quicker to carry out all monetary transactions in pence (or cents), assigning the result to a REAL variable just before final print-out. Even this is may be unnecessary, since

WRITE (result DIV 100 : 5, '.', result MOD 100 : 2)

may well be faster, but the point is often academic if the writing is to a printer or external file. The speed of such an operation is controlled by the external device, which will usually be much slower than quite slow internal calculations.

Memory size can be a limiting factor in small systems (mini- and micro-computers). Space has to be found in the internal memory for the operating system, for the program and for all those variables that are currently in scope. If a memory overflow occurs, it is usually best to see if it is possible to cut down on the size of arrays. Watch particularly arrays declared within procedures, especially if such procedures can call each other or themselves recursively. Each time a procedure is called, space is needed for all its declared variables until the end of its call. A procedure that calls itself recursively 10 times will have needed, by the last call, 10 times the space that it would have needed for one call. An integer variable (which term includes each component of an integer array) needs two bytes of memory store if MAXINT is 32 767 and four bytes if MAXINT is 2 147 483 647. A real variable typically occupies twice the space of an integer in the same system.

In some implementations, a multidimensional array with vectors whose magnitudes are widely disparate, for example

```
ARRAY [1..1000, 1..2] OF INTEGER
```

will occupy much less space if the vectors are transposed, thus:

```
ARRAY [1..2, 1..1000] OF INTEGER
```

In other implementations the reverse may be true. If the documentation does not tell you, the only way to find out will be to experiment. You may even find that it makes no difference, in which case your compiler is probably saving space at the cost of extra time whenever you access the array. The advice given above, to avoid multidimensional arrays where speed is important, is especially relevant with such compilers.

Using the program strategy and top-down approach of Chapter 11, your programs should run correctly the first time you load them. If errors do occur, they will be either *syntax* errors or *logic* errors. The former will usually be simple mistakes of wrong punctuation, omitting an END, forgetting to declare a variable or trying to use a part of the language that your implementation does not support. Such mistakes will all be picked up when you try to compile the program. Common errors are discussed later in this chapter.

Logic errors, however caused, are usually harder to find. If your program is not producing the results you intended, there is one golden rule. Get right away from the computer as a first step. Go right through your documentation, starting at level 1, and examine your reasoning stage by stage *top down*. Better still, get someone else to do it for you (another important reason for good program documentation!).

The following are errors that are commonly made and hard to identify: (a) attempting to access a global variable when a variable of the same name has been declared in a procedure that is in scope; (b) overlooking the fact that some implementations truncate identifiers, so that words that differ in their later characters are regarded as the same; (c) modifying a control variable within a **FOR** loop; (d) having a Boolean expression that never becomes FALSE at the start of a **WHILE** loop or TRUE at the end of a **REPEAT** loop. This last error often happens through rounding errors in real arithmetic. For example, if a is a REAL variable

```
UNTIL a = 2.0
```

is bad practice. There is a chance that the value of a that you expect to be 2.0 turns out, through successive rounding, to be, say, 2.000 000 000 01. The following might have avoided the risk of error:

```
UNTIL a >= 2
```

or

```
UNTIL (a >= 1.99999) AND (a <= 2.00001)
```

(e) Inadvertently using an array subscript that is out of range. For example, in the following search routine,

```
VAR
   itemNum : ARRAY [1 .. 100] OF INTEGER;
   . . .

n := 0;
REPEAT
   n := SUCC (n)
UNTIL (itemNum [n] = item) OR (n > 100);
```

if *item* is not found, *n* will reach a value of 101 and a test would be made of the Boolean expression

```
itemNum [101] = item
```

Since *itemNum [101]* does not exist, this would be an error. It would be no solution to this problem to reverse the two Boolean expressions after **UNTIL**, because the order in which such expressions are evaluated is not defined. (See the answer to Exercise 9.2, **FUNCTION** *location*, for one possible solution.)

If your examination of your program documentation fails to indicate a flaw, then study the program *listing* to ensure that the program you offered the computer did not differ from that which you developed on paper. Pascal is largely self-checking against one particular fault that commonly plagues users of some other languages where variables do not have to be declared. With these languages, if there is a misprint in spelling the name of a variable (the mis-keying of zero for letter O, for example; we all do it sometime!), the compiler assumes a new variable and acts accordingly. Such errors can take hours to spot. The same can happen in Pascal if two very similar names are used. This point is mentioned later.

If all else fails to find the error, you may have to resort to 'debugging' on the computer. Debugging is a time-consuming and frustrating process. How you do it will depend on the diagnostic facilities offered by your implementation. Let us assume that there are none and that you have to produce your own *diagnostics*. These are instructions that you insert at strategic points in a recalcitrant program which will write or print out information that you believe will help you solve the problem. Such information is usually of two types:

(a) 'Tracers' that indicate the point that has been reached in a program. This involves giving arbitrary names or numbers, which are used solely for the purpose of debugging, to strategic points in a program. Such points are usually the beginning or end of a loop, the entry to a procedure, etc.

(b) The current value of a certain variable or a number of variables. The variables chosen should, of course, have some bearing on the problem you are trying to solve. Typically, the control variable of a loop, the entry parameters of a procedure or the returned value of a function might be used.

Thus a diagnostic statement in a program might be

```
WRITELN ('@ 27  n=', n, '  p=', p )
```

Each time that point is reached in the program a message such as

```
@ 27  n=  13  p=  35
```

will be output.

If your normal output device is a VDU, the diagnostics will probably flash on and roll off the screen so fast that you will not be able to read them. In this case you have two choices. Either you can send the output to a printer, which may be slow but will give you information that you can study at your ease, or you can declare an additional CHAR variable (*dummy*, say) and change the diagnostic to

```
WRITE ('@ 27 n=', n, '  p=', p );
READ (dummy)
```

After each set of information appears on the screen, the program will halt until you press the <newline> key. You may thus be able to 'step' your way through the program faster, and more quietly, than with a printer.

Once you have cleared the bug, you may delete the diagnostic statement from the program, but it is sometimes wiser, until you are quite satisfied with the whole program, to put such statements in *comment* brackets, { } or (* *), for the time being. If another bug arises later, it may be quicker to delete the brackets than to retype the whole statement.

The following is a list, by no means exhaustive, of errors commonly made in programming. The first four are logic faults that might cause trouble at run-time but would not be picked up by the compiler. The rest are common syntax faults that would all, with the possible exception of number 17, be picked up during the compiling of the program.

(1) When comparing two variables for magnitude, it is sometimes the ABSolute values that should be compared and not the values themselves. This can happen, for example, when testing the convergence of a series.

(2) Watch out for potential 'illegal' operations such as division by zero, square root of a negative value, exceeding the maximum permitted absolute value for an integer or real number, logarithm of a negative value or of zero, subscript outside declared range. These will all give run-time errors that either halt the program or corrupt the results. If you want to avoid this, then it is advisable to insert a check such as

```
IF divisor = 0 THEN
BEGIN
   dividend :=
           (dividend DIV ABS (dividend) * MAXINT);
   WRITELN
           ('Attempted division by zero. Maxint used')
END
ELSE quotient := dividend DIV divisor
```

(3) Avoid using the name of any standard function or procedure when naming your constants, variables, functions or procedures, unless you specifically wish to redefine the standard identifier.

(4) Remember, when you call for the input of a letter character from the keyboard during run-time, that it may be in the opposite *case* or

shift to that which you were expecting. Check what your implementation does. If you intend your program to be transportable to other implementations, then it is best to cover yourself with a function such as *yesno* in Chapter 7.

(5) Do not omit the multiplication sign, '*'. This is a mistake easily made by newcomers to computer programming, particularly in expressions such as *(a + b) * (c + d)*.

(6) Remember to use the correct division operator: **DIV** for INTEGER operations, '/' for REAL.

(7) Check all punctuation, not least the final full stop. Some compilers reject the program if this is missing and it is infuriating to have to recompile the whole program for so trivial a mistake.

(8) Check on spaces and <newlines>. They must *not* appear in the middle of words, names or the combined symbols

$$<= \quad >= \quad <> \quad := \quad (**) \quad .. \quad \text{or} \quad ''$$

On the other hand, all words and names *must* be separated from each other and from numbers by a space, a <newline>, a symbol or a punctuation mark.

(9) Do not leave decimal points hanging in the air: 5, 5.0 and 0.5 are correct; 5. and .5 are not permitted.

(10) If you have any doubt about the order in which an expression will be evaluated, be liberal with the brackets. Brackets have a negligible time penalty at compile time and none at all at execution.

(11) Every '(' in an expression must have a corresponding ')'. In complicated expressions it is worthwhile to count them and not trust your eyesight.

(12) Every **BEGIN** must have an **END**.

(13) Every statement must be separated from the next by ';', **END**, **ELSE** or **UNTIL**. **END** must be followed by one of these separators or by a full stop.

(14) Every **CASE**, except in variants, must have an **END**. Some implementations do not permit a semicolon before this **END**.

(15) Watch for mis-typing, particularly for the use of '−' for '=' and vice versa. These are often on the same key and the error in the listing can easily be overlooked.

(16) Remember that

$$<label> : END$$

and

$$<label> : UNTIL$$

must be preceded by a separating semicolon.

(17) Be very careful not to omit the closing single quotation mark of a string or '}' or '*)' of a comment. The compiler will treat all the following program up to the next such marker as though it were a string or comment and may throw up an error message that has no relation either to the real nature of the fault or the place where it occurred.

As might be surmised, this list is compiled from bitter personal experience! And while on a personal note, remember that the format used for the program examples in this book is specific to the author's implementation. Some of it (the underlining of the Pascal reserved words) is specific to this book and unlikely to be found on any other implementation. Other points, particularly the use of lower case letters and the type of brackets to be used for array subscripts and comments may have to be modified for other implementations.

Pascal is generous in allowing identifiers of almost unlimited length. (Remember, however, that many implementations truncate identifiers.) Advantage should be taken of this generosity when choosing identifiers. It is a great help in following through a program if the identifier has some relevance to the variable it represents. Single letter identifiers should be used with care and where their meaning is clear.† For example, e as the base of Naperian logarithms is well known, but although a, b and c are commonly used as the three sides of a triangle, a program employing them would probably be clearer if *sideA*, *sideB* and *sideC* were used.

Try to avoid the use of the numerals 1 and zero in an identifier where the letters are in upper case. The following are four *different* identifiers. The differences would be very hard to spot in a long program.

RAT1O   RAT1O   RATIO   RATIO

One final word of advice. Re-read the documentation of your software at frequent intervals. Features for which there is no immediate need tend to be overlooked on first reading and their existence forgotten. It is common experience to bewail a shortcoming of the software, only to find later that it existed all the time! And this goes for this book too. If you have reached this point by a route that by-passed Chapters 14–18, it may be well worth your while to return to them in a few weeks or months, after you have gained some Pascal programming experience.

---

† The author defends the use of n and m as the control variables for **FOR** loops with the pathetically lame excuse that he has been doing it for 16 years! If you can think of more suitable names, then you should use them.

APPENDIX I

THE PASCAL RESERVED WORDS AND REQUIRED IDENTIFIERS

The following are the Pascal reserved words. Each has a special meaning and may not be redefined:

AND	ARRAY	BEGIN	CASE
CONST	DIV	DO	DOWNTO
ELSE	END	FILE	FOR
FUNCTION	GOTO	IF	IN
LABEL	MOD	NIL	NOT
OF	OR	PACKED	PROCEDURE
PROGRAM	RECORD	REPEAT	SET
THEN	TO	TYPE	UNTIL
VAR	WHILE	WITH	

The following are the 'required identifiers' of the Pascal language. It is possible, but inadvisable, to redefine them during a program.

INTEGER	REAL	CHAR	BOOLEAN
ABS	ARCTAN	CHR	COS
DISPOSE	EOF	EOLN	EXP
FALSE	GET	INPUT	LN
MAXINT	NEW	ODD	ORD
OUTPUT	PACK	PAGE	PRED
PUT	READ	READLN	RESET
REWRITE	ROUND	SIN	SQR
SQRT	SUCC	TEXT	TRUE
TRUNC	UNPACK	WRITE	WRITELN

The following word is a *required directive* and has also been assigned a special meaning in the language:

FORWARD

Some implementations have additional predefined functions and procedures.

SYNTAX DIAGRAMS

Pascal syntax should follow the route indicated in the following diagrams. In these diagrams the following rules hold:

(a) 'Letter' means any one of the 26 letters of the English alphabet. It may be in either upper case or lower case. The Pascal language does not differentiate between upper case and lower case letters except within character strings.

(b) 'Digit' means any one of the decimal digits 0 . . 9.

(c) 'Character' means any one letter or digit or other symbol. In theory this means any of the printable characters in a character set such as ASCII (see Appendix IV) but in practice there are often implementation limitations.

(d) All other tokens appearing within circles or boxes with semicircular ends should be reproduced in the program exactly as they appear in the diagram, except that letters may be in upper or lower case.

(e) All items in solid rectangular boxes are defined in this appendix.

program

block

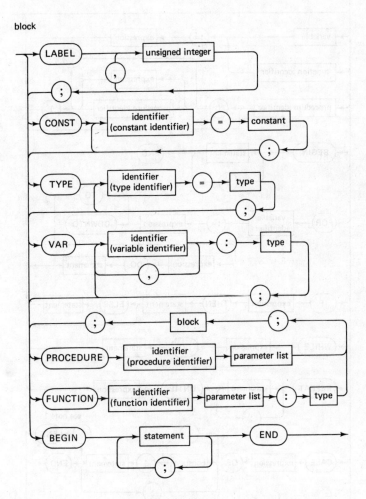

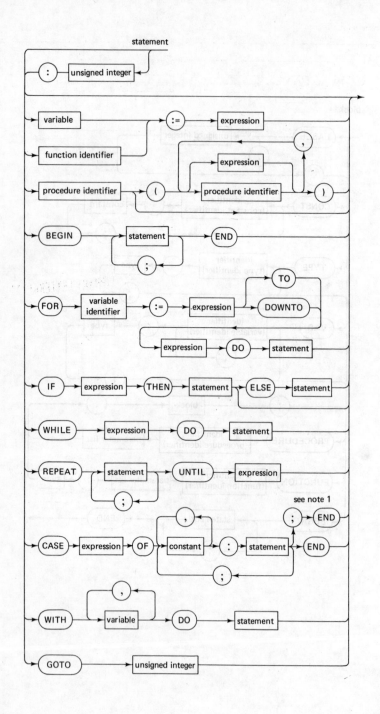

parameter list

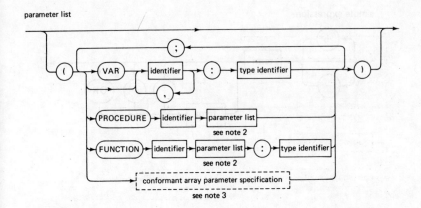

expression

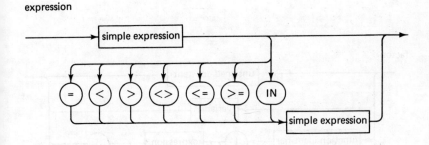

simple expression

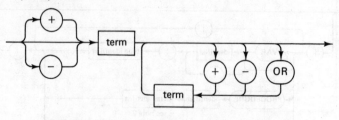

term

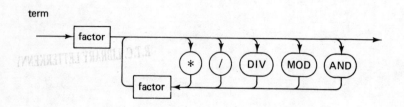

factor

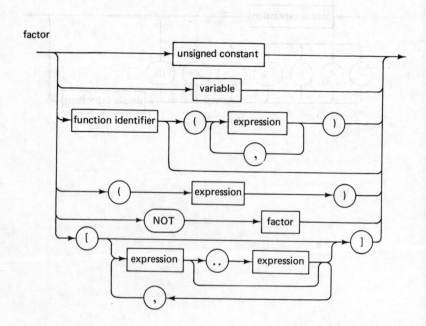

type

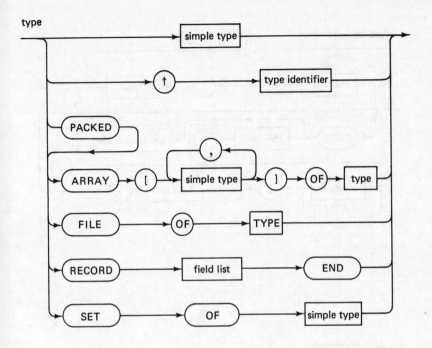

simple type

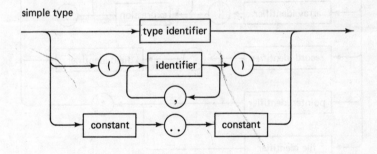

field list

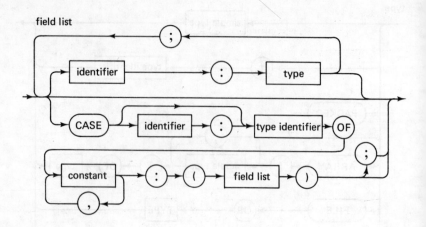

variable

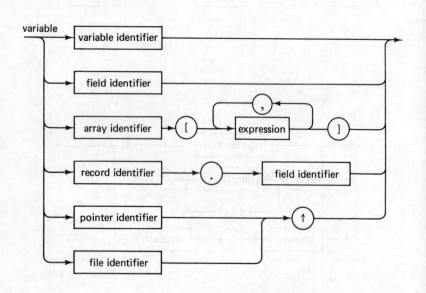

constant

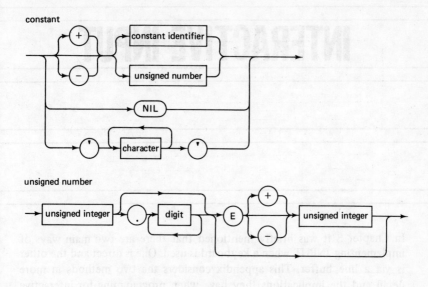

unsigned number

unsigned integer

identifier

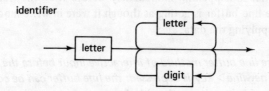

Note 1   The semi-colon before the **END** of a **CASE** statement was not permitted in some earlier Pascal implementations.

Note 2   The requirement for a parameter list in procedural and functional parameters was introduced in **BS 6192 : 1982**. It may not be permitted in some earlier implementations.

Note 3   Conformant array parameters are a feature of Level 1 of **BS 6192 : 1982**. They are not discussed in this book which claims to comply only with Level 0 of the Standard.

INTERACTIVE INPUT

In Chapter 8 it was briefly mentioned that there are two main ways of implementing INPUT when a keyboard is used. One is direct and the other is via a line buffer. This appendix considers the two methods in more detail and the implications they have when programming for interactive operation.

III.1 THE LINE BUFFER METHOD

The line buffer method requires that the <newline> key must be pressed after the called-for data has been entered. Figure III.1 shows diagrammatically what is happening immediately before the <newline> key is pressed. The line buffer is acting as though it were in write mode with the keyboard supplying the data.

Fig III.1 *the line buffer method of interactive input before the <newline> key is depressed: the line buffer can be considered as a file in write mode with the arrow representing the key-board's buffer variable*

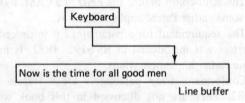

Keyboard

Now is the time for all good men

Line buffer

Figure III.2 shows the position immediately after pressing the <newline> key. The line buffer is now in read mode and the Pascal program's buffer variable is positioned to read the data.

Fig III.2 *the line buffer method of interactive inputs after the <newline> key is pressed; the line buffer is in read mode and the Pascal buffer variable is positioned to read the whole line*

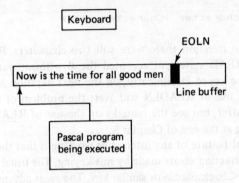

To see how this works in practice, let us look at a simple program:

```
PROGRAM CharHandling (INPUT, OUTPUT);

VAR
    character : CHAR;

BEGIN
  REPEAT
    WRITE ('Input a character >');
    READ (character);
    WRITELN ('Character is >', character);
    WRITELN
  UNTIL character = 'X'
END.
```

The result of running this program using the line buffer method is

```
Input a character >A←
Character is >A

Input a character >B←
Character is >B

Input a character >X←
Character is >X
```

Note that each character input has been followed by the pressing of the <newline> key.

The line buffer can introduce one feature that may be undesirable. Let us run the program again, but this time we shall supply more data than is needed to satisfy the first read list:

```
Input a character  >ABX←
Character is >A

Input a character  >Character is >B

Input a character  >Character is >X
```

On the second iteration there were still two characters, B and X, in the buffer. The READ statement accepted the B without waiting for a new character to be keyed in. Similarly, on the next iteration X was accepted. The judicious use of READLN will avert the problem of unwanted data left in the buffer, but see the remarks on the use of READLN for inter-active working at the end of Chapter 8.

An essential feature of any interactive working is that there should be a method of correcting errors made by mis-keying. The usual way to do this is by use of a <backspace> or similar key. The great advantage of the line buffer method is that such errors can usually be corrected before the <newline> key is pressed. The corrections are made in the line buffer by the computer's operating system and no special provision is needed in the Pascal program.

A disadvantage of the line buffer method is that <newline> always has to pressed. In many programs (games and computer drafting are examples) it is a definite disadvantage not to have some form of immediate single keystoke entry. For this reasons some implementations using a line buffer also provide an additional predefined function which scans the keyboard and, if a key is pressed, returns its value.

III.2 THE DIRECT METHOD

The direct method of interactive data entry is exemplified diagrammatically in Fig. III.3. Each character value is passed straight from the keyboard to the buffer variable.

If we run the above *CharHandling* program with this method we would get the following:

```
Input a character  >ACharacter is >A

Input a character  >BCharacter is >B

Input a character  >XCharacter is >X
```

This layout differs from that obtained with the line buffer method because we have not had to press the <newline> key after entering each character.

For games and similar programs the ability of the direct method to

Fig III.3 *the direct method of interactive input: each character is passed straight from the keyboard to the Pascal program; the programmer must write his or her own procedure for dealing with 'backspaced' corrections*

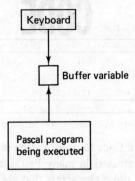

respond to the single entry of any key can be a distinct advantage. Also there is no line buffer to hold unwanted characters.

The main disadvantage of this method is that for certain applications the Pascal programmer may need to provide his own procedure for the correction of keying errors.

APPENDIX IV

A SUBSET OF THE ACSII

CODE

The American Standard Code for Information Interchange is used to define the ORD values of characters in many Pascal implementations. The table on the next page lists those characters that are likely to be used generally by Pascal programmers, together with their values.

Ord	Chr	Ord	Chr	Ord	Chr
32	\<space\>	64	@		
33	!	65	A	97	a
34	"	66	B	98	b
35	# or £	67	C	99	c
36	$	68	D	100	d
37	%	69	E	101	e
38	&	70	F	102	f
39	' (quote)	71	G	103	g
40	(	72	H	104	h
41	)	73	I	105	i
42	*	74	J	106	j
43	+	75	K	107	k
44	, (comma)	76	L	108	l
45	−	77	M	109	m
46	. (full stop)	78	N	110	n
47	/	79	O	111	o
48	0	80	P	112	p
49	1	81	Q	113	q
50	2	82	R	114	r
51	3	83	S	115	s
52	4	84	T	116	t
53	5	85	U	117	u
54	6	86	V	118	v
55	7	87	W	119	w
56	8	88	X	120	x
57	9	89	Y	121	y
58	:	90	Z	122	z
59	;	91	[	123	{
60	\<				
61	=	93	]	125	}
62	\>	94	↑		
63	?				

In addition to the above there are several control characters that, when output to some printers, have special significance. Among these are

      8 Back-space
      9 Horizontal tabulate
    10 Line feed
    12 Form feed (to the top of next page)
    13 Carriage return

REFERENCES

BS 6192: 1982 (1982). *Computer programming language Pascal*, British Standards Institution, London

Huggins, E. (1979). *Microprocessors and Microcomputers: Their Use and Programming*, Macmillan, London and Basingstoke

Jensen, K. and Wirth, N. (1975). *Pascal User Manual and Report*, Springer-Verlag, New York

Ledgard, H. F., Hueras, J. F. and Nagin, P. A. (1979). *Pascal with Style*, Hayden Book Co., Rochelle Park, N.J.

Moroney, M. J. (1951). *Facts from Figures*, Penguin Books, Harmondsworth, Middlesex

Vincent, G. and Gill, J. (1981). *Software Development*, 2nd edn, Texas Instruments, Bedford

Wirth, N., *see* Jensen

ANSWERS TO EXERCISES

CHAPTER 2

2.1

100   25   4   4   4   100.

Intermediate steps are

$j4 = -11, j3 = -4, j2 = 100, j3 = 4,$
$j4 = 4, r4 = 100, r3 = 4$ and $r2 = 25.$

2.2

```
PROGRAM ConvertInches (INPUT, OUTPUT);

VAR VAR miles, yards, feet, inches, length : INTEGER;

BEGIN
  WRITE('Length ? ');
  READ (length);
  inches := length MOD 12;
  length := length DIV 12;
  feet := length MOD 3;
  length := length DIV 3;
  yards := length MOD 1760;
  miles := length DIV 1760;
  WRITE('Miles =', miles, 'yards =', yards);
  WRITELN('feet =',feet, 'inches =', inches);
END.
```

CHAPTER 3

3.1 and 3.2 These exercises are discussed in Chapter 4.

3.3 (a) By reducing the value of *timeConst*.

(b) By nesting the **FOR** loop inside another thus

```
FOR m := 1 TO 1000 DO
  FOR n := 1 TO timeConst DO
```

etc.

(c) By making *timeConst* a variable of type INTEGER, instead of a constant and by READing its value at the start of the program.

CHAPTER 4

4.1

```
PROGRAM MultiplicationTables (OUTPUT);

VAR
  k, m, n : INTEGER;

BEGIN
  FOR k := 0 TO 2 DO
  BEGIN
    FOR m := 1 TO 12 DO
    BEGIN
      FOR n := 2 + (k * 3) TO 4 + (k * 3) DO
        WRITE (n : 2, ' x', m : 3, ' = ', n * m : 1);
      WRITELN
    END;
    WRITELN
  END
END.
```

4.2

```
BEGIN
  total := 0;
  WRITELN ( 'Number  Hours  Wagerate      Week''s pay');
  WRITELN;
  WRITE ('?');
  READ (num);
  WHILE num <> 0 DO
  BEGIN
    READ (hours, wageRate);
    weeksPay := hours * wageRate;
    WRITELN (weeksPay :38 :2);
    total := total + weeksPay;
    WRITE ('?');
    READ (num)
  END;
  WRITELN ('----------' :38);
  WRITELN ('Total wages for week = £' :29, total :9 :2);
  WRITELN ('==========' :38)
END.
```

```
BEGIN
  total := 0;
  WRITELN ( 'Number  Hours  Wagerate      Week''s pay');
  WRITELN;
  WRITE ('?');
  READ (num);
  REPEAT
    READ (hours, wageRate);
    weeksPay := hours * wageRate;
    WRITELN (weeksPay :38 :2);
    total := total + weeksPay;
    WRITE ('?');
    READ (num)
  UNTIL num = 0 ;
  WRITELN ('----------' :38);
  WRITELN ('Total wages for week = £' :29, total :9 :2);
  WRITELN ('==========' :38)
END.
```

```
BEGIN
  total := 0;
  WRITELN ( 'Number  Hours  Wagerate      Week''s pay');
  WRITELN;
  REPEAT
    WRITE ('?');
    READ (num);
    IF num <> 0 THEN
    BEGIN
      READ (hours, wageRate);
      weeksPay := hours * wageRate;
      WRITELN (weeksPay :38 :2);
      total := total + weeksPay
    END
  UNTIL num = 0 ;
  WRITELN ('---------' :38);
  WRITELN ('Total wages for week = £' :29, total :9 :2);
  WRITELN ('=========' :38)
END.
```

4.3

```
REPEAT
  FOR n := 1 TO 7 DO
  BEGIN
    seed := seed * 2;
    seed := seed MOD prime
  END;
  IF seed <= 9999 THEN
    etc
```

CHAPTER 6

6.1

```
PROGRAM Exercise61 (INPUT, OUTPUT);

VAR
  ch : CHAR;

BEGIN
  REPEAT
    READ (ch);
    WRITELN (ch : 2, ORD (ch) : 4)
  UNTIL ch = '.'
END.
```

6.2

```
BEGIN
  READ (ch);
  IF (ch >='0') AND (ch <='9') THEN
            WRITE ('digit')
  ELSE IF (ch >='A') AND (ch <='Z') THEN
          etc
```

6.3

```
WRITE ('You win ');
IF (number MOD 3 = 0) AND (number <> 0) THEN
  CASE number OF
    36                    : WRITELN ('first prize');
    6, 12, 18, 24, 30     : WRITELN ('second prize');
    3, 9, 15, 21, 27, 33  : WRITELN ('third prize')
  END
ELSE WRITELN ('nothing.  Bad luck!')
```

CHAPTER 8

8.1

```
PROGRAM CleanData (OUTPUT, MarksFile, Cleanfile);

CONST
   lineLength = 100;
   numForms = 6;

VAR
   ch : CHAR;
   lineCount : INTEGER;
   space : BOOLEAN;
   MarksFile, CleanFile : TEXT;

BEGIN
   RESET (MarksFile);
   REWRITE (CleanFile);
   space := FALSE;
   lineCount := 0;
   WHILE NOT EOF (MarksFile) DO
   BEGIN
      IF NOT EOLN (MarksFile) THEN
      BEGIN
         READ (MarksFile, ch);
         IF ch = ' ' THEN space := TRUE;
         IF (ch >= '0') AND (ch <= '9') THEN
            IF space = TRUE THEN
            BEGIN
               WRITE (CleanFile, ' ', ch);
               space := FALSE
            END
            ELSE WRITE (CleanFile, ch)
      END
      ELSE
      BEGIN
         WRITELN (CleanFile);
         space := FALSE;
         lineCount := SUCC (lineCount);
         READ (MarksFile, ch)   (* EOLN component *)
      END
   END;
   IF lineCount = numForms - 1 THEN
   BEGIN
      WRITELN (CleanFile);
      WRITELN ('Last EOLN missing.  Now supplied')
   END;
   IF lineCount < numForms - 1 THEN
                                 WRITELN ('Too few forms');
   WRITELN ('Completed');
   RESET (CleanFile)
END.
```

8.2 One solution to this problem is to read the file character by character instead of integer by integer. The integers can be formed by a statement:

```
mark := mark * 10 + digit
```

Each mark is complete when a space is read or when EOLN is detected. The resulting program would be a mixture of *AverageMarks* and *CleanData* above.

8.3 The exercise warns that a common error could be the omission of a relevant number. The effect of this would be to put the input 'out of step'. When this happens, real numbers might be read when integers were expected. If the program calls for READing an integer and the data offered is real, control could switch from the program to the implementation's diagnostics. This would probably halt the program before any desired error message had been output. In such circumstances it is probably better to read all numbers as real numbers and to test the integers with a statement such as

```
IF ABS (number) - TRUNC (ABS (number)) <> 0 THEN
```

In order to facilitate the location of errors, it is desirable to be able to output, in the error message, the last data that was apparently successfully read. In this exercise this would be the customer's number and the last pair of item/quantity. Thus each of these should be retained until its successor had been successfully read.

The other requirements of this exercise should present few difficulties.

CHAPTER 9

9.1

```
PROGRAM anagrams (INPUT,OUTPUT);

CONST wordsPerLine = 6;

VAR n, numLetters, wordCount : INTEGER;
    inBuffer, outBuffer : PACKED ARRAY [1 .. 7] OF CHAR;

PROCEDURE selectChar (charNum : INTEGER);

VAR n, m : INTEGER;

BEGIN
  FOR n := 1 TO numLetters DO
    IF inBuffer [n] <> ' ' THEN
    BEGIN
      outBuffer [charNum] := inBuffer [n];
      inBuffer [n] := ' ';
      IF charNum = numLetters THEN
      BEGIN
        FOR m := 1 TO numLetters DO WRITE (outBuffer [m]);
        FOR m := numLetters + 1 TO 10 DO WRITE (' ');
        wordCount := SUCC (wordCount);
        IF wordCount MOD wordsPerLine = 0 THEN WRITELN
      END
      ELSE selectChar (charNum + 1);   (* recursive call *)
      inBuffer [n] := outBuffer [charNum];
    END
END;

BEGIN
  n := 0;
  wordCount := 0;
  WRITELN ('Enter your word');
  WHILE (NOT EOLN (INPUT)) AND (n < 7) DO
  BEGIN
    n := SUCC (n);
    READ (inBuffer [n])
  END;
  numLetters := n;
  selectChar (1);
  WRITELN;
  WRITELN ('Number of anagrams =', wordcount : 5)
END.
```

9.2

```
PROGRAM InvoicePrep (OUTPUT, PriceList, CustPurchases);

VAR
   position : INTEGER;
   . . . .

   itemNum : ARRAY [1 .. 100] OF INTEGER;
   price : ARRAY [1..100] OF REAL;


FUNCTION location (number : INTEGER) : INTEGER;

VAR n : INTEGER;
       found : BOOLEAN;
BEGIN
found := FALSE;
   n := 1;
   REPEAT
      IF itemNum [n] = number THEN found := TRUE;
      n := SUCC (n)
   UNTIL found OR (n > 100);
   IF found THEN location := PRED (n)
   ELSE location := n
END;

   . . . .

   RESET (PriceList);  RESET (CustPurchases);
   FOR item := 1 TO 100 DO
      READ (PriceList, itemNum [item], price [item]);
      . . . .

   invTotal := 0;
   READ (CustPurchases, item);
   WHILE item <> 0 DO
   BEGIN
      READ (CustPurchases, qty);
      WRITE (item :4, qty :12 :3);
      position := location (item);
      IF (position > 0) AND (position <= 100) THEN
      BEGIN
         extension := qty * price [position];
         WRITELN (price [position] :12 :2, extension :12 :2);
         invTotal := invTotal + extension
      END
      ELSE WRITELN ('Item no', item, 'not recognised');
      . . . .
```

For the second approach, the following changes would have to be made to the above program:

```
   itemPrice : ARRAY [1 .. 2, 1 .. 100] OF INTEGER;

   . . . .

   REPEAT
      IF itemPrice [1, n] = number THEN found := TRUE;
      n := SUCC (n)
   UNTIL found OR (n > 100);
   location := n
END;

   . . . .

   RESET (PriceList);  RESET (CustPurchases);
   FOR item := 1 TO 100 DO
      FOR n := 1 TO 2 DO
         READ (PriceList, itemPrice [n, item]);
         . . . .
```

```
invTotal := 0;
READ (CustPurchases, item);
WHILE item <> 0 DO
BEGIN
  READ (CustPurchases, qty);
  WRITE (item :4, qty :12 :3);
  position := location (item);
  IF (position > 0) AND (position <= 100) THEN
  BEGIN
    extension := qty * itemPrice [2, position] / 100;
    WRITELN (itemPrice [2, position] / 100 :12 :2,
                          extension :12 :2);
```

CHAPTER 10

10.1 The solution to the first part of this exercise is similar to the *location* function of Exercise 9.2.

For the second part of this exercise, the Boolean declaration *found* could be replaced by two Boolean variables: *foundEqual* and *found-Greater*. The tests would be

```
IF itemNum [n] = number THEN foundEqual := TRUE;
IF itemNum [n] > number THEN foundGreater:= TRUE;
```

and the output would be

```
IF foundEqual THEN
  WRITELN ('Index = ', PRED (n)  : 1)
ELSE IF foundGreater AND (n > 2) THEN
  WRITELN ('Number is between indices ', n - 2 :1,
    ' and ',  PRED (n) : 1)
ELSE WRITELN ('Number out of range')
```

10.2 For these three solutions it is assumed that an integer array *list [1 .. 1000]* has been declared globally.

```
PROCEDURE bubbleSort (last : INTEGER);

VAR
  m, n, temp : INTEGER;

BEGIN

  FOR n := (last - 1) DOWNTO 1 DO
    FOR m := 1 TO n DO
      IF list[m] > list[m+1] THEN
      BEGIN
        temp := list[m];
        list[m] := list[m+1];
        list[m+1] := temp
      END
END;


PROCEDURE selectionSort (last : INTEGER);

VAR
  index, temp, k, m, n : INTEGER;

BEGIN
  FOR n := last DOWNTO 2 DO
```

```
    BEGIN
      temp := - MAXINT;
      FOR m := 1 TO n DO
        IF list [m] > temp THEN
          BEGIN
            temp := list [m];
            index := m
          END;
        FOR k := index TO n DO list [k] := list [k+1];
        list [n] := temp
    END
END;


PROCEDURE insertionSort (last : INTEGER);

VAR
  temp, k, m, n : INTEGER;

BEGIN
  FOR n := 2 TO last DO
    IF list [n] < list [n-1] THEN
    BEGIN
      temp := list [n];
      m := 1;
      WHILE temp > list [m] DO m := SUCC (m);
      FOR k := n DOWNTO m+1 DO list [k] := list [k-1];
      list [m] := temp
    END
END;
```

CHAPTER 11

11.1

```
PROGRAM Sorting (INPUT, OUTPUT, Results);

VAR
  list : ARRAY [1 .. 1000] OF INTEGER;
  seed, n, last : INTEGER;
  Results : TEXT;


PROCEDURE inSeed (VAR seed : INTEGER);

EXTERNAL;   (* Chapter 7 *)


FUNCTION random (VAR seed : INTEGER; max : INTEGER) :
INTEGER;

EXTERNAL;   (* Chapter 7 *)


PROCEDURE sort (last : INTEGER);

EXTERNAL;   (* Here insert the procedure under test *)

BEGIN
  inSeed (seed);
  REWRITE (Results);
  WRITE ('How many numbers ? ');
  READ (last);
  FOR n := 1 TO last DO
    list [n] := random (seed, 10000);
  WRITELN ('press <newline> to start');
  IF EOLN (INPUT) THEN sort (last);
  WRITELN ('stop');
  FOR n := 1 TO last DO WRITELN (Results, list [n]);
  (*  Writing the output to a Results file
      enables it to be checked  *)
  RESET (Results)
END.
```

11.2 This exercise is a matter of developing the program already outlined in the text.

CHAPTER 16

16.1 Because the function *deal* would be called when the pack was already empty. The expression

```
card IN cardPack
```

would never be true, however many random numbers were generated.

16.2

```
PROGRAM Shopping (INPUT, OUTPUT);

TYPE
   commodity = (apples, bread, cream, damsons, eggs, flour,
                gammon, ham, icecream, jam);
   commset = SET OF commodity;

VAR
   shop, aList, bList, cList,
   aBasket, bBasket, cBasket, dBasket,
   basket : commset;
   n : commodity;

PROCEDURE inputList (VAR list : commset; initial : CHAR);

VAR
   comm : commodity;

BEGIN
   list := [];
   WRITELN ('Enter ', initial,
                     '''s shopping list, numbers');
   WHILE NOT EOLN DO
   BEGIN
     READ (comm);
     list := list + [comm]
   END;
   WRITELN
END;
BEGIN
   shop := [damsons, eggs, flour, gammon, ham,
                icecream, jam];
   PAGE;
   WRITELN ('Commodities are:');
   WRITELN ('O. Apples   1. Bread   2. Cream   3. Damsons');
   WRITELN ('4. Eggs     5. Flour   6. Gammon  7. Ham');
   WRITELN ('8. Icecream     9. Jam');
   WRITELN;
   inputList (aList, 'A');
   inputList (bList, 'B');
   cList := [ gammon, ham, icecream, jam ];
   aBasket := aList * shop;
   bBasket := bList * shop;
   cBasket := cList * aBasket;
   aBasket := aBasket - cList;
   basket := cList * bBasket;
   cBasket := cBasket + basket;
   bBasket := bBasket - cList;
   IF aBasket = bBasket THEN dBasket := aBasket
     ELSE dBasket := shop - cBasket;
   WRITELN ('Diana''s basket contains:');
   IF dBasket = [] THEN WRITELN ('nothing') ELSE
```

```
    FOR n := damsons TO jam DO
       IF n IN dBasket THEN
          CASE n OF
          damsons  : WRITELN ('Damsons');
          eggs     : WRITELN ('Eggs');
          flour    : WRITELN ('Flour');
          gammon   : WRITELN ('Gammon');
          ham      : WRITELN ('Ham');
          icecream : WRITELN ('Icecream');
          jam      : WRITELN ('Jam')
          END
END.
```

INDEX

SYMBOLS IN ASCII ORDER

PROGRAMS, FUNCTIONS AND PROCEDURES

AA-1 program
P.O. Box 6000
Arlington
Va. 22218-0001
O.S.A.

IRELAND